Training:
Program Development
and Evaluation

BEHAVIORAL SCIENCE IN INDUSTRY SERIES

Edited by Victor H. Vroom
Yale University

☐ COMMUNICATION PROCESSES IN ORGANIZATIONS
Lyman W. Porter, University of California, Irvine
Karlene H. Roberts, University of California, Berkeley

☐ FOUNDATIONS OF BEHAVIORAL SCIENCE RESEARCH IN
ORGANIZATIONS
Sheldon Zedeck, University of California, Berkeley
Milton R. Blood, Georgia Institute of Technology

☐ INTERPERSONAL STRATEGIES FOR SYSTEM MANAGEMENT:
APPLICATIONS OF COUNSELING AND PARTICIPATIVE PRINCIPLES
Raymond G. Hunt, State University of New York at Buffalo

MAN-MACHINE ENGINEERING
Alphonse Chapanis, The Johns Hopkins University

☐ MANAGEMENT OF COMPENSATION
Allan N. Nash and Stephen J. Carroll, University of Maryland

☐ MOTIVATION IN WORK ORGANIZATIONS
Edward E. Lawler III, The University of Michigan

OCCUPATIONAL PSYCHOLOGY
Donald E. Super, Teachers College, Columbia University
Martin J. Bohn, Jr.

ORGANIZATIONAL ANALYSIS: A SOCIOLOGICAL VIEW
Charles B. Perrow, State University of New York at Stony Brook

PERSONNEL SELECTION AND PLACEMENT
Marvin D. Dunnette, University of Minnesota

PSYCHOLOGY OF UNION-MANAGEMENT RELATIONS
Ross Stagner and Hjalmar Rosen, Wayne State University

SOCIAL PSYCHOLOGY OF THE WORK ORGANIZATION
Arnold S. Tannenbaum, The University of Michigan

TRAINING IN INDUSTRY: THE MANAGEMENT OF LEARNING
Bernard M. Bass, The University of Rochester
James A. Vaughan

☐ TRAINING: PROGRAM DEVELOPMENT AND EVALUATION
Irwin L. Goldstein, University of Maryland

☐ = II

Training:
Program Development and Evaluation

Irwin L. Goldstein

University of Maryland

Brooks/Cole Publishing Company
Monterey, California
A Division of Wadsworth Publishing Company, Inc.

**To Micki, Beth, and Harold.
Their love makes this
book a family affair.**

ISBN: 0-8185-01324
L.C. Catalog Card No.: 74-82036
Printed in the United States of America
10 9 8 7 6 5 4 3 2 1

Production Editor: Meredith Mullins
Interior & Cover Design: Linda Marcetti
Illustrations: Creative Repro, Monterey, California
Typesetting: Holmes Composition Service, San Jose, California
Printing & Binding: Colonial Press, Clinton, Massachusetts

Preface

This book is written for undergraduate and graduate students as well as practitioners who are concerned with the systematic development and evaluation of training programs in a variety of organizational settings. Hopefully, the book provides a framework for both scrutinizing present efforts and establishing new and viable instructional programs in education, business, and government environments.

Part One emphasizes the belief that once instructional needs are assessed and objectives determined, evaluation provides information useful in modifying the training program. The first two chapters present an instructional-systems approach that emphasizes the important interacting components in the development and evaluation of training programs. The next three chapters describe the necessary components for the establishment of any instructional program: specifying the objectives in direct relation to need-assessment (Chapter 3), establishing criteria that will effectively measure success (Chapter 4), and designing the program only after careful research that includes considerations of threats to validity and of the degree of control exerted by the various experimental designs (Chapter 5).

Part Two presents the theoretical and empirical bases of learning, which provide the foundation for the design of instructional environments. Chapter 6 emphasizes the more basic principles of learning that have often served as stimuli for innovations in the design of training programs (for example, behavior modification and programed learning). Chapter 7 attends to the more complex determinants of transfer of learning, including material on the components of practice and motivational factors.

Part Three includes topics relating to serious attempts to face social problems such as training the hard-core unemployed and training those looking for second careers. Also included (in the multitreatment category) are studies of individual differences in which investigators have attempted to match the aptitudes of the learner with a variety of instructional approaches. In addition, there is material devoted to specific techniques, such as computer-assisted instruction, films, laboratory training, and role-playing. This part discusses approaches that elaborate on the need-assessment, evaluation, and learning material presented in the first two parts of the book. For each approach, I have provided a general description and discussion of the evaluation data, with particular emphasis on the questions that must be answered, and summaries of the advantages and disadvantages of each approach. There is little to be gained by the enormous efforts placed on the development of instructional programs unless there are data to tell the implementers where to revise and where to proceed. Stake (1967) expressed this viewpoint with the following statement.

> Folklore is not a sufficient repository. In our data banks we should document the causes and effects, the congruence of intent and accomplishment, and the panorama of judgments of those concerned. Such records should be kept to promote educational action, not obstruct it. The countenance of evaluation should be one of data gathering that leads to decision making, not to trouble making [p. 539].

My book is written with the hope that it will contribute information and ideas to those individuals who wish to partake in the decision-making process.

This manuscript is a result of the efforts of many generous people. I am especially indebted to all the authors and researchers who took time from their busy schedules to graciously share their articles, data, and manuscripts. I am also grateful to the organizations that contributed materials and ideas: American Institutes for Research; Applied Science Associates; HumRRO; Department of Training, U. S. Civil Service Commission; and Westinghouse Behavioral Safety Center. My special thanks to Sharon Dorfman, who used letters, phones, and charm to obtain copies of all relevant material. Many of the topics developed in the book appeared in conversations with Jack Bartlett, Peter Dachler, Ben Schneider, and the graduate students of our industrial psychology group at Maryland. They all served as sensitive critics for various sections of the manuscript. I am especially indebted to Jack Bartlett, who assumed many of my responsibilities so that I could complete the manuscript. I would also like to thank reviewers Garlie A. Forehand of Carnegie Mellon University, Sheldon Zedeck of the University of California, Berkeley, William C. Howell of Rice University, Norman W. Heimstra of the University of South Dakota, James Naylor of Purdue University, and Victor H. Vroom of Yale University, as well as the unusually supportive and efficient staff of Brooks/Cole Publishing Company, especially Bill Hicks and Meredith Mullins. My everlasting gratitude is extended to Sharon Johnson, who typed, obtained author permissions, typed some more, edited, and typed even more. Most of all, this book is a result of an environment designed by my children, Beth and Harold, and my wife, Micki, that enabled me to work quietly in the refuge of my home. Engineering psychologists concerned with the design of environments as work settings should hire them as consultants.

Irwin L. Goldstein

Contents

Part One

Assessment and Evaluation

Chapter One

Introduction

Throughout our lives, learning experiences are a potent source of stimulation. This text emphasizes the systematic modes of instruction designed to produce environments that shape behavior to satisfy stated objectives. From this point of view, *training and education are defined as the systematic acquisition of skills, rules, concepts, or attitudes that results in improved performance in another environment*. The school environment is designed to enable primary-school children to read books, newspapers, and magazines in their homes or the dental student to repair cavities in an office. Similarly, training programs are planned to produce a more considerate foreman or a more competent technician in working environments.

TRAINING AND EDUCATION

Both training and education are instructional processes designed to modify human behavior. As such, their basic foundations are dependent on learning and transfer processes. In the past, professionals emphasized differences between training and education based on the specificity of their program objectives. Thus, industrial training objectives were easily specified and were designed to produce uniform terminal behavior. But as our society becomes more concerned with providing services and managing human resources, as well as with nuts-and-bolts machinery, management has begun to recognize that uniform behavior by all trainees is not necessarily a desirable goal. This realization has led to management-training programs designed to enhance individual modes of behavior. On the other hand, education has become concerned with setting minimum acceptable levels of performance, resulting in a greater degree of uniformity. Some investigators trace this development to the beginning of programed instruction, which requires the specification of the final behavioral outcomes before the program can be constructed.

Determining educational and training objectives is a complex issue. Critics of educational programs have noted the continual changes in educational curricula with growing alarm. Puzzled parents have commented on the demise of specified university requirements, like math, English, and foreign languages, and there are constant disagreements among educators about the objectives to be achieved at the primary grade levels. These uncertainties reflect real difficulties in determining the objectives of educational programs. Similar problems have been encountered in human-relations training in industry. Trainers have been frustrated by programs with vague objectives—for example, to develop managers with more self-insight, self-awareness, and sensitivity to the behavior of their families and fellow employees.

Training and education should be recognized as part of the same instructional process. Each of these disciplines has similar problems related to the specification of objectives, design of the environment, and evaluation of the instructional process. Each field will profit from research that reduces the deplorable gulf between the basic psychology of learning and the understanding of how learning variables affect performance in complex instructional settings, and each will benefit from an exchange of research rather than an emphasis on uniqueness.

SCOPE OF THE INSTRUCTIONAL PROCESS

The design of instructional programs has developed into a large enterprise for educational systems, government units, military groups, and private corporations. The scope of these programs is clear from the following items:

1. Estimates for the fiscal year 1967 show that the U.S. Office of Education spent over 800 million dollars on instructional materials and media (Grayson, 1972). The 1973 budget proposed total outlays of over 6 billion dollars for Office of Education programs.
2. Surveys indicate that over 90 percent of private corporations have some type of systematic training program. One large corporation reported spending over 75 million dollars annually on the salaries of nonmanagement employees undergoing training. This figure did not include the costs of the training program or the facilities involved (Holt, 1963).
3. A catalog released by the U.S. Civil Service Commission (1971) presenting training programs for educationally disadvantaged employees lists over 50 basic reading programs. There are similar lists for language arts, mathematics, business, and consumer education.
4. The American Society for Training and Development had 15 members in 1943, 5000 members in 1967, and over 9500 members in 1972. The society estimates that there are over 50,000 professionals in the training area, excluding private and public educational systems (Jenness, 1972).
5. A basic undergraduate course in pilot training is 53 weeks long, with 240 hours devoted to training in the aircraft, 375 hours to academic training, and 236 hours to officer training (Smode & Meyer, 1966).

None of these activities suggests the startling innovations that may soon be upon us as well as a tongue-in-cheek article by humorist Art Buchwald, which was reprinted in the *Training and Development Journal* (Feifer, 1970, p. 43). In this article, Buchwald discusses a continuing education plan developed by Feifer.

Mass transportation is definitely one of the major problems of the next decade. The ideal solution would be faster, cleaner and safer transportation for everyone. But since this is impossible, other solutions must be found to make commuting worthwhile.

Irwin Feifer, who specializes in manpower problems, has come up with an idea which certainly deserves consideration.

Mr. Feifer says that as a commuter on the Long Island Railroad, he has been able to give hours of time to studying the transportation nightmare of the '70s.

On the basis of his own experience he has applied a systems-analysis approach to commuting which, when boiled down to layman's language, can be put this way: "How can time now used to look at your watch be otherwise employed constructively and productively to further the welfare of the country?"

The Feifer Solution is to incorporate all railroads as universities and allow commuters to take courses for bona fide college or graduate credits.

While the Long Island and Penn Central trains made their way slowly toward their destinations, each car would become a classroom where commuters could do their lesson, listen to guest lectures by experts who are stuck on the trains, and be graded by the conductors who punched their tickets.

A delay would no longer mean an inconvenience, but would actually be credited to the student as an hour or two hours of classroom work.

In order not to confuse the courses, each car would specialize in a different field of study and would be so marked on the outside. When buying your ticket at the gate you would specify what subject you would like to take for the month and the agent would issue you books at the same time he sold you a ticket.

The Feifer Plan is not without incentives and subsidies. One of the major provisions of the plan is to get a grant from the federal Office of Education which would be used as an inducement for commuters to take the courses.

Each month a true-or-false test would be given by the conductor. Those who received 90 or over would be granted a $5.50 reduction on their commuter tickets for the following months. Those scoring 80 or above would get a $3.25 reduction and those who passed with a 65 would not be given a money reduction, but would be assured a seat on the train for the next four weeks.

The Feifer Plan is not necessarily aimed just at people who take railroads (a subway educational plan where people can study while being delayed in tunnels is now being worked out), but could also be applied to people driving to work in the morning.

Those signing up for credits would listen to lectures on the radio in the morning and evening rush hours, and do their book studying at traffic bottlenecks and red lights.

The driver-students would hand in their tests and toll collectors would grade them as they made change.

Most people would not mind traffic delays as it would give them more time to get their homework done.

The Feifer Plan would provide for graduation exercises every six months. In the case of the railroads, the ceremonies would be held at the railroad stations with the Secretary of Transportation handing out the diplomas.

Automobile college graduates would receive their diplomas from the license bureau, and each license plate would indicate how many degrees the driver possessed.

The plan, if put into effect, would make Americans the most educated people in the world. It would also turn train delays and traffic jams into a profit. But more important, with everyone going to school, the generation gap could become a thing of the past.[1]

Another facet of the ever-increasing emphasis on instructional systems is the number of training techniques that are available to instructors and training directors. Various texts and articles list from 15 to 25 different techniques. A survey of 112 firms by Utgaard and Dawis (see Table 1-1) indicated that job-instruction training, conference or discussion, apprenticeship, and job rotation were the most frequently used techniques. These authors also found that certain techniques (for example, films, programed instruction, simulators, and television) were more likely to be utilized by organizations that had over 500 employees and a net revenue of over 1 million dollars.

TRAINING CAN WORK

The emphasis on instructional programs is based on the belief that they can achieve specific goals. The goals may vary from those of a school district that desires to raise the scores of its students above the national average to an industrial organization that expects quality goods produced in a shorter time period, a reduction in accidents with a corresponding decrease in insurance premiums, and a more satisfied work force, which in turn could help reduce turnover, absenteeism, sabotage, and grievances. The potential number of goals is unlimited. While training is not a panacea for all the ills of society, well-conceived training programs have achieved beneficial results. For example, Lindahl (1945) analyzed a disc-cutting operation and determined the correct foot patterns to use in a complex hand-foot coordination task. One measure utilized to evaluate this program was the number of wheels broken by the operator while operating the disc-cutting machine. Since the wheels were costly and as much as 30 minutes of production time was lost in changing each wheel, Lindahl

---

[1]From Buchwald, A. Training on the Train. Copyright 1970 by the Washington Post Company. Reprinted by permission.

Table 1-1. Rank Order of Frequency of Use of 18 Training Techniques, by Type of Firm

Training technique	Type of firm			
	Manufacturing[1]		Nonmanufacturing[2]	
	Rank order	Mean value[3]	Rank order	Mean value[3]
1. Job-instruction training	1	3.9	1	4.0
2. Conference or discussion	2	3.5	2	3.4
3. Apprentice training	3	3.1	6.5	2.5
4. Job rotation	4	2.8	3	2.8
5. Coaching	5	2.6	6.5	2.5
6. Lecture	6	2.4	5	2.6
7. Special study	7	2.3	4	2.7
8. Case study	8	2.1	10	2.2
9. Films	9	2.0	8.5	2.4
10. Programed instruction	10	1.9	8.5	2.4
11. Internships and assistantships	11	1.8	11	2.0
12. Simulation	12	1.7	12	1.9
13. Programed group exercises	13.5	1.6	16.5	1.3
14. Role playing	13.5	1.6	13	1.6
15. Laboratory training	15	1.5	16.5	1.3
16. Television	16	1.4	14.5	1.4
17. Vestibule training	17	1.2	14.5	1.4
18. Junior board	18	1.1	18	1.1

[1]Consists of 63 firms.
[2]Consists of 14 transportation, 13 finance, 10 retail, and 12 "other" firms.
[3]Computed from the following values: 5 = Always; 4 = Usually; 3 = Average; 2 = Seldom; 1 = Never.
From Utgaard, S. B. & Dawis, R. V. The most frequently-used training techniques. *Training and Development Journal,* 1970, **24,** 40–43. Reprinted by permission of the American Society for Training and Development.

considered this to be an important measure of the success of his program. Figure 1-1 shows that the trainees damaged 24 percent of their wheels during the first week. By the third week they were breaking less than were operators with nine months' experience. Lindahl reported similar data using other measures of performance from operators already on the job.

Unfortunately, most organizations do not have information available to determine the utility of their own instructional programs. Their techniques remain unevaluated, except for the high esteem placed upon them by training personnel. For example, the Civil Service Catalog of Basic Education Systems (1971) lists 55 basic reading programs for educationally disadvantaged employees. For these programs, 4 publishers list some type of validation program, 2 publishers offer case studies, and the other 49 indi-

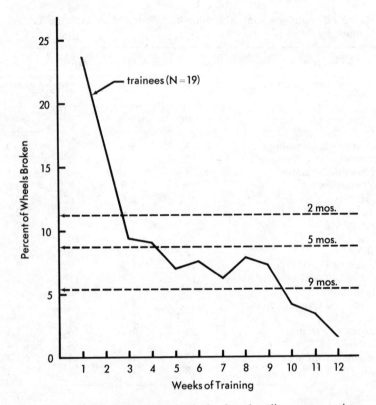

Figure 1-1. Percentage of wheels broken by disc-cutter trainees. Dotted lines represent average percentage of wheels broken for first 2 weeks by groups with an average of 2, 5, and 9 months' experience at start of training. From Lindahl, L. G. Movement analysis as an industrial training method. *Journal of Applied Psychology,* 1945, **29,** 430.

cate that validation data are not available. Other surveys of instructional programs echo these findings, with perhaps one in 40 firms performing systematic evaluation of any sort. Yet, when evaluation studies are completed, it is often found that the techniques are not achieving the desired results, and in many cases, the evaluation could provide clues to the modifications necessary to enable the program to work. Kozoll (1971) described a manpower-training program in an article with the unusually descriptive title "The Air Left the Bag—A Training Program That Failed." His analysis indicated that the program failed to develop jobs for the hard-core unemployed trainees in the supermarket industry because the interest and involvement of the potential employers were ignored. Thus, Kozoll's analysis has provided valuable insights into one of the factors that helps establish successful training programs.

FADS AND A RIDDLE

Some authors have described training techniques as faddish. Campbell (1971) describes fads as following particular patterns.

1. A new technique appears with a group of followers who announce its success.
2. Another group develops modifications of the technique.
3. A few empirical studies appear supporting the technique.
4. There is a backlash. Critics question the usefulness of the new technique but rarely produce any data.
5. The technique survives until a new technique appears. Then, the whole procedure is repeated.

When there are no empirical data to evaluate techniques, the cycle of fads continues. Evaluation must be sold as a tool to provide information rather than as a technique to determine passing and failing. Then, we may be able to shift from the cycles of fads to the more mature question of which technique works for which individuals, behaviors, or organizational settings. There isn't any supertechnique that will work for all given situations. It is not even certain which learning variables support performance or which instructional media are best for learning particular types of behavior. The level of analysis rarely reaches the point at which different techniques are actually compared.

The difficulties that must be confronted in order to produce sound, effective training programs and research are best described in "The Riddle of Training in Business and Industry" (DePhillips, Berliner, & Cribbin, 1960, pp. 5–6).

Few organizations would admit that they can survive without it—yet some act as though they could.

Everyone knows what it is—yet management, unions, and workers often interpret it in light of their own job conditions.

It is going on all the time—yet much of it is done haphazardly.

It is futile to attempt it without the needed time and facilities—yet often those responsible for it lack either or both.

It costs money—yet at times there is not adequate budgetary appropriation for it.

It should take place at all levels—yet sometimes it is limited to the lowest operating levels.

It can help everyone do a better job—yet those selected for it often fear it.

It is foolish to start it without clearly defined objectives—yet this is occasionally done.

It cannot be ignored without costing the company money—yet some managers seem blind to this reality.

It should permeate the entire organization and be derived from the firm's theory and practice of management—yet sometimes it is shunted off to one department that operates more or less in isolation from the rest of the business.[2]

Observers of instructional programs would agree that the riddle is equally applicable to educational and industrial programs. They might also concur that the riddle would be more complete by adding: "It is accepted as working—yet there is rarely any evidence to support this viewpoint." One of the goals of this book is to present information that will convince the reader that the conditions described by the riddle are worth changing. Hopefully, the text will also serve as a source of information and techniques necessary to design and evaluate instructional programs.

THE FUTURE OF INSTRUCTIONAL PROGRAMS

The time spent in learning occupies a significant portion of our lives. Predictions suggest that instructional technology will play an increasing role in influencing the lives of all members of our society. Some of the evidence and reasons for these predictions should include the following considerations.

THE REVOLUTION IN EDUCATION

Developments in technology have such vast potential that prognosticators (Abelson, 1972) are predicting a revolution in education. These predictions are based on the effects of new electronics—computers, cable television, and video cassettes—on full-time students. The changes produced by these techniques for off-campus instruction of adults and industrial training programs should be even greater.

TECHNOLOGY AND INDUSTRY

Advances in computer technology and work techniques have already led to changes in training requirements for many jobs in industrial enterprises. Each new advance has the potential to change job requirements as well as to create or abolish entire job categories. Automation generally requires higher levels of skill for the operator who desires to continue in his present job, but more jobs are created with requirements related to systems control, monitoring, and electronics maintenance. The effects on the organization are not always predictable. In almost all cases, however, the

---

[2]From DePhillips, F. A., Berliner, W. M., & Cribbin, J. J. *Management of Training Programs.* ©1960 by Richard D. Irwin, Inc. Reprinted by permission.

need for training and retraining increases. Usually, the training is limited to those concerned with immediate work requirements, but it is likely that the increasing complexity of the organization will lead to the necessity of retraining at all levels within the organization.

SPECIAL GROUPS

Minority groups and hard-core unemployment. Instructional programs have been offered as a possible solution to the problem of equal opportunities. All segments of our society, from the federal government to the local school system, have begun to offer programs that give previously unemployed individuals an opportunity to obtain the skills necessary for future employment. These programs include basic language skills, job skills, consumer information, and counseling. The design and implementation of these programs require a special sensitivity to the needs of the applicant population and the job requirements. As difficult as the initiation of these programs may be, there is little dispute that the need for such efforts will greatly increase in the next decade. In many cases, hard-core unemployed groups include large numbers of nonwhite trainees. These particular minority groups have faced problems of substantial unemployment as well as job discrimination related to promotional opportunities. While the Equal Employment Opportunities Commission (EEOC) has focused on those firms that have unfairly discriminated against minority employees in their selection practices, these cases represent just the tip of the iceberg. Future cases will likely involve firms that fail to provide opportunities to move up the corporate ladder. With this focus, the question of training programs and their fairness to minority groups (particularly those related to sex, race, and age) will quickly become an issue. A training technique that has not been validated and that is discriminatory in promotional and job opportunities will more than likely be ruled unfair by the courts.

Civil rights legislation has already recognized the large numbers of individuals who are over 45 years of age and cannot find work. Some of these individuals are victims of changing job requirements that left their skills obsolete. Employers have hired younger workers who have more recently developed skills and who cost the employer less in terms of payments for health insurance and pension plans. Many employers have quoted the old cliché "You can't teach an old dog new tricks" with no empirical evaluation data to support their viewpoint. Effective programs that can utilize older persons' years of experience must be developed.

Society has also become concerned with the teen-age unemployment problem. Many of these individuals are high school dropouts without basic job skills. Future training programs with the continuing impetus of federal and state grants will focus on training methodology to develop skills for these groups.

Selection programs and training. Many industrial psychologists have emphasized the use of various measuring instruments (for example, tests and interviews) to predict the future success of potential employees. Figure 1-2 presents a scatterplot of data illustrating the relationship between scores on a mathematical aptitude test and errors in dollars made by toll collectors at a hypothetical tunnel. One way of characterizing the relationships between two variables is by the statistical determination of the correlational coefficient (also known in personnel selection as the validity coefficient). The value of the correlational coefficient ranges from +1.00 for a perfect positive relationship to −1.00 for a perfect negative correlation. A .00 correlation indicates that there is no evidence that the two variables are associated. In this example, individuals with higher scores on the test tend toward a smaller number of errors in collecting tolls.

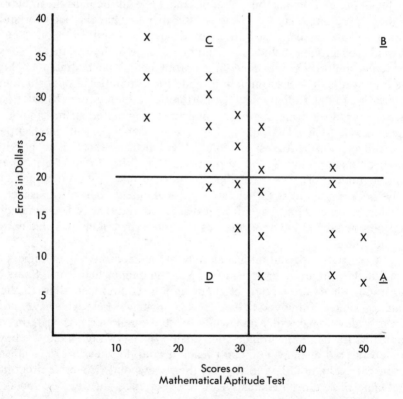

Figure 1-2. Hypothetical scores on a mathematical aptitude test and criterion measured in errors in dollars for toll collectors.

Assuming that proper procedures have been used and that the relationship is statistically significant, the negative correlation can be used to predict the performance of future applicants. The selection of individuals with higher scores on the mathematical aptitude test will result in employees who tend to make fewer errors collecting tolls.

The horizontal line at the $20 level is the cutoff for the measure of success.[3] This means that errors above that level are considered unacceptable and would lead to dismissal. The vertical line at the score of 31 on the mathematics test is the predictor cutoff. The setting of this cutoff is related to the selection ratio, which is the ratio of jobs available to the number of applicants. If there is a low selection ratio (that is, large numbers of applicants available and very few jobs), it is possible to move this cutoff to the right and thus accept applicants with higher aptitude scores who are likely to perform better on the criteria. However, if there are few applicants and many openings (a high selection ratio), it might become necessary to lower the cutoff score on the aptitude test in order to fill all of the positions. Further implications of this shift in cutoff scores will become clearer after a discussion of the four quadrants that result from the predictor and criterion cutoff points.

Group A. These are the applicants who have scored above the predictor cutoff and would meet the success level in terms of a low error rate. They would be hired and would be successful. Therefore, they represent a correct selection decision.

Group B. These individuals scored above the predictor cutoff. They would be hired, but their performance as measured by the criterion would be unsatisfactory. This group represents a selection error.

Group C. These applicants scored below the cutoff on the test and would also have performed poorly on the job. Thus, they represent a correct selection decision.

Group D. These individuals scored below the cutoff on the test, but they would have been satisfactory on the job. This group reflects a selection error.

An examination of the four quadrants indicates that shifts in the predictor and criterion cutoff affect the number of individuals in correct or incorrect decision categories. For example, if the selection ratio is favorable for the organization, it would be possible to raise the predictor cutoff. This new cutoff level would result in fewer failures on the job—that is, a higher proportion of Group A to Group B. However, this raise would also result in more Group Ds, in which persons who could perform well on the job would not be hired. A lowering of the predictor cutoff would result in missing fewer successful workers (Group D).

[3]The measure of success is also known as the criterion. For a more complete discussion of criterion issues, see Chapter 4.

It is interesting to speculate on the implications of the four quadrants for instructional programs (Bartlett, 1973). Training issues interact with the problems of all four groups. Even those individuals who are selected and are successful (Group A) will have to undergo some training before being admitted to the job. The problems of Group B are especially interesting. In these cases, the employee is hired but is unsuccessful. This failure causes difficulties for both the organization and the employee. Often, labor-union agreements have clauses that prevent an organization from firing an employee after a short trial period (usually six to eight weeks). From the other point of view, the employee may be dissatisfied with his lack of progress. One solution to the problem of unsuccessful employees may be the institution of retraining programs that are directed either toward improvement of skills or toward the development of new potential for different jobs in the organization.

Group D represents a severe loss for both the corporation and the individual. This group includes applicants who would be successful if given the opportunity. Some organizations that are unable to afford the loss of this group have instituted programs in which all potential employees are invited to preliminary training programs. During these programs, those individuals who have performed poorly on the selection tests are carefully trained on job-related tasks in an attempt to distinguish members of Group D from those of Group C. This technique often becomes a complex multiple-level cutoff program. Those scoring very poorly on the selection test (for example, 20 or below) are immediately eliminated, while others (scores from 30 to 40) are invited to the training program for a trial period. Performance in the training program is then used as a predictor of job performance for these groups.

Group C represents a special problem for society. They have been eliminated from job consideration and indeed would not succeed. There is increasing concern for these individuals who have been *selected out*. Too often, they are members of the previously discussed minority groups and the hard-core unemployed. Group C places a tremendous responsibility on the instructional community to develop valid training programs that will lead to the skills and attitudes necessary for the employment of all who desire to work.

Admittedly, there is a degree of speculation relating selection and training programs. The point is that these types of programs interact and have a role in organizational settings. It is unrealistic to consider a selection program isolated from training in most industrial, government, and military organizations. The situation in educational organizations is not so easily catalogued. From the primary grades through high school, the selection ratio (all applicants must be accepted) precludes the use of selection techniques. Thus, the emphasis must be on instructional programs. At the university level, selection ratios do operate, and there is considerable discussion of admission standards, minority applicants, and all varieties of instructional programs.

ACCOUNTABILITY

The tremendous costs of instructional programs have naturally resulted in questions about their effectiveness. It is not unusual for companies to accept contracts with school systems whereby their payment is directly related to the degree of improvement by the student on nationally standardized achievement tests. In management circles, it is becoming more conventional to question the effects of expensive training and development programs. This is a healthy trend that will test the ingenuity of training analysts to determine the effectiveness of their programs in terms of performance improvements, costs, and other subsidiary benefits through the establishment of systematic evaluation programs.

A PRECAUTIONARY STATEMENT

While this book is devoted to the topic of instructional programs, any program—training or otherwise—that exists in a vacuum and does not consider the influence of a multitude of other factors is doomed to failure. Many investigators have been disappointed with the results of their training programs because they assumed that success would always follow the implementation of a well-conceived program. In some instances, they didn't recognize that their programs failed because the human-factor design was inappropriate for the operator. Poor lighting, improper labeling of displays, and other incompatible factors sometimes made it impossible for the trainee to perform the job no matter how well he was trained. In other instances, social pressure prevented the trainee from using what he had learned because he feared retribution from his fellow employees or his employer. The complexity of these interactions is illustrated by the *black box phenomenon*, which relates to the fact that society does not quickly accept innovative ideas, especially those that are not understood. For example, we might consider the concerns of parents who are witnesses to the new forms of social interactions present in classes utilizing computer-assisted instruction. They remember sitting at a desk listening to lectures; therefore, they find it difficult to accept a classroom where children move freely around the room communicating with each other, picking up supplies, and working on computer terminals.

Most of society's systems have been resistant to change. Early studies in the 1930s (Grayson, 1972) estimated that it would take 57 years for technical innovation to become diffused through school systems. A later study in 1946 revised the estimate to 25 years. Of course, new techniques must be carefully examined, but proven innovations should be accepted and utilized.

Developers of new training approaches cannot move from fad to fad and expect society to pick up the pieces. They must take the responsibility to create programs carefully and systematically and to evaluate their research. Then, perhaps, the public will be more receptive to these necessary changes. The purpose of this book is to provide some of the information necessary to begin the long process of systematic development and evaluation.

The next chapter presents an instructional model that outlines the various factors to be considered in the design of systematic programs. The description of these interacting components should clearly indicate that there is no easy technique or gadget that can be used in the development of well-conceived programs. Instructional materials will have a profound effect on everyone's life. Present knowledge should be utilized in the development of new programs, and, hopefully, these new efforts will contribute more information to our existing state of knowledge.

Chapter Two

A Systematic Approach to Training

INSTRUCTIONAL TECHNOLOGY

While the term *technology* commonly refers to the development of hardware, *instructional technology* refers to the systematic development of programs in training and education. The systems approach to instruction emphasizes the specification of instructional objectives, precisely controlled learning experiences to achieve these objectives, criteria for performance, and evaluative information. Other characteristics of instructional technology would include the following:

1. The systems approach uses feedback to continually modify instructional processes. From this perspective, training programs are never finished products; they are continually adaptive to information that indicates whether the program is meeting its stated objectives.

2. The instructional-systems approach recognizes the complex interaction among the components of the system. For example, one particular medium, like television, might be effective in achieving one set of objectives, while another medium might be preferable for a second set of objectives. Similar interactions could involve learning variables and specific individual characteristics of the learner. The systems view stresses a concern with the total system rather than with the objectives of any single component.

3. Systematic analysis provides a frame of reference for planning and for remaining on target. In this framework, a research approach is necessary to determine which programs are meeting their objectives.

4. The instructional-systems view is just one of a whole set of interacting systems. Training programs interact with and are directly affected by a larger system involving corporate policies (for example, selection and management philosophy). Similarly, educational programs like the *Sesame Street* TV program are affected by the social values of society.

The various components of the instructional-systems approach are not new. Evaluation was a byword years before systems approaches were in vogue. Thus, the systems approach cannot be considered a magic wand for all the problems that were unsolved before its inception. If the training designer were convinced that his program worked, a systems approach would be unlikely to convince him that his program required examination. However, the systems approach does provide a model that emphasizes important components and their interactions, and there is good evidence that this model is an important impetus for the establishment of objectives and evaluation procedures. As such, it is a useful tool that enables designers of instructional programs (as well as authors of books like this one) to examine the total training process.

Figure 2-1 presents one model of an instructional system. Most of the components of this model (for example, derive objectives and develop criteria) are considered important to any instructional system, although the degree of emphasis changes for different programs. The chapters that follow discuss material related to each of these model components. This chapter provides an overview of the complete system and the relationships among the components.

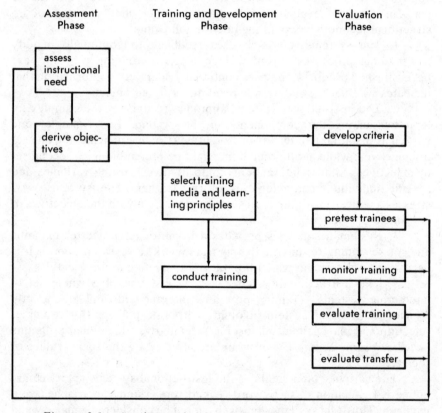

Figure 2-1. An instructional system. There are many other instructional-system models for military, business, and educational systems. Some of the components of this model were suggested by these other systems.

ASSESSMENT PHASE

ASSESSMENT OF INSTRUCTIONAL NEED

This phase of the instructional process provides the information necessary to design the entire program. An examination of the model indicates that the training and evaluation phases are dependent upon the input from the development phase. Unfortunately, many programs are doomed to failure because trainers are more interested in conducting the training program than in assessing the needs of their organizations. Educators have been seduced by programed instruction and industrial trainers by sensitivity training before they have determined the needs of their organization and the way the techniques will meet those needs. The need-assessment phase consists of organization analysis, task analysis, and person analysis.

Organizational analysis. Organizational analysis begins with an examination of the short- and long-term goals of the organization, as well as of the trends that are likely to affect these goals. Often, this analysis requires that upper-level management examine their own expectations concerning their training programs. Training designed to produce proficient sales personnel must be structured differently from programs to train sales personnel who are capable of moving up the corporate ladder to managerial positions. As school systems examine their goals, they recognize that their programs are designed for academically oriented students, and it becomes clearer why vocationally oriented students feel like second-class citizens. When organizational analysis is ignored, planning difficulties abound. Many corporations have spent considerable sums of money retraining personnel because the original training programs and decisions on performance capabilities were based on a system that soon became obsolete. Another aspect of the organizational analysis focuses on training programs and supporting systems—for example, selection, human-factors engineering, and work procedures. Particular operating problems might best be resolved by changes in selection standards or redesign of the work environment.

Task analysis. The second part of the need-assessment program is a careful analysis of the job to be performed by the trainees upon completion of the training program. The task analysis is usually divided into two separate procedures. The first step is a *job description* in behavioral terms. It is not a description of the worker. The narrative specifies the individual's duties and the special conditions under which the job is performed. The second procedure, most commonly referred to as *task specification*, further denotes all the tasks required on the job so that eventually the particular skills, knowledge, and attitudes required to perform the job will become clear. Thus, a brief description of the job of a gas-station attendant might state that the employee supplies cars and trucks with oil, water, air, and gas, changes oil, and lubricates autos and trucks. The task specification provides a list of tasks that includes: collects money, makes change, and provides directions to customers. These statements supply information about the behaviors required regardless of the individual performing the task.

Person analysis. The organizational analysis and task analysis provide a picture of the task and the organizational setting. One critical consideration is missing—that is, the behaviors required of the individual who will be in the training program. Job requirements must be translated into the human attributes necessary to perform the task. This is a difficult but necessary job that must be based on inferences drawn from the analysis of the organizational and task components. The determination of the learning environment and instructional media is directly dependent on the particular types of behavior necessary to perform the task.

Another facet of person analysis is the examination of the performance standards and the capabilities of the target population. It is important to determine which necessary behavioral characteristics have already been learned by the prospective trainees. Too many training programs are exercises in boredom, because they focus on skills already acquired. The determination of the target population is also necessary. Some training programs are designed for individuals who are already in the system, while others are for trainees who are not yet part of the organization. In any case, it is senseless to design the training environment without acknowledging the characteristics of the groups to be trained.

BEHAVIORAL OBJECTIVES

From information obtained in the assessment of instructional needs, a blueprint emerges that describes the behavioral objectives to be achieved by the trainee upon completion of the training program. These behavioral objectives provide the input for the design of the training program as well as for the measures of success (criteria) that will be used to judge the program's adequacy. The following is an example of one behavioral objective for our gas-station attendant.

By reading the gasoline pump, the employee can determine the cost of the product and provide correct change to the customer without resorting to paper and pencil for computations. Performance will be judged adequate if the employee:

1. always provides correct change for single items (for example, gas) up to the total cost of $10;

2. always provides correct change when the customer pays cash ranging up to $100;
3. successfully completes 20 trials by providing the correct change.

Similar statements could be designed for instructional systems in a variety of settings. For example, the following behavioral objective is appropriate to the solution of a particular servicing aspect of a Xerox machine (Cicero, 1973).

> Given a tool kit and a service manual, the technical representative will be able to adjust the registration (black line along paper edges) on a Xerox 2400 duplicator within 20 minutes according to the specifications stated in the manual [p. 15].

Well-written behavioral objectives specify what the trainee will be able to accomplish when he successfully completes the instructional program. They also indicate the conditions under which the performance must be maintained and the standards by which the trainee will be evaluated (Mager, 1962). Thus, objectives communicate the goals of the program to both the learner and the training designer. From these goals, the designers can determine the appropriate learning environment and the criteria for examining the achievement of the objectives.

Chapter 3 examines the assessment phase, which includes organizational, task, and person analyses as well as the development of behavioral objectives.

TRAINING-DEVELOPMENT PHASE

THE TRAINING ENVIRONMENT

Once the objectives have been specified, the next step is designing the environment to achieve the objectives. This is a delicate process that requires a blend of learning principles and media selection, based on the tasks that the trainee is eventually expected to perform. Gilbert (1960) described the temptations that often lead to a poor environment.

> If you don't have a gadget called a teaching machine, don't get one. Don't buy one; don't borrow one; don't steal one. If you have such a gadget, get rid of it. Don't give it away, for someone else might use it. This is a most practical rule, based on empirical facts from considerable observation. If you begin with a device of any kind, you will try to develop the teaching program to fit that device [p. 478].

Gilbert's remarks are equally appropriate for any device or method, from airline simulators to educational television.

From the assessment of instructional need, the skills and knowledge necessary to perform the job become apparent. Now the performance required must be matched with the characteristics of the various media. "The best available basis for the needed matching of media with objectives . . . is a rationale by which the kind of learning involved in each educational objective is stated in terms of the learning conditions required" (Briggs, Campeau, Gagné, May, 1967, p. 3). This is the same process that gardeners use when they choose a certain tool for a certain job. In the same manner, trainers choose airline simulators that create the characteristics of flight in order to teach pilots; however, the simulator is not usually considered appropriate to teach an adult a foreign language. The analysis of job tasks and performance requirements, and the matching of these behaviors to those produced by the training environment, is, at this point, as much an art as a technology. Although the preceding examples of pilot training and language learning are misleading because they represent obvious differences between tasks, there could be significant improvements in the design of training environments if more emphasis were placed on this matching of training environments to required behaviors.

LEARNING PRINCIPLES

In training environments, the instructional process involves the acquisition of skills, concepts, and attitudes that are transferred to a second setting (for example, on the job or in another classroom). The acquisition phase emphasizes learning a new task. Performance on the job and in the next environment focuses on transfer of learning to a second setting. Both theoretical and empirical sources of information are available to aid in the design of environments to improve worker performance. Unfortunately, a definitive list of principles from the learning environment that could be adapted to the training setting has not completely emerged. The learning literature is weak in describing the variables that affect man, especially those pertaining to various forms of skilled behavior. Basic research has centered on the more simple behaviors for which there are available laboratory tasks. However, learning theorists have progressed to a stage of development at which it is clear that the choice of the proper learning variable or level of that variable cannot be based on random option. Learning variables interact with the training environment. Thus, it is not appropriate to ignore the information from the learning literature or to accept a particular variable (for example, feedback or knowledge of results) as useful for all tasks. An illustration of these interactions is provided in a review by Gagné (1962), which suggests that feedback—one of the most sacred variables—is not effective in improving performance on some types of motor-skill training. This does not mean that feedback is not a potent variable for some tasks. It does, however, imply that there are complex interactions that will require consistent research before definitive answers can be found.

Chapters 6 and 7 discuss the learning principles that underlie training processes. The two chapters include discussions about the acquisition and transfer process, as well as about the learning variables that interact with the training environment. Chapters 8 through 10 examine some major training techniques prevalent in education and industry. These chapters discuss the objectives of a particular environment, provide illustrations, note the learning principles involved, and discuss the evaluation techniques that are employed to determine the value of these training procedures.

EVALUATION PHASE

Since the development of a training program involves an assessment of needs and a careful design of the training environment, the trainee is expected to perform his job at acceptable criterion levels. Unfortunately, this statement of faith displays a sense of self-confidence that is far from justified. Careful examinations of the instructional process disclose numerous pitfalls resulting from mistakes or deficiencies in our present state of knowledge. The assessment of the instructional need might have omitted important job components, or the job itself might have changed since the program was designed. In other instances, there are uncertainties about the most appropriate training technique to establish the required behaviors.

Unfortunately, few programs are evaluated. Indeed, the word *evaluation* raises all sorts of emotional defense reactions. In many cases, the difficulties seem related to a failure to understand that instructional programs are research efforts that must be massaged and treated until the required results are produced. An experience of mine may illuminate this problem.

A community agency was offering a program for previously unemployed individuals to help them obtain jobs. A colleague and I were invited to visit and offer suggestions about improvements to the program. Our questions about the success of the program were answered by reference to the excellent curricula and the high attendance rate of the participants. A frank discussion ensued related to the objectives of the program, with particular emphasis on the criteria being utilized to measure the adequacy of the program—that is, how successful the participants were in obtaining and holding jobs. This discussion led to the revelation that the success level simply was not known, because such data had never been collected. Of course, it was possible that the program was working successfully, but the information to make such a judgment was unavailable. Thus, there was no way to judge the effectiveness of the program or to provide information that could lead to improvements.

The evaluation process centers around two procedures —establishing measures of success (criteria) and using experimental and nonexperimental designs to determine what changes have occurred during the training and transfer process. The criteria are based on the behavioral objectives, which were determined by the assessment of instructional need. As standards of performance, these criteria should describe: the behavior required to demonstrate the trainee's skill, the conditions under which the trainee is to perform, and the lowest limit of acceptable performance (Mager, 1962).

Criteria must be established for both the evaluation of trainees at the conclusion of the training program and the evaluation of on-the-job performance (referred to as transfer evaluation in the model). In educational settings, the criteria must pertain to performance in later courses as well as to performance in the original environment where the instructional program was instituted. One classification (Kirkpatrick, 1959, 1960) for this purpose suggests that several different measures are necessary, including reaction of participants, learning of participants in training, behavior changes on the job, and final results of the total program. Other serious issues pertain to the integration of the large number of criteria often needed to evaluate a program and to the difficulties (for example, biased estimates of performance) associated with the collection of criterion information. These issues are discussed in Chapter 4.

In addition to criterion development, the evaluation phase must also focus on the necessary design to assess the training program. Some designs use proficiency measures before and after training (pre- and post-tests) as well as continual monitoring to be certain that the program is being implemented as originally designed. Other designs include control groups to determine if any of the training effects could be caused by factors that are unrelated to the training program. For instance, some startled trainers have discovered that their control group performed as well as trainees enrolled in an elaborately designed training program. This often occurred because the control groups could not be permitted to do the job without training. Thus, they either had on-the-job training or were instructed through a program that existed before the implementation of the new instructional system. Chapter 5 shows that the rigor of the design affects the quality and quantity of information available for evaluation.

There are situations in which it is not possible to use the most rigorous design because of cost or because of the particular setting. In these cases, it is important to use the best design available and to recognize those factors that affect the validity of the information.

A training program should be a closed-loop system in which the evaluation process provides for continual modification of the program. An open-loop system, in contrast, either does not have any feedback or is not responsive to such information. In order to develop training programs that achieve their purpose, it is necessary to obtain the evaluative information and to use this information for program modifications.

The information may become available at many different stages in the evaluation process. For example, an effective monitoring program might show that the training program has not been implemented as originally planned. In other instances, different conclusions might be supported by comparing data obtained from the training evaluation or transfer evaluation. If the participant performs well in training but poorly in the transfer setting, the adequacy of the entire program must be assessed. As indicated by the feedback loops in the model (refer again to Figure 2-1), the information derived from the evaluation process is utilized to reassess the instructional need, thus creating input for the next stage of development.

Even in those instances in which the training program achieves its stated objectives, there are continual developments that can affect the program, including the addition of new media techniques and changes in the characteristics of trainees. These changes often cause previous objectives to become obsolete. The development of training programs must be viewed as a continually evolving process.

One purpose of this overview of the instructional process is to provide the reader with a model that can be used to organize the material in the following chapters. We shall begin the more comprehensive discussion of the components of instructional programs in the next chapter by examining the first step—assessment of instructional need.

Chapter Three

The Assessment Phase

Training programs are designed to achieve goals that meet instructional needs. There is always the temptation to begin training without a thorough analysis of these needs; however, a re-examination of the instructional model introduced in Chapter 2 will emphasize the danger of beginning any program without a complete assessment of tasks, behaviors, and environment. The model shows that the objectives, criteria, and design of the program all stem from these analyses. Goals and objectives are the key steps in determining a training environment, and unless they are specified, there is no way to measure success. Machinists don't choose their tools before they examine their job; builders don't order their materials or plan their schedules until they have their blueprints (Mager, 1962). Why is it, then, that trainers and teachers argue over the merits of particular teaching aids without even specifying what the aid is to accomplish?

Perhaps the following example will illustrate the dangers of a "let's do it in our heads" approach. This outlandish memo was intercepted by a student as it made the rounds of the federal office buildings in Washington, D. C.

Memorandum for the Director of Personnel

Proposed: Allocation of a position titled:
Director of Personnel, Industrial and Agrarian Priorities
Description of duties and responsibilities.

(1) Without direct or intermediate supervision, and with a broad latitude for independent judgment and discretion, the incumbent directs, controls, and regulates the movement of the wealth of the American economy.

(2) The decisions of the incumbent are important since they affect with great finality the movement of agricultural products, forest products, minerals, manufacturers' goods, machine tools, construction equipment, military personnel, defense materials, raw materials and products, finished goods, semi-finished products, small business, large business, public utilities, and government agencies.

(3) In the effective implementation of these responsibilities the incumbent must exercise initiative, ingenuity, imagination, intelligence, industry, and discerning versatility. The incumbent must be able to deal effectively with all types of personalities and all levels of education from college president to industrial tycoon to truck driver. Above all, the

incumbent must possess decisiveness and the ability to implement motivation on the part of others consistent with the decision the incumbent had indicated. An erroneous judgment, or a failure to properly appraise the nuance of an unfolding development, could create a complete obfuscation of personnel and equipment generating an untold loss of mental equilibrium on the parts of innumerable personnel of American Industry who are responsible for the formulation of day-to-day policy and guidance implementation of the conveyances of transportation both intra-state and inter-state.

(4)   In short, on highway construction projects where only one-way traffic is possible, the incumbent waves a red flag and tells which car to go first.

Many analysts insist that job descriptions dictated by this "let's do it in our heads" approach or by a "we know it all already" approach can be just as far from practical application as our illustration. Certainly, it would be hard to design a training program based on the flowing descriptors in this document. Carefully described objectives that set forth required behavior are needed to plan effective training programs; moreover, there should be a direct relationship between these objectives and the type of instruction. A doctor diagnoses illness using X rays and laboratory tests before he attempts to prescribe a cure through medication, surgery, or other techniques. The training analyst also makes a diagnosis using organizational analysis, task analysis, and person analysis to determine if a cure is necessary and which cure is most likely to produce the desired result. While each of these analyses is discussed separately, they all interact with each other; for example, information for task analyses often results from organizational analyses.

ORGANIZATIONAL ANALYSIS

Data from an organizational analysis should be available before any instructional program is designed. This analysis consists of an examination of the entire organization, including its goals, resources, and the environment in which it exists. The statements, "start training at the top" and "I wish my boss had been exposed to this training program" indicate real differences between the approach or values of the training program and those of upper-level supervisors. However, to compare the goals of upper-level supervision with those of the training program after the instructional program has been instituted is too late. Training programs that are in conflict with the goals of the organization are likely to produce confused and dissatisfied workers. A study by Fleishman, Harris, and Burtt (1955) illustrates the difficulties that arise when the training program and the working environment promote different values. These researchers designed a training program to increase the amount of consider-ation (friendship, mutual trust) in foremen. The initial results, collected at the end of the training program, indicated success (as shown by the training scores). However, a follow-up of the program showed that the consideration factor was not maintained on the job. The researchers discovered that the day-to-day social climate, influenced by the super-visors, was not sympathetic to the new values. This study illustrates the need to examine transfer behavior (from the training program to the job) and the importance of experimental designs that enable researchers to specify effects. Just as important, however, the study provides an example of a training program that did not achieve the expected result because its goals and those of the organization were not consistent.

Some organizations have recognized that there are other goals and objectives besides those related to the behavior of a particular student or trainee. Lynton and Pareek (1967) describe a program that successfully trains foreign engineers but does not meet the goals of the organization.

> Perhaps the most striking example of the dangers of paying inadequate attention to this dimension is the cumulative residue in industrially ad-vanced countries of newly trained managerial and technical personnel from overseas. In the last 20 years, 30,000 foreign engineers alone have remained in the United States after completing their training. That they are able to make a living in competition with native Americans confirms their indi-vidual competence. Even if many stayed on because of attractive living standards, others did so because they were trained "out" of their country in the same way that school in a less developed country such as India seems to educate young people "out of their villages." The training qualified them for settings and conditions that do not (yet) exist at home. This may be good for the individual, i.e., good education. As training, that is, for achieving development in their home organizations, such overseas training has obviously been unrealistic and unsuitable [p. 32].[1]

When organizational goals are not considered in the implementation of training programs, objectives and criteria that ensue from the need-assessment process are not appraised. Later, the organizations are not able to specify their achievements, because they have not collected the necessary criterion information. Beginning in the 1960s, the federal government instituted social-action programs like Project Headstart, Title I, and Project Follow-Through, designed to help millions of children. Investigations of a number of innovative programs funded under the Title I program indicated that the achievement level of the students was not improved under the auspices of the various programs. This finding led to conclusions that Title I was not working. Cohen (1970)

[1]From Lynton, R. P., & Pareek, U. *Training for Development*. ©1967 by Richard D. Irwin, Inc. Reprinted by permission.

objected to this interpretation for two reasons. First, Title I was not created just to raise achievement scores. Intermediate measures, such as tests, do not necessarily reflect the program's ultimate criterion —improved social and economic conditions leading to adult success. A resolution of this issue must await complete data. (The difficulties associated with waiting for data from ultimate criteria will be discussed in Chapter 4.) Cohen's second point is more critical to the discussion of organizational objectives. He notes that the original Congressional Act had many goals besides improvements in individual performance. One such goal was related to the reduction of differences in per-pupil expenditure between the cities and their suburbs. Thus, the purpose here was:

> ...to deliver more resources to the poor, whether they are districts, schools, children or states. It is, therefore, essential to know how much more and for whom. It is important because citizens should know the extent to which official intentions have been realized, and because without much knowledge on that score it is hard to decide what more should be done [pp. 222–223].

Other programs fail because their instructional design is too narrow to reflect the organizational objectives. Students have been withdrawn from computer-assisted instruction programs because their parents were uncomfortable when they discovered that "Johnny" was not sitting quietly, as they had done, listening to a teacher's lecture. If one of the organizational goals was to achieve acceptance of this new medium in education, the training program should have provided for implementation of that objective. In this instance, orientation was important for the parent as well as the child. The components of organizational analysis are dependent on the type of program being instituted and the characteristics of the organization. However, there are certain general categories that can be suggested (McGehee & Thayer, 1961).

THE SPECIFICATION OF GOALS

This analysis should consider all long- and short-term goals of the organization—even those that do not seem related to the training program. In the training of foreign engineers in the United States discussed earlier, if the goals of the trainee's home country included the return of the trainee, the program was a failure. The program may have failed because there was no job commensurate with the skills developed, but the specification of the goals would have provided the first step toward a solution. It is a formidable task to require upper-level personnel to express their goals. However, such a requirement will ensure that important measures of success are not overlooked, and it will become clearer whether the program has achieved its goals.

RESOURCE ANALYSIS

It is difficult to establish working objectives without determining the human and physical resources that are available. This analysis should include a description of the layout of the establishment, the type of equipment available, and the financial resources. Even more important, human-resource needs must include manpower planning that projects future requirements. Too often, organizations respond to manpower needs only in a crisis situation—for example, when they realize they are losing 5 percent of their work force through retirement. Some academic institutions have sabbatical systems whereby faculty may take a six-month leave after six consecutive years of employment. These institutions often fail to realize that potentially 1/7 of their faculty will be on leave for six months each year. When undergraduate programs that specify the required number of course offerings are designed, this information is not taken into account. Thus, department chairmen often discover that they do not have the manpower to meet the needs of their programs. Table 3-1, designed by McGehee and Thayer (1961), presents some important manpower questions. Similar resource questions related

Table 3-1.   Data Required for Manpower Inventory

1. Number of employees in the job classification
2. Number of employees needed in the job classification
3. Age of each employee in the job classification
4. Level of skill required by the job of each employee
5. Level of knowledge required by the job of each employee
6. Attitude of each employee toward job and company
7. Level of job performance, quality and quantity, of each employee
8. Level of skills and knowledge of each employee for other jobs
9. Potential replacements for this job outside company
10. Potential replacements for this job within company
11. Training time required for potential replacements
12. Training time required for a novice
13. Rate of absenteeism from this job
14. Turnover in this job for specified period of time
15. Job specification for the job

From McGehee, W., & Thayer, P. W. *Training in Business and Industry.* ©1961 by John Wiley & Sons, Inc. Reproduced by permission.

to the cost of labor and materials, quality of goods and services, and distribution costs should also be considered.

INTERNAL AND EXTERNAL FACTORS

The design of instructional programs is affected by social, economic, and political factors, as well as by the policies of internal units. Inter-relationships of these variables should be carefully specified during organizational analysis. The importance of internal units in the organization is well illustrated by the role of the personnel department and its hiring philosophy (for example, attitudes toward minorities and handicapped workers). Schneider (1973) suggests that the philosophy of the organization, whether or not it is formally stated, has an impact on the way employees perceive their work conditions. Thus, the *organizational climate* for motivation, leadership, turnover, or accidents is utilized by employees as a frame of reference to judge their own behavior. In order to understand the behavior of individuals, we must gain some insight into the behavior of organizations.

Similarly, external factors, like public policy, interact with the functions of training and educational units. Certainly, the expectation that our judicial system will soon be hearing discrimination suits based on failures to provide training and promotional opportunities for minority-group members has important implications for future training programs. Berlak (1970) developed a model that specifies public-policy outcomes and program outcomes as two major facets of analysis. A profile by Byers (1970) (see Table 3-2) specifies some of the many factors that should be included in organizational analyses. While this profile is a good foundation, it is important to remember that each organization is different and that a thorough investigation requires a tailor-made profile.

TASK ANALYSIS

Just as an organizational analysis is necessary to determine the organizational objectives, a task analysis is necessary to determine the objectives related to performance standards for skills, knowledge, and attitudes needed to successfully perform the task. The task analysis consists of several components, each of which further delineates the performance required to succeed at the task. Thus, the analysis begins with a task description, followed by a detailed specification of behaviors necessary to perform each task.

Table 3-2.   Organizational Training-Needs Profile

Organization or Unit			*Fiscal Year*	
	Problems?[1]		*Training Indicated?*	
	Yes	*No*	*Yes*	*No*

I. MISSION STATEMENT—(From mission documents and supplemented through interviews with managers and supervisors.)

   A. _____

   B. _____

   C. _____
      etc.

II. UNITS AND SUBUNITS—(This section summarizes the objectives and functions of organizational components to define the role of components in carrying out mission. Information is obtained from unit documents and interviews.)

   A. _____

   1. Objectives: 2. Functions;
      (a)_____   (a)_____
      (b) _____   (b) _____
      (c)_____   (c)_____

   B. _____

   1. Objectives: 2. Functions:
      (a)_____   (a)_____
      (b) _____   (b) _____
      (c)_____   (c)_____

III. CONSTRAINTS—Factors inhibiting accomplishment of goals. (Describes environmental factors, limitations, and constraints, obtained from interviews with managers and employees. Includes motivational, attitudinal, and other environmental factors.)

---

[1]Major problems related to organizational missions can be explored on the basis of information from records, reports, and interviews. Indicate which missions are affected by identified problems.

From Byers, K. T. (Ed.) *Employee Training and Development in the Public Service.* Chicago: Public Personnel Association, 1970. Reproduced by permission of the International Personnel Management Association.

Table 3-2. Organizational Training-Needs Profile

Organization or Unit	Fiscal Year			
	Problems?[1]		Training Indicated?	
	Yes	No	Yes	No

IV. TRAINING-NEEDS SUMMARY—List of organizational training needs. (The basic data for listing of organizational needs will be gathered through analysis of information obtained from data sources listed in Part IV. Data should be put together in context of information outlined in Parts I, II, and III. The major purpose of this format is to relate requirements to mission and objectives of the organization.)

V. DATA SOURCES
   A. Records and report data
      1. Employee records
         (a) Turnover
         (b) Safety records
         (c) Absenteeism and sick leave
         (d) Complaints and grievances
         (e) Disciplinary action
      2. Production reports
         (a) Backlogs
         (b) Quality control—high cost, rejects, etc.
         (c) Bottlenecks
      3. Management audits
      4. Feedback from training evaluation
   B. Interview and/or questionnaire data
      1. Morale and interest data—questionnaire and employee interviews
      2. Interviews and observations
         (a) Managers:
            (1) What areas in your group's mission performance need most improvement?
            (2) How would you characterize the performance of the staff under your management?
            (3) What should your staff be able to perform better than they do at present? Why?
            (4) What are the effects on mission or objectives accomplishment?
            (5) What are the major constraints that inhibit mission accomplishment?
            (6) What do you consider your major personnel needs now and in the future?
            (7) Can you specify problems that can be alleviated by training and/or education?
            (8) What functions do you have the most difficulty keeping adequately staffed?
            (9) In what way might training aid in overcoming these problems?

Table 3-2. Organizational Training-Needs Profile

    (b) Supervisors:

        (1) What are the functions in which your group needs most to improve?

        (2) Which of these might be improved by additional training?

        (3) Which of these are most important to you in getting your job done?

        (4) Are there any of these functions on which you receive pressure from your boss?

        (5) What would you like your staff to be able to do that it is not now doing?

        (6) Have you made a task analysis of your group to identify training needs? If so, what major needs did it indicate?

        (7) What are you doing to help employees improve? What else needs to be done?

    (c) Employees:

        (1) What part of your job gives you the most difficulty?

        (2) Are there demands made on you that you don't feel qualified to fulfill?

        (3) What is being done to help you in improving your performance?

        (4) What additional training do you think would help you meet the demands made on you?

        (5) Are you generally satisfied with your job?

C. Observations

During interviews and visits to various parts of the organization, notes should be kept of your observations of activities in the organization. They might include the following:

    1. Communication failures (Do you get different stories in different parts of the organization?)

    2. Interpersonal conflicts

    3. Complaints

    4. Evidence of lack of concern about work

    5. Supervisory effectiveness

    6. Lack of sense of purpose

    7. Failure to understand mission and/or objectives

    8. Lack of interest or attention to work

    9. Poor management practices

TASK DESCRIPTION

The task description is a statement of the activities performed on the job and the conditions under which the job is performed. It is not a description of the worker. The statement should completely describe all the essential activities of the job, including the "worker's actions and the results accomplished; the machines, tools, equipment, and/or work aids used; materials, products, subject matter, or services involved; and the requirements made of the worker" *(Handbook for Analyzing Jobs, 1972,* p. 30). The statement includes the characteristics of the environment (for example, noise or extreme temperature variations) and any special features (for instance, stress) that further delineate the job. A short list of some of the environmental conditions that could potentially affect many jobs is presented in Table 3-3. As Thorndike (1949) summarizes, "A job description should provide an accurate picture of significant factors in the physical, social, and psychological environment in which the work must be carved out" (p. 15). The description should contain material about each of the kinds of activities involved, either in order of their importance or in the chronological order in which they are performed. Thus, the job description of a gas-station attendant might state: performs services

Table 3-3. Environmental Conditions and Physical Demands

Environmental conditions	*Physical demands*
1. Environment	1. Strength (lifting, carrying, pushing, and/or pulling)
Teamwork_____%	
Inside_____%	
Proximity_____%	Sedentary work
Outside_____%	Light work
Isolation_____%	Medium work
2. Extreme cold with or without temperature changes	Heavy work
3. Extreme heat with or without temperature changes	Very heavy work
4. Wet and/or humid	2. Climbing and/or balancing
5. Noise	3. Stooping, kneeling, crouching, and/or crawling
Estimated maximum number of decibels	
6. Vibration	4. Reaching, handling, fingering, and/or feeling
7. Hazards	
Mechanical	
Electrical	5. Talking and/or hearing
Burns	6. Seeing
Explosives	
Radiant Energy	
Other	
8. Atmospheric conditions	
Fumes	
Odors	
Dusts	
Mists	
Gases	
Poor Ventilation	
Other	

From Manpower Administration, U. S. Department of Labor. *Handbook for Analyzing Jobs.* Washington, D.C.: U. S. Government Printing Office, 1972.

requested by the customer; supplies cars or trucks with oil, water, air, and gas; changes oil and greases autos and trucks; sells and installs such accessories as windshield wipers, air filters, spark plugs, and tires; changes and repairs tires.

The Department of Labor *Handbook for Analyzing Jobs* (1972) suggests that the descriptions be terse, in the present tense, and started with an action verb. Each word should give necessary information, and words that have more than one meaning should be avoided.

TASK SPECIFICATION

The next phase in the task analysis is to specify the tasks performed, determine their importance, and detail the actual steps necessary to perform each important task. As an illustration (see Table 3-4) of this procedure, Mager and Beach (1967) offer a list of tasks performed by a service-station attendant. As indicated in the table, three criteria are used to measure their importance.

1. Frequency of performance.
2. Importance of the activity in terms of the potential consequences (negative or positive) of the worker's not being capable of performing the activity.
3. Learning difficulty.[2]

The determination of the importance of the task often requires the use of several different approaches to task analyses. Several of these procedures are discussed later in this chapter. Specifying the measures of importance is critical in the ultimate design of the training program. A task that is not very important, frequently performed, and easy to learn would not require the attention that should be given to an infrequent but critical task that is difficult to learn.

The final phase involves breaking down the components of the tasks into the steps involved in performance. Thus, the gas-station attendant would do the following to clean and replace spark plugs:

1. Note plug location relative to the cylinder; remove plug cover and leads.
2. Remove all spark plugs.
3. Identify the type of plugs.
4. Decide whether to clean, adjust, and/or replace plugs.

[2]This criterion should be used in conjunction with the analyses of worker characteristics and the determination of target-population attributes that are described later in this chapter.

5. Adjust and clean plugs, if appropriate.
6. Reinsert plugs in engine.
7. Connect ignition wire to appropriate plugs.
8. Check engine firing for maximum performance.
9. Clean and replace equipment and tools [Mager & Beach, 1967, p. 17].

From the specification of tasks and determination of their importance, it's possible to begin viewing behavioral objectives and criteria that will be used to measure performance. It should also be possible to start considering what types of behavior are necessary to perform the job and which instructional media and learning variables best support those types of behavior. While such analysis is clearly easier to complete on a service-station attendant than on a corporation executive, the proper design of a training program requires similar analyses for each case.

Table 3-4. Task-Listing Sheet

No.	Task	Frequency of performance	Importance	Learning difficulty
	Vocation:_____			
1.	Cleans or replaces spark plugs.			
2.	Adjusts and bleeds brakes.			
3.	Replaces wheel cylinders.			
4.	Inspects and flushes radiators.			
5.	Tests antifreeze.			
6.	Repairs tube or tubeless tires.			
7.	Rotates tires.			
8.	Lubricates vehicles.			
9.	Balances tires.			
10.	Replaces air cleaners.			
11.	Cleans or replaces gas filters.			
12.	Washes and waxes autos.			
13.	Sells auto accessories.			
14.	Replaces oil filters.			
15.	Checks oil, brake fluid, power steering, etc.			
16.	Washes windshields, replaces blades.			
17.	Fills gas tanks, radiators.			
18.	Keeps daily records of sales, inventory changes.			
19.	Orders supplies.			
20.	Opens and closes station.			

Adapted from Mager, R. F., & Beach, K. M. *Developing Vocational Instruction.* ©1967 by Fearon Publishers. Reprinted by permission of Fearon Publishers/Lear Siegler, Inc.

PERSON ANALYSIS

The organizational analysis and the task analysis provide a picture of the task and the environmental setting. However, the task analysis provides a specification of the required behaviors regardless of the individual performing the task. There remains a very critical part of the total process—the human being. Two populations must be considered; the first consists of those persons who are already performing the job, while the second involves those persons who will be trained. In some instances, these are the same individuals, but other cases involve new trainees. Since these new individuals differ from those already performing the task, it is necessary to examine this second population. This analysis includes: specification of human traits, performance analysis, and analysis of the target population.

SPECIFICATION OF HUMAN TRAITS

This part of the analysis is an interpretation of the job in terms of human attributes necessary for success. This difficult specification is based on inferences drawn from the analyses of organization and task components. Thorndike (1949) notes that a sound set of categories is required to describe the qualities of behavior. He suggests that these categories should have the following characteristics:

1. They should be comprehensive and systematic in covering the complete range of traits or qualities.
2. Whenever possible, they should be independent.
3. They should be psychologically meaningful in terms of behavior.
4. They should suggest testing operations for their measurement.

The *Handbook for Analyzing Jobs* (1972) includes a general list of worker traits, with a series of behavioral descriptions related to different levels of performance for each of the traits. These traits include categories based on training time, aptitudes, temperaments, and interests. As an example of these groupings, the aptitude and temperament categories are presented in Table 3-5. To illustrate the details of each aptitude, Table 3-6 presents the levels of numerical aptitude.

PERFORMANCE ANALYSIS

The purpose of this analysis is to determine whether a task performance is acceptable or substandard—if there is a significant difference between what the worker is able to do and what he is expected to do.

The results of this analysis, in conjunction with information from the trait analysis, provides important clues to the proper strategy for developing training programs. If the performance is substandard and the analyses

Table 3-5. Worker Traits

Aptitudes are the specific capacities or abilities required of an individual in order to facilitate the learning of some task or job duty. The following are the aptitudes included in this component:

G	Intelligence
V	Verbal
N	Numerical
S	Spatial
P	Form Perception
Q	Clerical Perception
K	Motor Coordination
F	Finger Dexterity
M	Manual Dexterity
E	Eye-Hand-Foot Coordination
C	Color Discrimination

Temperaments, for the purpose of collecting occupational data, are defined as "personal traits" required of a worker by specific job-worker situations. This component consists of the following 10 factors:

D-DCP	Adaptability to accepting responsibility for the direction, control, or planning of an activity.
F-FIF	Adaptability to situations involving the interpretation of feelings, ideas, or facts in terms of personal viewpoint.
I-INFLU	Adaptability to influencing people in their opinions, attitudes, or judgments about ideas or things.
J-SJC	Adaptability to making generalizations, evaluations, or decisions based on sensory or judgmental criteria.
M-MVC	Adaptability to making generalizations, evaluations, or decisions based on measurable or verifiable criteria.
P-DEPL	Adaptability to dealing with people beyond giving and receiving instructions.
R-REPCON	Adaptability to performing repetitive work, or to performing continuously the same work, according to set procedures, sequence, or pace.
S-PUS	Adaptability to performing under stress when confronted with emergency, critical, unusual, or dangerous situations or situations in which working speed and sustained attention are make-or-break aspects of the job.
T-STS	Adaptability to situations requiring the precise attainment of set limits, tolerances, or standards.
V-VARCH	Adaptability to performing a variety of duties, often changing from one task to another of a different nature without loss of efficiency or composure.

Adapted from Manpower Administration, U. S. Department of Labor. *Handbook for Analyzing Jobs*. Washington, D.C.: U. S. Government Printing Office, 1972.

Table 3-6.   Numerical Aptitude—The Ability to Perform Arithmetic
Operations Quickly and Accurately

Level 1

Conducts research in fundamental mathematics, in application of mathematics, and in application of mathematical techniques to science, management, and other fields; solves or directs solutions to problems in various fields by mathematical methods.

Tests hypotheses and alternative theories.

Level 2

Applies principle of accounting to install and maintain operation of general accounting system.

Applies numerical reasoning to design or modify systems to provide records of assets, liabilities, and financial transactions; applies arithmetic principles to prepare accounts, records, and reports based on them; audits contracts, orders, and vouchers; and prepares tax returns and other reports to government agencies.

Level 3

Sets up and operates X-ray unit to obtain photographs of internal structure of body, using standard formulas based on principles of algebra and geometry to compute amperage and voltage settings, exposure time, and distances of film from object and X-ray tube.

Level 4

Makes women's garments such as dresses, coats, and suits according to customer specifications and measurements.

Measures customer to determine dimensions of garment; adds and subtracts to adjust pattern to customer's dimensions.

From Manpower Administration, U. S. Department of Labor. *Handbook for Analyzing Jobs.* Washington, D.C.: U. S. Government Printing Office, 1972.

indicate that the personnel do not have the specific vocational preparation specified for the task in the trait analysis, the training personnel must decide whether training could provide a solution to the problem or whether new personnel are needed. These analyses and the decisions that come from them are complex, and they interact with the information obtained throughout the entire need-assessment program. Few, if any, organizations can afford instructional programs on every aspect of the task. Performance analysis is used to determine where the resources should be spent. The knowledge tests, performance reports, supervisory evaluation, and observation techniques (explained in the next section) utilized to obtain performance measures also help specify which objectives are important to achieve and what criteria or measures of success are useful in determining whether the objectives have been achieved.

ANALYSIS OF THE TARGET POPULATION

An instructional program must be based on the characteristics of the group that will be placed in the training environment. If the program is intended for those persons already on the job, the data from the performance analysis and the specification of traits provide the required information for an analysis of the target population. However, if the target population is a new group of students or employees, the analyses are incomplete. Observers have commented on the differences in values between those students entering school and work situations today and those of preceding generations. Such differences must be considered in program design. For example, particular errors may occur on a job due to difficulties related to mathematical ability. However, entering trainees may have the prerequisite skills in mathematics and not need emphasis in that particular area. Thus, the organization may need different training programs for persons presently employed and those coming to the job.

Unfortunately, it is difficult to analyze the incoming target population, because they are not presently employed. Potential solutions might consist of examining employees who have recently been hired or consulting with similar organizations that have recently hired trainees. The latter procedure must be performed carefully, because small differences between firms can radically change the characteristics of the entering population. Thus, two corporations or two schools with the same characteristics but from differing locales (for example, rural versus urban) may draw significantly different employees. It is necessary to match the characteristics of the target population to the traits required for successful performance. Some of the methods and techniques that can be utilized are described in the following section.

GATHERING TASK INFORMATION

SOURCES OF TASK INFORMATION

A number of available sources contain information that is potentially useful in need-assessment analyses. The material is organized into two major categories—previous analyses of tasks and documentary materials.

Previous analyses of tasks. Information on any series of tasks is usually available from government sources. For industrial tasks, the Manpower Administration (U. S. Department of Labor) has extensive materials related to worker functions, task requirements, and worker traits, as well as information related to the proper procedures for performing task analyses. The *Dictionary of Occupational Titles* (1965) presents brief analyses of job tasks and worker requirements for a large number of different occupations. Similar information is available in military and educational technical reports through the National Technical Information Service (for military documents) and the ERIC Clearinghouse on Educational Media and Technology (for educational documents).

Documentary materials. There is also a substantial literature describing training programs and other aspects of organizations. It includes catalogs and descriptions prepared by the organization itself; technical literature prepared by trade associations, labor unions, and professional societies; pamphlets and books prepared by federal, state, and municipal departments in the appropriate field (health, education, or labor); and books and pamphlets generally related to the subject.

Previous task analyses and documentary materials provide useful introductions to tasks being investigated. However, they are not substitutes for the extensive analysis that must be performed each time a training program is designed. Although the analysis of previous tasks describes the tasks as they are generally found in any setting, the literature search is not likely to produce the particular task, conditions, and target population required by the training analyst. In many cases, careful examination shows that only the names of the task or the job are the same. Even if the tasks are similar, organizational characteristics may demand a completely different program. These problems are often compounded in the examination of documentary material in which particular viewpoints may affect the report. Documents published by different organizations (for example, labor or management) may make the same job sound very different. Thus, these sources provide information that is useful in the initial examination of the task, but the final analysis must be performed on the organization and task of immediate concern.

METHODS OF COLLECTING TASK INFORMATION

There are many different methods for collecting information about the task and the organization. The purpose of these methods is to provide valid and reliable information; therefore, it is important to make sure an individual method does not bias the quality of the information. Unfortunately, this is more easily said than done. Each method has unique characteristics that can affect both the kinds and the quality of information obtained. An interview is dependent on the interviewer's skills and biases, while a mail questionnaire is subject to the sampling biases that occur when a substantial number of participants do not return the survey. It is important to be aware of these difficulties and to carefully design methodology to avoid potential sources of biased information. Morsh (1964) has described some of these methods and indicated their advantages and disadvantages. Most analyses utilize several of these techniques.

Questionnaire method. The questionnaire method is most often used to obtain occupational information through a mail survey. The respondent provides identifying data and describes his position in his own words. This method can be difficult for individuals who are not used to writing or preparing reports. Thus, supervisory personnel may have little difficulty with the technique, but it may be especially burdensome for some production and maintenance workers. Organizing large amounts of handwritten information presents a difficult problem for the job analyst. Also, this method depends on the recall of the participants, which may lead to incomplete descriptions of the job. However, a careful analysis of these open-ended responses often provides the initial information necessary for some of the other analysis techniques.

Checklist method. With this technique, the respondent chooses the tasks he performs from a list of tasks provided by the analyst. This method requires extensive preliminary work (often involving other methods such as questionnaires or interviews) to identify the potential list of tasks. The checklist method, requiring recognition rather than recall, is easier for the respondent and is not as time consuming as the questionnaire method. However, the information obtained from this method is limited, especially in relation to the sequencing of tasks, relationships of different tasks, and interactions between employees and machines. These data are easily adaptable to machine tabulation.

Individual interview. The individual interview is usually based on a standardized format that has been designed on the basis of previously collected job information. The analyst selects "representative" individuals and interviews them away from the job. The results are then combined to provide a composite picture of the task. This method is especially time consuming and dependent on the recall of the interviewee and the skill of the interviewer; thus, the method is not practical for obtaining information from large samples. However, the interview is a useful technique for small samples and for jobs on which it is difficult to obtain information by direct observation (for example, upper-level managerial personnel). In some cases, a group interview is used to offset the costs of the single-interview method and to increase sample size. The interviewer guides the group into a discussion of their work activities utilizing a standardized format designed from other job-information sources. This technique requires a skilled interviewer who is trained to handle the interpersonal dynamics of a group. At the conclusion of the group interview, the interviewer combines the various sources of information into a composite analysis.

Observation interview. In observation interviews, the analyst combines interview and observation techniques. He observes the worker performing the task and then questions him. If the participants and the tasks are representative, this particular technique avoids the recall problems associated with the interviewing technique. The disadvantages are that the method interferes with normal work activities and is slow and costly. Thus, it is not practical for the collection of large amounts of data.

Work-participation method. The work-participation method permits the analyst to gain first-hand experiences by performing the job. The technique has clear advantages when the job is relatively simple or easily learned. However, for any job that is highly technical or complex, the method is impractical, time consuming, and expensive. Even in those cases in which the job can be performed by the analyst, this method will not suffice by itself because there are many factors about the work situation (for example, organizational characteristics and changing tasks) that will not become apparent in a short trial period.

Technical-conference method. In this method, experts chosen for their knowledge and experience work as a group to determine the activities needed for the task. These experts are usually supervisors who have previously performed the jobs and were promoted because of their skill; thus, their knowledge is a valuable resource. However, the findings must be tempered by the fact that these experts no longer perform the jobs and may present a misleading analysis of the skill components necessary to perform the job.

Diary method. This method requires the participants to maintain logs of their daily activities according to a predetermined schedule. The tasks are often precoded to facilitate statistical organization. Although this method readily establishes the frequency of task performance, it does not necessarily establish the importance of the various components and in some cases can be time consuming and disruptive. One U.S. government agency asked its members to clock their work at 12-minute intervals and provided them with a dictionary of 125 code numbers to describe their tasks. At the suggestion of the employees, this study was abruptly terminated.

Critical-incident method. This method (Flanagan, 1954) consists of direct observation of behavior that might lead to particularly excellent or unsatisfactory performance. These observations provide behavioral information about the critical components of the task that often lead to success or failure. Thus, this analysis is often useful in determining which components of a training program require extensive attention. However, the critical-incident method does not include a complete description of all of the components of the job or the interactive sequences necessary in performing the task.

DERIVATION OF OBJECTIVES

The organizational analyses, task analyses, and person analyses provide the information necessary for the assessment of instructional need. This assessment makes it possible to specify the objectives of the training program. The objectives provide direct input for the design of the training program and help specify the criterion measures that will be used to evaluate the performance of the trainee at the end of the training program and in the transfer setting (on the job, in the next program, and so on). The assessment of instructional need tells the trainer where to begin, and the specification of the objectives tells him the completion point of the program.

Mager and Beach (1967) describe the characteristics of objectives in the following manner:

1. An objective is a statement about a student; it is not a text or teacher.
2. The objective refers to the behavior of the student. It not only specifies what he is to know but also defines *knowing* by indicating how the student will demonstrate his knowledge.
3. An objective is stated in terms of terminal performance. Thus, it is a description of the end product, not the method for reaching the end product.
4. An objective describes the conditions under which the student will perform. Thus, if the student is expected to perform with the use of a training aid (for example, a calculator), the objective specifies its use.
5. An instructional objective indicates the level of performance necessary to achieve that objective. Thus, statements related to the number of errors permitted and the speed of performance are included as part of the objective.

Sound objectives communicate to the learner what he is expected to be able to do when he finishes the program. Some trainers have suggested (not without a note of sarcasm) that if the instructor communicated these objectives, the success of the program would be assured. The difficulties in specifying behavioral objectives are well documented by Mager's (1962) example of the objective *to appreciate music*. A close examination of this objective indicates that it does not state what the learner is doing when he appreciates music and does not indicate the desired terminal behavior or the conditions under which the behavior will be performed. As a matter of fact, the objective, as stated, would permit any of the following behaviors to be considered as meeting the goal, although it is doubtful that most instructors would be willing to assign passing grades on that basis.

1. The learner sighs in ecstasy when listening to Bach.
2. The learner buys a hi-fi system and $500 worth of records.
3. The learner correctly answers 95 multiple-choice questions on the history of music.
4. The learner writes an eloquent essay on the meanings of 37 operas.
5. The learner says "Oh, man, this is the most. It's just too much" [Mager, 1962, p. 15].

Certainly, the design of the training program should be dependent on the definition of *appreciation of music*. The following example specifies the educational intent; communicates to the learner what he will be doing; and describes the terminal behavior, conditions, and criteria of successful performance.

The student must be able to write a musical composition with a single tonal base. The composition must be at least 16 bars in length and contain at least 24 notes. The student must demonstrate his understanding of the rules of good composition by applying at least three of them in the development of his score. The student is to complete his composition within four hours [Mager, 1962, p. 50].

Similar objectives can be written for all the important aspects of a training program. In many cases, the trainer will discover that the objectives of the training program are not exactly the same as those for successful job performance. When the job is complex, the trainee cannot be expected to exhibit the same behavior as persons who have been performing the task for many years. Thus, one set of objectives and criteria is designed for the initial training analyses, and other objectives and criteria are designed to be used at a later time on the job. These issues are discussed further in the next chapter, on criterion development. However, the specification of these different objectives will, in itself, clear up many misunderstandings about trainee requirements upon completion of the program.

Thus far, the objectives discussed have been related to specific aspects of trainee behavior. They represent only one level of analysis. There are also objectives that are concerned with the performance of a system as a whole, rather than behaviors of individual trainees. Some observers (Cogan, 1971) have suggested that two organizational objectives of educational systems should be to individualize instruction and to prevent "dropouts." These objectives must also be specified through behavioral outcomes, performance conditions, and criteria of successful performance. Although this is difficult, the determination of the achievement of policy and organizational objectives is dependent on these specifications.

One specification program, typically called "management by objectives" (MBO), has been recognized by industry for a number of years. Strauss (1972, p. 11) states that:

> MBO (at least when it works as it should) requires management to define exactly what it wants to accomplish and to specify all important objectives, especially those commonly ignored. It reduces the emphasis on short-run profits, increases the number of managerial goals and forces the explicit consideration of exactly what steps must be taken if these goals are to be fulfilled. In this way, it helps subordinates learn what is required of them, thus reducing their need for guesswork. As a result, it makes decision-making more rational, for both boss and subordinate. In sum, MBO can become a coordinated process of planning which involves every management level in determining both the goals that it will meet and the means by which they are to be met.

There are several difficulties associated with the MBO process. One group of conflicts is related to the procedures used in implementing the system. There are complaints about the amount of paperwork required, as well as about the great flourish with which objectives and goals are announced—only to be forgotten six months later. These complaints appear to be related to the failure to properly implement the program. Another more serious criticism is related to who designs the objectives and how the objectives are used—procedures that often lead to conflict between personal and corporate goals. Often the information gathered is used simply to exercise a greater degree of control over the organization. These controversies pertain to participative action, in which all individuals have an opportunity to help in the determination of goals and objectives. Whether the system is participative or not, goals and objectives are ultimately designed by someone at the policy level. It is as important to determine the success of the policies as it is to determine the success of an individual worker performing his task. Certainly, the specification of the goals provides information that can also lead to changes in the objectives as well as measures of their achievement.

CONCLUDING STATEMENTS

The purpose of need-assessment analyses is to obtain the information that is necessary to design the training environment and evaluate the training program. At the conclusion of the planning phase, the performance objectives should be apparent. As mentioned before, "The best available basis for the needed matching of media with objectives is a rationale by which the kind of learning involved in each educational objective is stated in terms of the learning conditions required'' (Briggs, Campeau, Gagné, & May, 1967, p. 3). The process of going from task analysis to systematic identification of the behaviors to be learned remains one of the most difficult phases in the design of training programs. Some of the techniques being used in this process will be discussed in Chapter 6.

The other aspect of our training program that follows from the analyses discussed in this chapter is the evaluation process. The criteria and methods for evaluating programs cannot be conveniently added onto the end of the project without disrupting the training program. In addition, some of the data must be collected before and during the training program, as well as some time after the student has completed training. The evaluation design is an integral part of the entire program but is often a neglected function. The next two chapters discuss the evaluation phase.

Chapter Four

The Criterion Choices: Introduction to Evaluation

Evaluation consists of procedures designed to systematically collect the descriptive and judgmental information necessary to make effective training and educational decisions. Decision makers are concerned with questions related to the selection, adoption, and value of various training activities. The objectives of instructional programs reflect many different types of goals, ranging from student progress to organizational goals; thus, the evaluation must examine the total complexity of the program. Evaluations began, in school systems, as nothing more than the administration and interpretation of achievement tests (Stake, 1967). Evaluations now involve thorough examinations of objectives related to developing attitudes, motivations, as well as knowledge, and skills.

There have been many innovations in instructional processes in the past decade, ranging from programed instruction to training programs for the hard-core unemployed. Little is to be gained from these programs unless there are evaluative data to tell the program directors how to make effective revisions.

> Folklore is not a sufficient repository. In our data banks we should document the causes and effects, the congruence of intent and accomplishment, and the panorama of judgments of those concerned. Such records should be kept to promote educational action, not obstruct it. The countenance of evaluation should be one of data gathering that leads to decision making, not to trouble making [Stake, 1967, p. 539].

While the intentions of those concerned with evaluation are admirable, the effort devoted to evaluations and the state of evaluation methodology leave much to be desired. A review by French in 1953 indicated that only 1 company in 40 made any scientific evaluation of supervisory training programs, and an examination of 476 studies by Castle in 1952 failed to find any research that examined both pretraining and on-the-job performance. During the next 20 years, rhetoric concerning the necessity for evaluation increased, no doubt spurred by increasing sums of money being spent on federally sponsored programs in schools and industry. However, in 1961, Shafer found that most companies spent less than 5 percent of their time and training budgets on evaluation. In

1970, Cohen, commenting on evaluation reports of the federally financed school program known as Title I, stated that the national evaluations of these programs were little more than annual reports—not evaluations. Similar commentary on the lack of sound empirical data for managerial training programs is also available (Campbell, Dunnette, Lawler, & Weick, 1970).

While there are a variety of reasons for the lack of adequate evaluation, there is remarkable consistency in the views of researchers in different organizational settings—that is, schools, government training laboratories, military establishments, and private industry. These views include the following:

1. There has been considerable difficulty in finding acceptable criteria (MacKinney, 1957). This problem becomes more serious as researchers attempt to measure the achievement of organizational objectives. However, as we shall see, the measurement of behavior in any setting is difficult.
2. There is a serious lack of personnel trained in the methodology of evaluation. Guba (1969, p. 37) quotes a director of a research and development center.

   We are having trouble finding people... with sufficient sophistication so that they can help with technical problems. We need an evaluator interested in measuring change, who is statistically competent and has all the characteristics of a stereotype methodologist in evaluation but who has a willingness to look at new kinds of problems.
3. Wallace and Twichell (1953) have lamented the difficulties in establishing meaningful relationships in industrial settings. Guba (1969) noted that school evaluation studies are frequently incapable of securing any significant information. Studies of different alternatives most often find no statistically significant differences, and, even when differences are established, researchers are uncertain about the variables that determine the effect.
4. The personnel responsible for training and educational research are often not responsive to the need for evaluation or are fearful of the entire process. In some cases, management is reluctant to expend effort to evaluate a program that it considers to be more than adequate (Wallace & Twichell, 1953). In other cases, the training or educational director is afraid of evaluation because, if his program were found to need modification, it might jeopardize the continuance of the program as well as his position as director (Howell & Goldstein, 1971). The latter view assumes that training programs that are not immediately successful will be dissolved; the theory that training programs should be continually evaluated in order to modify and improve the product is not recognized.

The criterion problem and the establishment of evaluation methodology constitute the core of the dilemma. An evaluation study will not solve all training problems, but it is an important step forward. In many instances, the utilization of a simple procedure—for example, giving participants a pretest that can be used in later comparisons—will dramatically improve the validity of the obtained information. The complexities of evaluation should not be underestimated; however, the most serious problem has been the failure to even consider examining the instructional methods. The following material focuses on the various components of evaluation. This chapter discusses the criteria, and the following chapter presents methods and designs of evaluation approaches. Clearly, there are numerous interactions between the two topics; thus, the chapters should be treated not as separate entities but as two parts of the same evaluation process.

INTRODUCTION TO CRITERION DEVELOPMENT

Industrial psychologists concerned with the selection of personnel have developed programs based on instruments (for example, paper-and-pencil tests) that predict a standard of success or criterion of the job. The last decade of research has attempted to resolve questions related to these measures of success. Unfortunately, designers of training and educational programs are still faced with the same questions—that is, the choice of measures against which they can determine the viability of their program. In some cases, the training program is the instrument utilized to predict job success. In this situation, the evaluator attempts to establish the relationship between performance in the training program and performance on the job. In a different model, the training evaluator attempts to determine if persons undergoing one form of training perform better on the job than those persons who have either been trained in another program or simply been placed on the job. In all of these situations, the measures of success are standards by which the value of the program can be judged. The most carefully designed study, employing all the sophisticated methodology that can be mustered, will stand or fall on the basis of the adequacy of the criteria chosen.

In Chapter 3, we traced the development of objectives through the techniques of organizational, task, and person analyses. These objectives stated the terminal behavior, the conditions under which the terminal behavior is expected, and the standard below which the performance is unacceptable. In other words, good instructional objectives clearly state the criteria by which the student is judged. At this point, it would be tempting to declare the problem solved and proceed to the next chapter. Unfortunately, that is not possible. First, the choice of the criteria is complex. Finding adequate measures of the success of a training program begins with the specification of the objectives. Just because there is a measure of success does not mean that it is reliable or free from bias. It is one matter to measure success in a training program that has a degree of control, but quite another to measure success on the job, where the environment often makes the collection of valid criteria a demanding chore. There is also the question of the relationship between the measures chosen in training and performance on the job. Wallace (1965) described life-insurance programs in which it was possible to predict training-school grades with considerable accuracy; however, the scores had no relation to selling performance on the job.

In addition, there is little doubt that the complex goals represented by organizational objectives are even more difficult to measure. Guion (1961) describes with pointed humor the whole sequence of criterion selection. The following is an abbreviated version.

1. The psychologist has a hunch (or insight) that a problem exists and that he can help solve it.
2. He reads a vague, ambiguous description of the job.
3. From these faint stimuli, he formulates a fuzzy concept of an ultimate criterion.
4. He formulates a combination of measures that will give him a satisfactory composite for the criterion he desires.
5. He judges the relevance of this measure—that is, the extent to which it is neither deficient nor contaminated.
6. He then finds that the data required for his carefully built composite are not available in the company files, and there is no immediate prospect of having such records reliably kept.
7. Therefore, he selects the *best available criterion*.

Similar difficulties plague all forms of organizational and educational research. Stake (1967) suggests that the more formal evaluations specify few criteria, with little concern for standards of acceptability. He notes that even the best-trained evaluators have used a microscope rather than a panoramic viewfinder in their examination of instructional methods. Stake laments the difficulty of finding adequate criteria to study the total complexity of the educational goals. However, he is also suffering from the evaluator's decision to choose the most available criterion. Wherry (1957) further warns us that this choice is often dictated by measurement considerations that are no more valid than an arbitrary choice. He notes that selecting a criterion just because it can be measured says "We don't know what we are doing, but we are doing it very carefully, and hope you are pleased with our unintelligent diligence" (pp. 1-2). Little understanding can be gained by carefully measuring the wrong thing. Thus, these researchers suggest that criteria must also be carefully evaluated so that a good indicant of the impact of our instructional program may be obtained. The following section considers these issues of criterion evaluation.

THE EVALUATION OF CRITERIA

CRITERION RELEVANCY

The closer the relationship between the criterion measure and the true criterion, the more relevant the criterion measure (Nagle, 1953). Relevancy can then be thought of as a relationship between the operational measures (criteria) and the true values that will hopefully be represented. The true values are sometimes referred to as ultimate criteria, because they represent a complete array of the aspects that determine success. In a sense, they are the final goals of a training or educational program. The psychologist uses true values as his standards when he attempts to determine the relevance of the actual criteria that he is required to use. Thus, ultimate success of a graduate student is not indicated by whether he finishes his Ph.D. but by whether he achieves success in his given field. However, the criteria chosen to evaluate the adequacy of graduate instructional methods usually involve the achievement of certain grades or the Ph.D. degree. These criteria are chosen because it is difficult to agree on measures of ultimate success and because many programs cannot afford to wait for these ultimate measures.

The chosen criteria are judged relevant to the degree that the components (knowledge, skills, attitudes) required to succeed in the training program are the same as those required to succeed at the ultimate task (Thorndike, 1949). It is important to recognize that evaluators often choose a criterion because of its immediate availability, so it must be examined for relevance, the fundamental requirement that transcends all other considerations related to criterion development. Accurate job analysis and the ensuing behavioral objectives suggest more clearly the actual criteria to be employed in achieving the behavioral objectives. This relationship between the objectives and the criteria is an exercise in determining relevance.

Figure 4-1 presents the relationship between the ultimate and actual criteria, as well as some of the variables that affect criterion relevancy. The term *criteria* refers to the many measures of success that must be utilized to evaluate instructional programs and to the numerous objectives of training programs, from individual achievement to organizational goals. The degree of overlap between the actual and ultimate criteria determines the degree of relevance. As previously mentioned, the difficulties in obtaining measures of ultimate criteria make empirical estimates of relevance difficult to achieve. However, it is possible to work toward the achievement of more relevant criteria by reducing the other two components—criterion deficiency and criterion contamination.

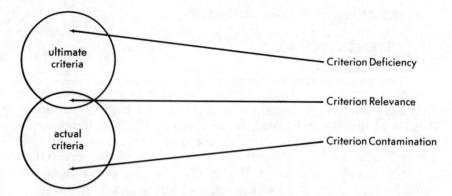

Figure 4-1. The constructs of deficiency, relevance, and contamination. Adapted from *Industrial Psychology: Its Theoretical and Social Foundations,* Rev. ed. by Milton L. Blum & James C. Naylor. ©1968 by Harper & Row, Publishers, Inc. Used by permission.

CRITERION DEFICIENCY

Criterion deficiency is the degree to which there are components in the ultimate criteria that are not present in the actual criteria. The more learned through need assessment about the components that determine ultimate success, the easier it will be to identify more immediate criteria that provide for the measurement of all the required behaviors. Sometimes, ultimate criteria are also known as "theoretical criteria," because their measurement can never be fully achieved. This term is not often used because the attitudes it fosters are detrimental to efforts necessary to develop training criteria at all levels. Thus, training analysts do not develop complete criteria for entry-level positions, because it is too difficult to discover what determines success, even in the first six months on the job. The evaluator then discovers that individuals who perform extremely well on their training criteria perform poorly on the job, and he shakes his head in amazement. In some of these cases, the training criteria are deficient, and since the criteria stem from objectives that determine the training program, the program itself is also likely to be deficient.

The only solution is to determine, through the methodology of need assessment, the most appropriate multiple criteria to measure success. The complexity of these on-the-job criteria should be represented in those criteria chosen to judge the initial success of individuals in the training program while recognizing that there will be many instances in which the trainee will not be able to perform with the same skill as an experienced worker. Thus, relevance for a training program consists of two sets of circles—one describing the relationship between the actual job criteria and the ultimate criteria and the second describing the relationship between the training criteria and the ultimate criteria.

The issues related to deficient criteria are just as important to the measurement of organizational objectives—adding a degree of complexity that some evaluators would prefer to avoid. It is one matter to specify all the components that determine the success of an individual on required tasks, but it is quite another matter to insist that all the components that determine the success of an entire training program also be specified in criteria that can be measured and evaluated. However, it should be clear that criteria representing organizational objectives provide information that is critical for the feedback and decision processes.

CRITERION CONTAMINATION

Figure 4-1 presents a third construct—criterion contamination. This construct pertains to extraneous elements present in the actual criteria that are not part of the ultimate criteria. The existence of these elements that contaminate the criteria can lead to incorrect conclusions regarding the validity of the training program. For example, a supervisor may give better work stations to those individuals who have participated in the new training program because they are "better equipped" to handle the assignment than those persons who have simply been placed on the job. In this case, the training program may demonstrate its validity because the participants have better assignments, but it is just as easy to describe situations in which the opposite phenomenon occurs. Bellows (1941) described some of the factors that contribute to criterion contamination. The following presentation adapts his concepts, as well as Blum and Naylor's approach (1968), to issues concerning instructional procedures.

Opportunity bias. This type of bias refers to situations in which individuals have differing opportunities for success, unrelated to the skills developed through their training program. The previous illustration concerning work assignments is an example of opportunity bias. In other instances, educators may provide more or less opportunity for students who have previously been instructed through innovative media like computer-assisted instruction (CAI). Thus, data may indicate that students from a CAI program do not perform well in a second course utilizing more traditional techniques because the educator does not provide the same opportunities for them as for students educated traditionally. On the other hand, some educators have extraordinary faith in media like CAI and do not offer equal remedial help to more traditionally trained students. Any approach that treats individuals from various instructional conditions differentially will contaminate the criteria and lead to improper evaluation of the program. A study by Dorcus in 1940 demonstrated that criteria-contamination problems were a serious concern even in the relatively simple job of door-to-door sales of bakery products. In order to reduce opportunity bias, Dorcus constructed economic maps of the city based on rental values of homes so that he could have an estimate of the effect of sales territory on sales volume. Another investigation by Ohmann (1941) underscores the large number of variables that could lead to opportunity bias. In order to establish territories with equal potential for each salesman of construction materials, Ohmann considered the following factors:

1. sales volume for 1937
2. average number of calls per day
3. number of years worked at Tremco
4. salesman's net commission earnings for 1937
5. average size of order
6. average number of new accounts per month
7. average sales volume per year for length of time employed
8. sales volume for the first six months on the job
9. trend of sales volume over a period of years
10. amount of allowances to customers
11. amount of returned merchandise
12. classes of trade called on
13. classes of products sold [p. 19].

Similar factors must be considered for any environment in which there is variability in the transfer setting.

Group-characteristic bias. Another type of bias can result from the characteristics of the group in the transfer setting. In some instances, the trainee is not permitted to demonstrate the skills he has gained from the training program because of informal or formal regulations that do not permit him to work at capacity levels. Thus, experienced personnel often socially ostracize workers who produce at too rapid a rate, or regulations often restrict the use of particular equipment that might raise the level of production.

Knowledge of training performance. The contamination arises here because the person responsible for judging the capabilities of the trainee allows his knowledge of the training performance of the individual to bias his judgment of the individual's capabilities in the transfer setting—that is, on the job or in the next class. Thus, individuals who performed well in the training setting would be evaluated correspondingly well on the job. This problem becomes particularly serious when more subjective measures of performance, like rating scales, are used to determine capabilities.

It is important to be continually aware of the potential danger of criterion contamination because, in many instances, control is possible. For example, training designers should keep the scores of trainees confidential and should control for factors like trainee work assignments. There are other factors that interrelate with the criteria measures, including the experimental design utilized in the evaluation. These issues will be examined in the next chapter.

CRITERION RELIABILITY

Reliability refers to the consistency of the criteria measures. If the criteria are ratings of performance, and there is little agreement between two raters, then there is low reliability. Correspondingly, consistently different performance scores by the same individual at different times also reflect low consistency and thus low reliability. Reliability is a necessary condition for stable criteria measures, but it is important to recognize that it will not replace the need for relevant criteria. Because reliability can be measured statistically, some evaluators emphasize it rather than relevance, but, as mentioned earlier there is no utility in carefully measuring the wrong indicant of success.

Nagle (1953) suggests that the instability of a given activity is the main limitation in achieving reliable criteria. He lists the following factors that affect the reliability of measures.

1. the size of the sample of performance
2. the range of ability among the subjects
3. ambiguity of instructions
4. variation in conditions during measurement periods
5. the amount of aid provided by instruments [p. 277].

In addition, Nagle lists sources of unreliability that are peculiar to those situations in which ratings are used as criteria.

1. the competency of the judges
2. the simplicity of the behavior
3. the degree to which the behavior is overt
4. the opportunity to observe
5. the degree to which the rating task is defined [p. 277].

OTHER CONSIDERATIONS

In addition to relevancy and reliability, there are several other considerations in the evaluation of criteria. These include acceptability to the organization, cost, and realistic measures. These factors cannot replace relevancy and reliability; they are of consequence only after the relevancy and reliability have been determined. If these latter factors have been established, the training analyst knows he is convincing the organization to accept criteria that may be costly but that are the most valid measures to judge the adequacy of the training program.

THE MANY DIMENSIONS OF CRITERIA

There are few, if any, single measures that can adequately reflect the complexity of most training programs and transfer performance. When all the facets of man's behavior are considered, including satisfaction, motivation, and achievement, it is clear that there is a series of ultimate criteria from which actual criteria that are relevant and reliable must be obtained. A study by O'Leary (1972) further illustrates the importance of considering the many different dimensions of the criteria. She utilized a program of role-playing and group-problem-solving sessions with hard-core unemployed women. At the conclusion of the program, the trainees had developed positive changes in attitude toward self, but these were not accompanied by positive attitudes toward tedious, structured jobs. Rather, these trainees apparently raised their levels of aspiration and subsequently sought employment in a work setting consistent with their newly found expectations. In this instance, it was obvious that the trainees were leaving the job as well as experiencing positive changes in attitude. However, there are many other cases in which the collection of a variety of criteria related to the objectives is the only way to effectively evaluate the training program.

One treatment of criterion development argues that performance can best be approximated by a single measure or a group of measures combined into a single measure. This is known as the *composite view* of the criterion. The other side of the issue, known as the *multiple-criteria approach*, states that the various performance measures must be treated independently. Advocates of the multiple-criteria approach believe a single composite measure is invalid; criteria are multidimensional. Considering that training programs must be examined with a multitude of measures, including participant reactions, learning, performance, and organizational objectives, it is necessary for training evaluators to view the criteria as multidimensional. Training can best be evaluated by examining many independent performance dimensions. However, the relationship between measures of success should be closely scrutinized, as the inconsistencies that occur often provide important insights into training procedures. The collection of different criteria reflecting the many objectives of an organization leads to a more difficult decision process than the collection of a single criterion of performance. However, judgment and feedback processes depend on the availability of all sources of information. For instance, a particular instructional program might lead to increased achievement but dissatisfied participants. It is important to find out why the program is not viewed favorably so changes that might improve the reactions of the trainees may be considered. If the decision makers are more concerned with achievement than with reaction, they might not be willing to institute changes. However, the decision makers do have the information available to make the choice and can consider the possible consequences.

There are many different dimensions by which criteria can vary, including the time the criteria are collected and the type of criteria data collected. These dimensions are not independent. For example, learning criteria and behavior on the job not only are different types of criteria but also vary according to the time of collection. Some of the more important dimensions that should be considered are discussed in the following section.

LEVELS OF CRITERIA

Kirkpatrick (1959) suggests that evaluation procedures should consider four levels of criteria—reaction, learning, behavior, and results.

Reaction

Kirkpatrick defines reaction as what the trainees thought of the particular program. It does not include a measure of the learning that takes place. The following are suggested guidelines for determining participant reaction.

1. Design a questionnaire based on information obtained during the need-assessment phase. The questionnaire should be validated by carefully standardized procedures to be certain that the responses reflect the opinions of the participants.
2. Design the instrument so that the responses can be tabulated and quantified.
3. To obtain more honest opinions, provide for the anonymity of the participants. Often, it is best to provide for anonymity with a coding procedure that protects the individual participant but permits the data to be related to other criteria, like learning measures and performance on the job.
4. Provide space for opinions about items that are not covered in the questionnaire. This procedure often leads to the collection of important information that is useful in the redesign of the questionnaire.

5. Pretest the questionnaire on a sample of participants to determine its completeness, the time necessary for completion, and participant reactions.

The reaction of the participants is often a critical factor in the continuance of training programs. Responses on these types of questionnaires help ensure against decisions based on the comments of a few very satisfied or disgruntled participants. Most trainers believe that initial receptivity provides a good atmosphere for learning the material in the instructional program but does not necessarily cause high levels of learning.

Learning

Here, the training analyst is concerned with measuring the learning of principles, facts, techniques, and attitudes that were specified as training objectives. The measures must be objective and quantifiable indicants of the learning that has taken place in the training program. They are not measures of performance on the job. There are many different measures of learning performance, including paper-and-pencil test, learning curves, and job components. The objectives determine the choice of the most appropriate measure.

Behavior

Kirkpatrick uses the term *behavior* in reference to the measurement of job performance. Just as favorable reaction does not necessarily mean that learning will occur in the training program, superior training performance does not always result in similar behavior in the transfer setting. For example, it is important to examine the learning that takes place in a special reading lab and then to examine the trainee's behavior in the classroom, where that learning is expected to produce a variety of changes. The significance of these criteria is emphasized by a review that examined research studies from 1906 to 1952. In this investigation, Severin (1952) found that the median correlation between production records and training grades was .11. He concluded that training records did not always accurately represent performance on the job and should not be substituted for studies of on-the-job behavior without first determining that a strong relationship exists.

Results

Kirkpatrick uses this category to relate the results of the training program to organizational objectives. Some of the results that could be examined include costs, turnover, absenteeism, grievances, and morale.

The previous chapter, on need assessment, described the various components of organizational analyses, including goals and objectives, which in turn should suggest relevant organizational criteria.

While all four categories of criteria are important, research indicates that these data are usually not collected. One investigation (Catalanello & Kirkpatrick, 1968) found that of 154 companies surveyed, the largest number (77 percent) stressed studies related to reactions. Even in those instances in which reaction data are collected, some investigators (Mindak & Anderson, 1971) have suggested that most of these measures are *eyeball* attempts to measure reactions. Few investigations have bothered to measure learning, behavior, or results, and those that have done so rarely stress proper evaluation procedures (for example, control groups). It is probably not unreasonable to suspect that these investigations also do not consider criterion relevance and reliability.

Kirkpatrick's analysis of criteria represents just one approach to different levels that could be examined. Other categories have been developed that are more specific to the particular program being evaluated. Thus, Lindbom and Osterberg (1954) suggest that three effective levels for examining the results of supervisory training are: (1) supervisor's classroom behavior, (2) supervisor's behavior on the job, and (3) employee's behavior on the job.

PROCESS AND OUTCOME MEASURES

Outcome measures refer to criteria, like learning and performance, that represent various levels of achievement. While these measures are critical in determining the viability of the instructional programs, strict reliance on outcome measures often makes it difficult to determine why the criteria were achieved. Thus, some authors (for example, Cronbach, 1963) have stressed the importance of process measures that examine what happens during instruction. It is not unusual for a training program to bear little relationship to the originally conceived format. In one instance, which occurred in a basic-learning laboratory, a pigeon was trained to peck at a key for food. Later in the experiment, the researcher noted that the response rate of the animal was surprisingly low. The researcher decided to observe the pigeon and discovered that it was not pecking the key to earn reinforcement. Instead, it was running across the cage and smashing into the wall that held the key, thereby setting off the mechanism and earning food! Other researchers, including myself, have discovered that classes utilizing new CAI systems have often spent large percentages of time watching frustrated instructors attempting to get the system on the air. In such instances, low achievement scores may result from a program that simply isn't operating as originally specified. The evaluation phase specifies that training must be monitored in order to obtain process measures that will permit the analyst to explore the meaning of his outcome measures.

INTENDED AND UNINTENDED OUTCOMES

An especially interesting approach to criteria examination suggests studying both the intended and the unintended outcomes at each criterion level. Most of the previous discussion has focused on the necessity for developing criteria to measure the intended outcomes of reaction, learning, behavior, and results. Fitzpatrick (1970) noted that there is a whole set of unintended outcomes, either wanted or unwanted, associated with most programs. This view stresses the concern for side effects that is familiar to researchers in medicine but is ignored by most training researchers. For example, criteria might be established to measure the side effects of a training program for hard-core unemployed workers. Since such a program would place more minority-group workers on the job, it might have the unintended and unwanted effect of increasing racial tensions by introducing workers with a different set of personal and social values. Criteria should be established to measure these unintended outcomes so that information is available to determine side effects. In many cases, these criteria data become important elements in shaping policy and determining future objectives.

TIME DIMENSION

Criteria also vary according to time of collection. Thus, learning-criteria measures are taken early in training, and behavior-criteria measures are taken after the individual has completed his training program and transferred to his new activity. Figure 4-2 depicts the time dimension of criteria. In this diagram, immediate criteria refer to those measures that are available during the training program. Proximal criteria are measures that are available shortly after the initial training program. They might include performance in an advanced section of the training program or initial success on the job. Distal criteria are available after considerable time in the transfer setting. There are no exact rules that tell when to measure or when a proximal criterion becomes a distal criterion.

Ghiselli (1956) introduced the concepts of *static* and *dynamic* dimensions to account for the changes in criteria that occur during the passage of time. The static dimension is used to describe criteria that do not change over time. The dynamic dimension indicates that successful

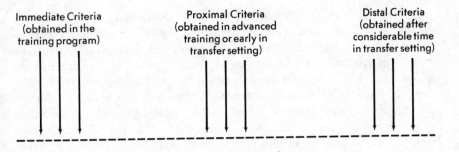

Figure 4-2. The time dimensions of criteria.

performance is affected by factors that change with time. Thus, organizational objectives might change, in which case new criteria become necessary. The initial objectives might be growth and acquisition of new clients, while the later objectives might be stability and cultivation of present clients (Prien, 1966). New criteria will have to be developed to measure these objectives. A further implication is that the relationship between training performance and transfer performance is dependent on the time of measurement.

TYPES OF CRITERIA

This section provides a few general criteria categories that are meaningful for training research but have not been emphasized in previous sections. These categories include norm- and criterion-referenced measures and objective and subjective measures.

CRITERION- AND NORM-REFERENCED MEASURES

Criterion-referenced measures are dependent on an absolute standard of quality, while norm-referenced measures are dependent on a relative standard. Criterion-referenced measures provide a standard of achievement for the individual as compared with specific behavioral objectives and therefore provide an indicant of the degree of competence attained by the trainee. Norm-referenced measures compare the capabilities of an individual to those of other trainees. Thus, schools administer nationally standardized exams that determine the individual's standing in comparison with a national sample. The norm-referenced measures tell us that one student is more proficient than another, but they do not provide much information about the degree of proficiency in relationship to the tasks involved. Unfortunately, many training evaluations have employed norm-referenced measures to the exclusion of other forms of measurement. In order to properly evaluate training programs, it is necessary to obtain criterion-referenced measures that provide information about the skill level of the trainee in relationship to the expected program achievement levels. Data informing us that the student is equal to or above 60 percent of the population provide little information about his specific capabilities; thus, it is difficult to design modifications to improve the program.

OBJECTIVE AND SUBJECTIVE MEASURES

Measures that require the statement of opinions, beliefs, or judgments are considered subjective. For example, rating scales are subjective measures, while measures of absenteeism are more objective. (However, supervisors' ratings of the absenteeism level of employees could turn that measure into a subjective criterion.) Objective measures—for example, rate of production—are especially vulnerable to criterion contamination based on opportunity bias, whereas subjective measures are affected by the difficulties that one individual has in rating another without bias. The rating scale is the measure most commonly employed in applied settings. Guion (1965), in a survey of several psychological journals published between 1950 and 1955, found that 81 percent of the studies utilized ratings as a criterion measure. The choice of criteria should be based on the most relevant and reliable measure available to examine the stated objectives.

UNOBTRUSIVE MEASURES

Recent research (Webb, Campbell, Schwartz, & Sechrest, 1966) has seriously questioned the reliance of social-science work on interviews and questionnaires. In comments relevant to training research, Webb and his associates suggest that these techniques create as well as measure attitudes and that they are chosen solely on the basis of accessibility and availability. While these authors agree that any method is subject to serious flaws, they are especially concerned because these methods are the only techniques being employed. Thus, they suggest that some measures that do not require the cooperation of a respondent and do not themselves contaminate the response should be examined. They offer two examples.

1. The floor tiles around the hatching chick exhibit at Chicago's Museum of Science and Industry must be replaced every six weeks. Tiles in other parts of the museum need not be replaced for years. The selective erosion of tiles, indexed by their replacement rate, is a measure of the relative popularity of exhibits.
2. Library withdrawals were used to demonstrate the effect of the introduction of television into a community. Fiction titles dropped; nonfiction titles were unaffected [p. 2].

Although it is difficult to imagine the use of the first example's measure as a criterion for a training program, the second example does suggest an interesting way to examine the implications of educational and training programs offered through television.

These methods are not without their own drawbacks and sources of biases. This is clearly indicated by D. T. Campbell's (1969) discussion of the use of archival methods.

> Those who advocate the use of archival measures of social indicators must face up not only to their high degree of chaotic error and systematic bias, but also to the politically motivated changes in record keeping that will follow upon their public use as social indicators [p. 415].

With that warning taken into consideration, it still appears that the solution to the criterion problem will depend on the effective use of the analyst's imagination and willingness to work to uncover relevant measures of success.

CONCLUSION

In summary, the following suggestions about the determination of criteria appear relevant.

1. Place the greatest degree of effort on the selection of relevant criteria. While relevance cannot be measured empirically, it can be conceptualized as a relationship between the operational measures (criteria) and the true values that will hopefully be represented. Thus, several suggestions can aid in the selection of relevant criteria. First, carefully examine the behavioral objectives established from the need-assessment procedures. Since the objectives are statements about terminal performance, they suggest potential criteria. Next, carefully examine all the components suggested by the need assessment so that the criteria are not deficient. For example, criteria utilized to measure the performance of grocery cashiers include not only measures of register skills but also ratings of various aspects of customer service. Finally, carefully reduce the extraneous elements that often cause criterion contamination.

As described earlier, two contaminating factors that can be effectively eliminated are opportunity bias and preknowledge of training performance.

2. After establishing relevant criteria, statistically determine the reliability or the consistency of the measure. If the criteria are not measured reliably, they are useless as indicants of success. Several of the factors that affect the reliability of the measure are listed on page 57. Since ratings are often used as measures of success, consider the difficulties in rating a bus driver on his ability to slow and stop his vehicle. The following rating statements are utilized by Continental Safeway Trails.

Slowing and Stopping
1. stops and restarts without rolling back
2. tests brakes at top of hills
3. uses mirrors to check traffic to rear
4. signals following traffic
5. stops before crossing sidewalk when coming out of driveway or alley
6. stops clear of pedestrian crosswalks

Note that the behaviors are overt, easy to observe, and well defined. Certainly, more reliable measures could be expected by utilizing these statements than by simply rating "slowing and stopping" without further defining the behaviors.

Because of the complexity of most training programs and the corresponding evaluation efforts, criterion selection should be influenced by several different levels. One especially useful paradigm is suggested by Kirkpatrick's (1959) measures of reaction, learning, behavior, and results. This particular analysis provides for measures of training performance, transfer performance, and organizational objectives. Depending on the situation, the analyst might also consider a variety of other measures, such as unintended outcomes and unobtrusive measures.

Chapter Five

Evaluation Procedures

Rational decisions related to the selection, adoption, support, and worth of the various training activities require some basis for determining that the instructional program was responsible for whatever changes occurred. Instructional analysts should be able to respond to the following questions:

1. Does an examination of the various criteria indicate that a change has occurred?
2. Can the changes be attributed to the instructional program?
3. Is it likely that similar changes will occur for new participants in the same program?

These questions could be asked about measures at each criterion level (for example, reaction, learning, behavior, results). Thus, evaluations of training programs are not likely to produce dichotomous answers. However, training analysts who expect results to lead to a value or no-value judgment are unrealistically imposing a simplistic structure and are raising false expectations among the recipients and sponsors of training research.

The unique objectives and constraints of each instructional setting make attempts to generalize results to other programs extremely hazardous. Kirkpatrick (1959) expressed this view by suggesting ". . . that one training director cannot borrow evaluation results from another; he can, however, borrow evaluation techniques" (p. 3). Before discussing particular methodologies for training evaluation, it is important to recognize that there are many different viewpoints about the desirability of evaluation, the approach to evaluation, and the effects of evaluation. The following sections discuss the most prominent of these viewpoints.

VIEWS OF THE EVALUATION PROCESS

NEGATIVISTS, POSITIVISTS, AND FRUSTRATES

One continuum of thought revolves around the necessity for evaluation. As expressed by Randall (1960), negativists are those individuals who feel that evaluation of training is either impossible or unnecessary—that the value of formal instructional programs cannot be demonstrated by quantitative analysis. They feel that learning in an instructional setting is irrelevant and that improved performance in the transfer setting will be obvious without evaluation techniques. On the other end of the continuum are the positivists, who believe that scientific evaluation of training is the only worthwhile approach. This group suggests that instructional analysts should not waste time and money on anything other than a controlled study. In the center of these two groups are the frustrates, who recognize that training programs must be evaluated but are concerned with the methodology necessary to perform the evaluation. This group recognizes that all programs will be evaluated, either formally or informally; thus, it is concerned with the quality of the evaluation rather than with the decision whether to evaluate or not.

Each group's generalizations have a degree of validity. This text supports the view that the evaluation process is difficult but that the potential worth of evaluation remains undetermined because few evaluation studies are conducted. The negativist's viewpoint treats evaluation of programs in extremes—the program is either good or bad. Instead, training programs should be considered dynamic entities that slowly accomplish their purpose in meeting predesigned objectives. Without systematic evaluation, there is no feedback to provide the information necessary to improve programs or quality information to make decisions. It is also difficult to accept the negativist's view that trainee improvements in the transfer setting will be obvious. A consideration of the difficulties associated with criterion contamination alone makes it clear that casual observations are not likely to provide much more than the observer's biased opinion. The positivists, on the other hand, would not permit a study except under completely controlled conditions. This view, if carried to an extreme, could result in research only in academic laboratories where systematic control of the environment can be maintained. While the data collected in these settings are important, the approach could have the undesired effect of reducing our understanding of instructional programs in real settings. The most reasonable approach is offered by the frustrates (the appropriate category for those participating in training research today). It is important to use the most systematic procedures available that fit the particular setting being investigated, to control as many of the extraneous variables as possible, and to recognize the limitations of the design being utilized. Thus, the better experimental procedures control more variables, permitting a greater degree of confidence in specifying program effects. While the constraints of the environment may make a perfect evaluation impossible, an awareness of the important factors in experimental design makes it possible to avoid a useless evaluation. The job of the training analyst is to choose the most rigorous design possible and to be aware of its limitations. These limitations should be taken into account in data interpretation and in reports to program sponsors.

TYPES OF EVALUATION

There are also varying opinions about the most appropriate type of evaluation. One dimension, discussed in this section, includes formative and summative evaluation. Another dimension, discussed in the next section, includes formal instructional research, action research, and casual research.

FORMATIVE AND SUMMATIVE EVALUATION

As originally conceived by Scriven (1967), formative evaluation is utilized to determine if the program is operating as originally planned or if improvements are necessary before the program is implemented. The major concern of summative evaluation is the evaluation of the final product with the major emphasis being program appraisal. Thus, formative evaluation stresses tryout and revision processes, primarily using process criteria, while summative evaluation uses outcome criteria to appraise the instructional program. However, process criteria (such as daily logs of activities) are also important in summative evaluation, because they supply the information necessary to interpret the data. Of course, both formative and summative evaluations can lead to feedback and program improvements. Design changes based on summative evaluations are determined by the degree to which program objectives are achieved. Improvements based on formative evaluations are more related to how closely the program is operating to the original design. The formative evaluation should be completed and judged adequate before summative evaluations are begun. Many research problems result from one-shot evaluation studies that attempt to combine formative and summative evaluations. Thus, the program is often appraised as if it is a completed product when it has not been implemented as originally designed.

A false concern with formative evaluations is that methodological difficulties might be caused by the continual changes adopted from collected data. But that constant modification is exactly the purpose of the formative period, and experimental design considerations should not prevent the necessary changes. Once the formative evaluation is completed, experimental design provides the foundation for the summative evaluation. On the other hand, satisfactory formative data indicating that the program is operating as designed do not mean that summative evaluations are unnecessary, just as the satisfaction of the personnel responsible for the implementation of the program does not mean that the program is meeting the stated objectives.

FORMAL INSTRUCTIONAL RESEARCH, ACTION RESEARCH, AND CASUAL RESEARCH

Borg (1963) developed an interesting comparison of these three types of research in educational settings. Table 5-1 shows that most of the categories are appropriate for all types of instructional settings. Since the remainder of this chapter will consider the methodological factors of these types of research (for example, sampling and design), this discussion will concentrate on more general considerations.

Practical, statistical, and scientific significance. Analysts sometimes overemphasize the importance of statistically significant changes. It is quite possible to achieve statistically significant changes so small that they have virtually no meaning to the organization's objectives. On the other hand, the achievement of practical significant changes assumes that the differences are indeed reliable and will recur when the next instructional group is exposed to the treatment. Interacting with both ideas is the concept of scientific significance—that is, the establishment of meaningful results that permit generalizations about training procedures beyond the immediate setting being investigated. As Campbell, Dunnette, Lawler, and Weick (1970) suggest for managerial training, "Once the effects of such a program are mapped out for different kinds of trainees and for different types of criterion problems under various organizational situations, the general body of knowledge concerning management training has been enriched" (p. 284). If the instructional program is well designed, it should contribute to the solution of organizational goals, as well as add to the body of instructional knowledge.

METHODOLOGICAL CONSIDERATIONS

Each research design has different assets and liabilities in controlling extraneous factors that might threaten the evaluator's ability to determine: (1) if a real change has occurred, (2) whether the change is attributable to the instructional program, and (3) whether the change is likely to occur again with a new sample of subjects. Specific research designs will be discussed in a later section, but several general design

Table 5-1. Differences among Formal Instructional Research, Action Research, and the Casual Approach to Problem Solving in Education

Area	Formal educational research	Action research	Casual or "common sense" approach
1. Goals	To obtain knowledge that will be generalizable to a broad population and to develop and test instructional theories.	To obtain knowledge that can be applied directly to the local classroom situation and to give the participating teachers inservice training.	To make changes in the current procedure that appear likely to improve the situation.
2. Sampling	Research worker attempts to obtain a random or otherwise unbiased sample of the population being studied but is usually not completely successful.	Pupils available in the class of the teacher or teachers doing the research are used as subjects.	Some casual observation of pupil behavior may be made by the teacher after the change decided upon has been in effect for a while.
3. Experimental design	Design is carefully planned in detail prior to start of the study and adhered to as closely as possible. Major attention is given to maintaining comparable conditions and reducing error bias. Control of extraneous variables is important.	Procedures are planned in general terms prior to start of study. Changes are made during the study if they seem likely to improve the teaching situation. Little attention is paid to control of the experimental conditions or reduction of error. Because participating teachers are ego-involved in the research situation, bias is usually present.	If classroom-testing of the decision is attempted, procedures are planned only in the most general terms. No attempt is made to establish common definitions or procedures among participating teachers.

Table 5-1. Differences among Formal Instructional Research, Action Research, and the Casual Approach to Problem Solving in Education (cont.)

Area	Formal educational research	Action research	Casual or "common sense" approach
4. Measurement	An effort is made to obtain the most valid measures available. A thorough evaluation of available measures and a trial of these measures usually precede their use in the research.	Less rigorous evaluation of measures than in scientific research. Participants often lack training in the use and evaluation of educational measures but can do satisfactory job with help of a consultant.	Usually no evaluation is made except for the casual observations of the teachers participating. The teacher's opinion as to whether the new procedure is an improvement or not depends almost entirely on whether the teacher approves the change.
5. Analysis of data	Complex analysis often called for. Inasmuch as generalizability of results is a goal, statistical significance is usually emphasized.	Simple analysis procedures usually are sufficient. Practical significance rather than statistical significance is emphasized. Subjective opinion of participating teachers is often weighted heavily.	Subjective opinion of the participants is usually the only procedure used. No attempt made at objective analysis.
6. Application of results	Results are generalizable, but many useful findings are not applied in educational practice. Differences in training and experience between research workers and teachers generate a serious communication problem.	Findings are applied immediately to the classes of participating teachers and often lead to permanent improvement. Application of results beyond the participating teachers is usually slight.	Decisions reached are applied immediately in classes of participating teachers. Even if the decision leads to improvement, it is often changed later because no evidence is available to support its continuance. This approach leads to educational fads and "change for the sake of change."

Adapted from Borg, W. R. *Educational Research.* Copyright©1963, 1971 by David McKay Co., Inc. Reprinted by permission of the publisher.

concepts, including control groups and pre/post-testing, are mentioned here as background for the presentation of the sources of error that can affect the validity of the experimental design.

PRE/POST-TESTING

The first question is whether the participants, after exposure to the instructional program, change their performance in a significant way. A design to answer this question would use a pretest administered before the instructional program begins and a post-test given after exposure to the instructional program. The timing of the post-test for the evaluation of an instructional program is not easily specified. A post-test at the conclusion of the training program provides a measure of the changes that have occurred during instruction, but it does not give any indication of later transfer performance. Thus, other measures should be employed after the participant has been in the transfer situation for a reasonable time period. Comparisons can then be made between (1) the pretest and the first post-test, (2) the pretest and the second post-test, and (3) the first and second post-tests. For convenience, this section will refer only to pre- and post-tests, but it is important to remember that one post-test immediately after training will ordinarily not suffice. An additional factor in the analysis of pre- and post-test scores is how scores on the pretest affect the degree of success on the post-test. One possibility is that the participant who initially scored highest on the pretest will perform best on the post-test. In order to examine this effect, some researchers (Mayo & DuBois, 1963) have suggested that the pretest scores should be partialed out of the post-test.

The variables measured in the pre- and post-tests must be associated with the objectives of the training program. The expected changes .associated with the instructional program should be specified so that statistically reliable differences between the pre- and post-tests can confirm the degree to which the objectives have been achieved. This text does not attempt to treat the statistical considerations in instructional evaluation analyses except to warn the reader that statistical expertise is necessary to properly evaluate programs.

CONTROL GROUPS

The specification of changes indicated by pre- and postmeasurement is only one consideration. It must be determined that these changes occurred because of the instructional treatment. To eliminate the possibility of other explanations for the changes between the pre- and post-test, a control group is used (treated like the experimental group on all variables that might contribute to pre/post differences except for the actual instructional program). With control procedures, it is possible to specify whether the changes in the experimental group were due to the instructional treatment or to other factors, like the passage of time, maturation factors, or events in the outside world. The particular kinds of errors that can occur will be specified in the next section, but, as an example of the necessity for control groups, we can consider the placebo effect. In medical research, the placebo is an inert substance administered to the control group so that the subject cannot distinguish whether he is a member of the experimental or the control group. This allows the researcher to separate the effects of the actual drug from the reactions induced by the subject's expectations and suggestibility. In instructional research, similar cautions must be taken to separate the background effects sometimes employed in the experimental setting and the actual treatment. It is possible that treatment effects in an experimental group in which videotape feedback is being investigated are caused by the presence of recording equipment and numerous observers (Isaac & Michael, 1971). Thus, the control group should be presented with similar attention. In medical and psychological research, there is concern about experimenters who unknowingly interact with subjects and shape their behavior, through subtle cues, toward the predicted results. While control groups do not provide a solution for this latter problem, researchers should be aware of these potential dangers.

Before discussing specific research designs, it is necessary to consider those factors that contribute sources of error. D. T. Campbell and J. C. Stanley (1963) have organized and specified these threats to experimental design, and, for the most part, their labels and organization are utilized.

INTERNAL AND EXTERNAL VALIDITY

Internal validity asks the basic question "Did the treatment make a difference in this particular situation?" Unless internal validity has been established, it is not possible to interpret the effects of any experiment, training or otherwise. External validity refers to the generalizability or representativeness of the data. The evaluator is concerned with generalizability of his results to other populations, settings, and treatment variables. External validity is always a matter of inference and thus can never be specified with complete confidence. However, the designs that control the most threats to internal and external validity are, of course, the most useful.

THREATS TO INTERNAL VALIDITY

These threats are variables other than the instructional program itself that can affect its results. The solution to this difficulty is to control these variables so that they may be cast aside as competing explanations for the experimental effect. Threats to internal validity include the following.

History. History refers to the specific events, other than the experimental treatment, occurring between the first and second measurements that could provide alternative explanations for results. When tests are given on different days, as is almost always the case in instructional programs, events occurring between the testing periods can contaminate the effects. For instance, an instructional program designed to produce positive attitudes toward safe practices in coal mines may produce significant differences that have no relationship to the material presented in the instructional program because a coal-mine disaster occurred between the pre- and post-test.

Maturation. Maturation includes all biological or psychological effects that systematically vary with the passage of time, independent of specific events like history. Participants become older, fatigued, or more or less interested in the program between the time of the pre-test and the time of the post-test. Thus, performance can change for reasons unrelated to the instructional material.

Testing. This variable refers to the influence of the pretest on the scores of the post-test. This is an especially serious problem for instructional programs in which the pretest can sensitize the participant to search for material or to ask friends for information that provides correct answers on the post-test. Thus, improved performance would occur simply by taking the pre- and post-tests, without any intervening instructional program.

Instrumentation. This threat to validity results from changes in the instruments that might result in differences between pre- and post-test scores. For example, fluctuations in mechanical instruments or changes in grading standards can lead to differences, regardless of the instructional program. Since rating scales are commonly employed as a criterion in training research, it is important to be sensitive to differences related to changes in the rater (for example, additional expertise in the second rating, bias, or carelessness) that can cause error effects.

Statistical regression. Participants for instructional research are often chosen on the basis of extreme scores. Thus, students with extremely low and extremely high intelligence-test scores may be chosen for participation in a course using programed instruction. In these cases, a phenomenon known as statistical regression often occurs. On the second testing, the scores for both groups regress toward the middle of the distribution. Thus, students with extremely high scores would tend toward lower scores, and those with extremely low scores would tend toward higher scores. This regression occurs because tests are not perfect measures; there will always be some change in scores from the first to the second testing simply because of measurement error. Since the first scores are at the extreme ends, the variability must move toward the center (the mean of the entire group). Students with extremely high scores might have had unusually good luck the day of the first testing, or students with extremely low scores may have been upset or careless that day. On the second administration, however, each group is likely to regress toward the mean.

Differential selection of participants. This effect stems from biases in choosing comparison groups. If volunteers are used in the instruction group and randomly chosen participants are used in the control group, differences could occur between the two groups simply because each was different before the program began. This variable is best controlled by random selection of all participants, with appropriate numbers of participants (as determined by statistical considerations) for each group. Random selection is a particular problem in educational settings where one class is chosen as the control group and another class as the experimental group. Establishing experimental and control groups by placing individuals with matched characteristics (for example, intelligence, age, sex) in each group is still not the best alternative. Often, the critical parameters that should be used to match the participants are not known, and thus selection biases can again affect the design. One alternative is a combination of matching and randomization in which participants are matched on important parameters; then, one member of each pair is assigned randomly to the treatment or control group.

Experimental mortality. This variable refers to the differential loss of participants from the treatment or control group. In a control group of volunteers, those persons who scored poorly on the pretest may drop out because they are discouraged. Thus, the group in the experimental program may appear to score higher than the control group, because the low-scoring performers have dropped out.

Interactions. Many of the above factors—for example, selection and maturation—can interact to produce threats to internal validity. When younger students are compared with older students over a period of a year, there are differences in initial selection and differences in maturation changes that could occur at varying rates for each of the different groups.

THREATS TO EXTERNAL VALIDITY

External validity refers to the generalizability of the study to other groups and situations. Internal validity is a prerequisite for external validity, since the results of the study must be valid for the group being examined before there can be concern over the validity for other groups. The representativeness of the investigation determines the degree of generalizability. For example, when the data are initially collected in a low socioeconomic setting, it is difficult to claim that the instructional program will work equally well for a high socioeconomic area. Campbell and Stanley list the following threats to external validity.

Reactive effect of pretesting. The effects of pretests often lead to increased sensitivity to the instructional procedure. Thus, the participant's responses to the training program might be different from the responses of individuals who are exposed to an established program without the pretest; the pretested participant might pay attention to certain material in the training program only because he knows it is covered in test items.

Interaction of selection and experimental treatment. The characteristics of the group selected for experimental treatment determine the generalizability of the findings to other participants. The characteristics of employees from one division of the firm may result in the treatment's being more or less effective for them, as compared to employees from another division with different characteristics. Similarly, characteristics of school students, like socioeconomic status or intelligence level, may make them more or less receptive to particular instructional programs.

Reactive effects of experimental settings. The procedures employed in the experimental setting may limit the generalizability of the study. Observers and experimental equipment often make the participants aware of their participation in an experiment, which can lead to changes in behavior that cannot be generalized to those individuals who will participate in the instructional treatment when it is nonexperimental. The Hawthorne studies have become the standard illustration for the "I'm a guinea pig" effect. This research shows that a group of employees continued to increase production regardless of the changes in working conditions designed to produce both increases and decreases in production. Interpreters believe that the experimental conditions resulted in the workers' behaving differently. Explanations for the Hawthorne effect include: novelty; awareness of being a participant in an experiment; changes in the environment due to observers, recording conditions, and social interaction; and daily feedback on production figures (Isaac & Michael, 1971). Since the factors that affect the treatment group will not be present in future training sessions, the performance obtained is not representative of that of future participants.

Multiple-treatment interference. The effects of previous treatments are not erasable; therefore, threats to external validity occur whenever there is an attempt to establish the effects of a single treatment from studies that actually examined multiple treatments. Thus, trainees exposed to role playing, films, and lectures may perform best during the lectures, but that does not mean they would perform in a similar manner if they were exposed to lectures all day long without the other techniques.

EXPERIMENTAL DESIGN

This section presents some of the many designs that examine the effects of experimental treatments. The previous sections on internal and external validity discussed some of the factors that make it difficult to determine whether the treatment produced the hypothesized results. As we shall see, these threats are differentially controlled by the various designs. Given a particular setting, the researcher should employ the design that has the greatest degree of control over threats to validity. Certainly, it is possible to avoid choosing a useless design. In many cases, the main difficulty has been the failure to plan for evaluation before the program was implemented. In these instances, the utilization of a few procedures—for example, pre/post-testing and control groups—could dramatically improve the quality of information.

For convenience in presenting the experimental designs, T_1 will represent the pretest, T_2 the post-test, X the treatment or instructional program, and R the random selection of subjects. Campbell and Stanley (1963) have organized a detailed examination of the variables that should be considered when choosing a research design. The designs in this text, organized into several different categories, provide examples of the numerous approaches available. The first category includes pre-experimental designs that do not have control procedures and are valueless in analyzing cause-and-effect relationships. Experimental designs, the second category, have varying degrees of power that permit some control of threats to validity. The third category includes quasi-experimental designs that are useful in many social-science settings where investigators lack the opportunity to exert full control over the environment.

PRE-EXPERIMENTAL DESIGNS

1. The one-shot case study:

In this method, commonly called the case-study approach, the subjects are exposed to the instructional treatment (without a pretest) and then are tested once. This design has a total absence of control, and all threats to internal validity are present. Thus, there is no scientific value to this approach. The only bases for comparisons are intuitions and impressions. As Campbell and Stanley have observed, these studies often involve a tedious collection of specific detailed data that cannot substitute for a more rigorous design. The only purpose that this design can serve is to collect preliminary information for a more thorough investigation.

2. The one-group pretest/post-test design:

```
┌─────────────────────────────┐
│  T₁        X        T₂       │
└─────────────────────────────┘
```

When this design is employed, the participants are given a pretest, presented with the instructional program, and then given a post-test. This design is widely utilized in the examination of instructional settings, because it provides a measure of comparison between the same group of subjects before and after treatment. Unfortunately, without a control group, it is difficult to establish whether the experimental treatment is the prime factor determining any differences that occur between the testing periods. Thus, the many threats to internal validity, including changes in history, maturation, testing effects, changes in instrumentation, and statistical regression, are not controlled. This design does, however, control biases due to subject mortality.

RESEARCH EXAMPLE OF PRE-EXPERIMENTAL DESIGNS

Golembiewski and Carrigan (1970) carried out a training program that utilized a pre/post design without a control group in one of a series of investigations designed to change the style of a sales unit in a business organization. They had a series of goals, including: the integration of a new management team, an increase in congruence between the behaviors required by the organization and those preferred by the men, and a greater congruence of individual needs and organizational demands. The training program consisted of a laboratory approach using sensitivity training to encourage the exploration of the participant's feelings and reactions to the organization. The program also included confrontations in which management of various levels were given an opportunity to discuss their ideas and feelings. The instrument used to measure pre- and postexperimental changes was Likert's profile of organizational characteristics, which includes items related to leadership, character of motivational forces, communication, interaction influence, decision making, goal setting, and control.

After statistical analyses, the authors concluded that the learning design had the intended effect in terms of the measured attitudes. Golembiewski and Carrigan indicated that they had included all the managers in the treatment and so did not have a control group. Thus, their design did not permit them to be certain that the effects were a result of the training program rather than of random factors or the passage of time. This design uncertainty is expressed by Becker (1970) in an article entitled "The Parable of the Pill":

There once was a land in which wisdom was revered. Thus there was great excitement in the land when one of its inhabitants announced that he had invented a pill which made people wiser. His claim was based on an experiment he conducted. The report of the experiment explained (1) that the experimenter secured a volunteer; (2) the volunteer was first given an IQ test; (3) then he swallowed a pill which he was told would make him more intelligent; (4) finally he was given another IQ test. The score on the second IQ test was higher than on the first, so the report concluded that the pill increased wisdom.

Alas, there were two skeptics in the land. One secured a volunteer; gave him an IQ test; waited an appropriate length of time; then gave him another IQ test. The volunteer's score on the second test exceeded that of the first. Skeptic One reported his experiment and concluded that taking the first test was an experience for the subject and that the time between the tests allowed the subject to assimilate and adjust to that experience so that when he encountered the situation again he responded more efficiently. Time alone, the skeptic argued, was sufficient to produce the increase in test score. The skeptic also pointed out that time alone could have produced the change in test score reported in the experiment on the Wisdom Pill.

Skeptic Two conducted a different experiment. He held the opinion that most people were to some extent suggestible or gullible and that they readily would accept a suggestion that they possessed a desired attribute. He further believed that people who accept such a suggestion might even behave in a way such as to make it appear, for a time at least, that they indeed did possess the suggested ability. Therefore, the skeptic secured a volunteer; gave him an IQ test; had him ingest a pill composed of inert ingredients; told him the pill would increase his intelligence; then gave him another IQ test. Skeptic Two dutifully reported his subject achieved a higher score on the second test and, based on his hypothesis, explained how the disparity arose. He also pointed out that the increase in test score in the Wisdom Pill experiment could have been due to the taking of the pill and expectations associated with taking the pill rather than to the ingredients in the pill.

The inventor of the wisdom pill drafted a reply to the two skeptics. He wrote that, although he did not employ a control group or a placebo group, he is confident that the pill's ingredients caused the observed change because that change is consistent with the theory from which he deduced the formula for his pill [p. 94].[1]

The point in the parable is that Skeptic One, Skeptic Two, or the inventor of the pill may be right. There is no way of being certain, given the present design, what was responsible for the effect.

Essentially, pre-experimental designs do not provide good information about the impact of the treatment. They should be used only to collect preliminary data. The next group of designs shows how easily many of the pre-experimental designs can be improved. Design 1 can be strengthened by adding a pretest, and both Design 1 and Design 2 can be improved by adding a control group. Even where the environment makes a control group impractical, these designs can be improved by using the time-series approach (described in the section on quasi-experimental designs).

EXPERIMENTAL DESIGNS

3. Pretest/post-test control-group design:

Experimental Group (R)	T_1	X	T_2
Control Group (R)	T_1		T_2

In this design, the subjects are chosen at random from the population and assigned randomly to the experimental group or control group. Each group is given a pre- and post-test, but only the experimental group is exposed to the instructional treatment. If there is more than one instructional treatment, it is possible to add additional experimental groups.

This design represents a considerable improvement over Designs 1 and 2, because many of the threats to internal validity are controlled. The differential selection of subjects is controlled by the random selection. Variables like history, maturation, and pretesting should affect the experimental group and the control group equally. Statistical regression based on extreme scores (if subjects are chosen that way) is not eliminated but should be equal for the two groups because of the random

[1]From Becker, S. W. The parable of the pill. *Administrative Science Quarterly*, 1970, 15, 94–96. Reprinted by permission of *Administrative Science Quarterly* and the author.

selection procedures. However, any effects not part of the instructional procedure that are due to differential treatment of subjects in the control and experimental groups must still be controlled by the experimenter. This design is affected by external threats to validity, which are not as easily specified as the threats to internal validity. The design does not control the effects of pretesting; thus, T_1 could have sensitized the participants to the experimental treatment in a way that makes generalizations to future participants difficult. Generalizations would also be hampered because subjects in the experiment might be different from those who will participate at later times and because the guinea-pig effect could lead to differences between the experimental and control groups. This latter concern is dependent on the ingenuity of the experimenter in reducing the differences between groups by treating the control group in the same manner as the experimental group (except for the specific instructional treatment).

The difficulties associated with external validity should not freeze the researcher into inactivity. While threats to internal validity are reasonably well handled by experimental designs, generalizations, which are the core of external validity, are always precarious. As Campbell and Stanley point out, experimenters try to generalize by scientifically guessing at laws and by trying out generalizations in other specific cases. Slowly, and somewhat painfully, they gain knowledge about factors that affect generalizations. (For example, there is now ample evidence that pretesting does sensitize and affect participants.) As shown in the following design, a control for pretest sensitization is relatively easy to achieve by adding a group to Design 3 that is exposed to the treatment without first being presented with the pretest.

4. Solomon four-group design:

Group

1 (R)	T_1	X	T_2
2 (R)	T_1		T_2
3 (R)		X	T_2
4 (R)			T_2

The Solomon four-group design represents the first specific procedure designed to consider external-validity factors. This design adds two groups that are not pretested. If the participants are randomly assigned to the four groups, this design makes it possible to compare the effects of pretesting. (Group 4 provides a control for pretesting without the instructional treatment.) It also permits the evaluator to determine the effects of some internal-validity factors. For example, a comparison of the post-test performance for Group 4, which was not exposed to pretesting or instructional treatments, to the pretest scores for Groups 1 and 2 permits the analysis of the combined effects of maturation and history.

RESEARCH EXAMPLE OF EXPERIMENTAL DESIGNS

Goodacre (1955) reported on an evaluative study of a supervisory training program at B. F. Goodrich Company that fits into the classification of experimental designs. The program consisted of conferences, lectures, and discussions for different supervisory and managerial personnel on topics related to the understanding of human behavior, decision making, employee selection, employee progress, and job evaluation. The experimental design was developed in conjunction with the program and built into the instructional procedure. The 800 participants were randomly placed into two groups—an experimental group and a control group. As Goodacre notes, random selection was necessary to assure that the groups would be comparable on variables like age, length of service, job level, and intelligence. The control group did not participate in the training program, but, in all other regards, it was treated similarly to the experimental group. Various criterion measures, including attitude scales, achievement tests, and ratings by immediate supervisors, were adminstered both before and after training.

As reported by J. P. Campbell et al. (1970), the control group did not show any significant changes, but the experimental group improved on the achievement tests, self-confidence ratings, and post-training performance measures. This is one of the few studies that not only used a rigorous design but also attempted to measure performance on the job and in the training program. Goodacre and Campbell et al. note that one problem with the performance ratings was that the raters knew who participated in the training program. Yet, even with that difficulty, the experimental design permitted the control of many threats to internal validity that plague pre-experimental design. However, it did not control for the external-validity threats of pretesting sensitization.

QUASI-EXPERIMENTAL DESIGNS

5. The time-series design:

$$T_1 \quad T_2 \quad T_3 \quad T_4 \quad X \quad T_5 \quad T_6 \quad T_7 \quad T_8$$

This design is similar to Design 1, except that a series of measurements are taken before and after the instructional treatment. This particular approach illustrates the possibilities of utilizing quasi-experimental designs in situations in which it is not possible to gain the full control required by experimental designs. An examination of the internal-validity threats shows that this design provides more control than Design 1. If there are no appreciable changes from pretests 1 to 4, it is unlikely that any effects will occur due to maturation, testing, or regression. The major internal-validity difficulty with this design is the history variable; that is, events that may happen between T_4 and T_5 (such as environmental changes and historical occurrences) are not controlled by this procedure.

The use of the time-series design does not control most of the external-validity threats. Thus, it is necessary to be sensitive to any relationships between the treatment and particular subject groups (like volunteers) that might make results difficult to generalize to other groups, and it is also necessary to be aware that subjects might be sensitized to particular aspects of the instructional program through the use of pretests.

6. The nonequivalent control-group design:

Experimental Group	T_1	X	T_2
Control Group	T_1		T_2

The nonequivalent control-group design is the same as Design 3, except that the participants are not assigned to the groups at random. (The choice of the group to receive the instructional treatment is made randomly.) This design is often used in educational settings where there are naturally assembled groups, such as classes. If there is no alternative, this design is well worth using and is certainly preferable to designs that do not include control groups (such as Design 2). The more similar the two groups and their scores on the pretest, the more effective the control becomes in accounting for extraneous influences—for instance, internal-validity factors like history, pretesting, maturation, and instrumentation. However, the investigator must be especially careful, because this design is vulnerable to interactions between selection factors and maturation, history, and testing. Since the participants were not chosen randomly, there is always the possibility that critical differences exist that were not revealed by the pretests. For example, some studies use volunteers who might react differently to the treatment because of motivational factors. Thus, the investigator must be sensitive to potential sources of differences between the groups. The dangers of instrumentation changes and of differential treatment of each group (unrelated to the treatment) remain a concern for this design as well as for Design 3.

Although the external-validity issues are similar to those for Design 3, the nonequivalent control-group design does have some advantages in the control of the reactive effects of experimental settings. The utilization of intact groups makes it easier to design the experiment as part of the normal routine, thus reducing some of the problems associated with the guinea-pig effect. Since this design is not as disruptive, it is also possible, in some settings (for example, educational systems), to have a larger subject population, thus increasing generalizability.

RESEARCH EXAMPLE OF QUASI-EXPERIMENTAL DESIGNS

A study by Canter (1951) illustrates a quasi-experimental design employing pre/post measures with nonequivalent control groups. The purpose of this investigation was to train supervisory personnel in human relations—that is, to establish facts and principles so that supervisors could become more competent in their knowledge and understanding of human behavior. The criteria consisted of a test battery including measures of supervisory behavior, social judgment, and logical reasoning.

The experimental group contained supervisors from one department, and the control group contained members from two other departments. Since the participants were not randomly chosen, Canter checked variables like age, sex, mental alertness, and years of service. While there were no statistical differences due to considerable variability in the scores, the author indicated that differences in number of years of service and mental alertness were discernible. The results of the study indicated that changes in performance favored the trained group.

While this design controls history and maturation factors reasonably well, there are problems related to selection interactions and factors like history and testing. The participants in this program worked under different supervisors and in different psychological and physical environments. The effects of these selection factors are unknown, but of special concern is the fact that the department heads for these participants did observe certain aspects of the training.

SUMMARY

Campbell and Stanley have summarized threats to validity for various designs (see Table 5-2). They warn us about using the summary table without a full understanding of the various designs and threats to

Table 5-2. Sources of Invalidity for Designs 1 through 6

	Sources of invalidity											
	Internal								External			
Design	History	Maturation	Testing	Instrumentation	Regression	Selection	Mortality	Interaction of selection and maturation, etc.	Interaction of testing and X	Interaction of selection and X	Reactive arrangements	Multiple-X interference
Pre-Experimental Designs:												
1. One-shot case study X T₂	–	–				–	–	–		–		
2. One-group pretest/post-test design T₁ X T₂	–	–	–	–	?	+	+	–	–	–	?	
True Experimental Designs:												
3. Pretest/post-test control-group design R T₁ X T₂ R T₁ T₂	+	+	+	+	+	+	+	+	–	?	?	
4. Solomon four-group design R T₁ X T₂ R T₁ T₂ R X T₂ R T₂	+	+	+	+	+	+	+	+	+	?	?	
Quasi-Experimental Designs:												
5. Time series T₁ T₂ T₃ T₄ X T₅ T₆ T₇ T₈	–	+	+	?	+	+	+	+	–	?	?	
6. Nonequivalent control-group design T₁ X T₂ T₁ T₂	+	+	+	+	?	+	+	–	–	?	?	

Note: A minus indicates a definite weakness, a plus indicates that the factor is controlled, a question mark indicates a possible source of concern, and a blank indicates that the factor is not relevant.

Adapted from Campbell, D. T., & Stanley, J. C. *Experimental and Quasi-Experimental Designs for Research*. Chicago: Rand McNally, 1963.©1963 by the American Educational Research Association, Washington, D. C. Used by permission.

validity. While it is often best to use regularly employed personnel in operating the training program, the design of the program and the statistical analyses require adept professionals. Experts working closely with the regular staff will create the most productive program, design, and analyses.

A FINAL WORD

In summary, it is important to note that the literature abounds with studies of designs that do not justify the conclusions reached by their authors. Sadly, the majority of research utilizes pre-experimental designs (pre/post, no control; or post, no control). To add to the difficulties, most of this research employs criteria reflecting training performance (reactions and learning), with little attention to criteria that may be available at a later time in the transfer situation. The studies sometimes reflect a lack of sophistication, but, in most instances, the evaluators appear fully knowledgeable about the inadequacies of their design and even comment about the uncontrolled factors before going on to justify their conclusions. It is difficult to interpret data from training and educational settings because of the many possible contaminants. In many instances, the researchers simply could not impose strong experimental designs (such as Design 4). However, many of the quasi-experimental designs could have been utilized with little extra effort. The difficult process of properly evaluating our instructional programs must be undertaken. Dunnette and Campbell (1968) summarize the important minimum requirements for evaluation.

What needs to be done?
The *scientific* standards necessary for properly evaluating training experiences are few in number and disarmingly simple, but . . . they are almost never put into practice.
First, measures of trainees' status should be obtained *before* and *after* the training experience. Ideally, the measures should sample, as broadly as possible, trainee *behaviors* relevant to the organization's problems and/or to the aims of the training procedures, but attitudinal, perceptual, and other self-report measures may also prove useful. Second, measured changes shown by the trainees between pre- and post-training periods should be compared with changes, if any, occurring in a so-called control group of similar, but untrained, persons. Using control groups is the only way to assure that changes observed in the experimental (or trainee) groups are actually the result of training procedures instead of possible artifactual effects—such as the mere passage of time, poor reliability of measures, Hawthorne effects, or other spurious components. Finally, a third standard necessary for most training evaluation studies stems from the possibility of interaction between the evaluation measures and the behavior of the trainees during the program. For example, if trainees are asked beforehand

to answer questions about their supervisory "styles", they may be alerted to look for the "correct answers" during training in order to answer the same questions "more appropriately" (i.e., more in line with the desires of the trainer) when they are asked again after training. One way of estimating the degree of interaction between such measures and the training content is to provide a quasi-control group which takes part in the training program *without* first completing the measures. Then, comparisons between the two trained groups (experimental and quasi-control) on the after-measures may give estimates of the relative amounts of change actually due to training or due simply to having been alerted by prior exposure to the measures.

Unfortunately, these three rather simple standards for learning what training accomplishes are actually very difficult to meet, and they have been applied only rarely . . . [p. 8].[2]

The importance of the improvements that can be realized by rejecting pre-experimental designs and by considering the three factors stressed by Dunnette and Campbell—that is, pre- and post-tests, control groups, and a control for pretest sensitization—should be emphasized. In most instances, the inclusion of these procedures requires some planning, but it is well worth the effort in terms of the quality of information. Even in those cases in which it is not possible to implement all the procedures, a degree of forethought can provide dividends. Thus, in the situations in which a control group is not possible, a time-series design is preferable to a one-group pretest/post-test design. Thoughtful considerations can often provide solutions when the environment appears to dictate otherwise. For example, Rubin (1967) managed to obtain a control group for a sensitivity-training procedure while still providing the treatment for all participants. This was accomplished by having a selected number of trainees complete a pretest by mail several weeks before the treatment commenced. This group then completed the questionnaires again shortly before the treatment began for all participants. These pre- and post-test scores without an intervening treatment provided a control group that was later compared to pre- and post-test scores separated by the treatment condition.

[2]From Dunnette, M. D., & Campbell, J. P. Laboratory education: Impact on people and organizations. *Industrial Relations*, 1968, **8**, 1–45. Copyright 1968 by the Regents of the University of California, Berkeley. Reprinted by permission.

Part Two

The Learning Environment

Chapter Six

Basic Phenomena of Learning

A productive training environment is created by careful examination of the training objectives to determine the type of learning necessary for acquiring essential behaviors. There is still considerable controversy about the kinds of learning necessary to describe performance. In one system of examination, described more completely in Chapter 7, Gagné (1965, 1967, 1970) formulates eight types of learning, including concept learning, rule learning, and problem solving. Another system (Harmon, 1968) divides the objectives into three groups, including verbal, physical, and attitudinal performance. In each of these systems, the researcher analyzes his objectives and determines the required behaviors. Then, the behavior is matched to the most appropriate learning environment and instructional media. *Learning environment* refers to the dynamics of the instructional setting, with particular emphasis on learning variables—for example, knowledge of results or massed and spaced practice. *Instructional media* refers to particular devices and techniques, like simulators, programed instruction, films and lectures. In some cases, the instructional medium itself helps predetermine the learning variables. It is relatively easy to obtain individual feedback with a teaching machine, but it is difficult to do so with lecture material. In other cases, however, teaching machines can be used without individual feedback, and simulators may present the entire task (whole learning) or components of the task (part learning). In either case, it is important for the learning environment and instructional media to be determined by the objectives and the form of performance required.

Training sponsors understand, for instance, that simulators are not the best media available for learning a foreign language but that they may be excellent for learning driving skills. However, inappropriate techniques are often used because they are readily available. Unfortunately, the design of the learning environment and the selection of the appropriate instructional variables have not been treated with the same degree of awareness. Often a training designer insists that knowledge of results or feedback is necessary, without first determining what kinds of behavior are desired and whether feedback is appropriate for learning those particular behaviors. The approach emphasized in this text stresses the determination of objectives through need assessment and the analysis of those objectives to determine the behaviors required. After that has been accomplished, the proper learning environment, with appropriate learning variables, media, and techniques, can be selected.

LEARNING THEORY

The basic foundation for instructional programs is learning. The establishment of instructional procedures is based on the belief that it is possible to design an environment in which learning can take place and later be transferred to another setting. The close relationship between learning and instruction is suggested by most learning definitions.

> Learning is the process by which an activity originates or is changed through reacting to an encountered situation, provided that the characteristics of the change cannot be explained on the basis of native response tendencies, maturation, or temporary states of the organism (e.g., fatigue, drugs, etc.) [Hilgard & Bower, 1966, p. 2]

This definition implies that the change is relatively permanent, but it does not assume that all changes lead to improvements in behavior. Although most learning does lead to improvements, there is clear evidence that people can acquire behavioral tendencies toward drugs or racial hatred that might be injurious. It is also important to note that learning is an inferred process that is not directly observable. In some cases, learning becomes immediately observable through performance, but, in other cases, a considerable period of time passes before learning becomes apparent. The care with which the inference must be established is demonstrated by the effects of alcohol and other drugs on behavior. In many instances, the use of drugs can cause poor performance. However, it should not be inferred that learned behavior has been forgotten. When the effects of the drugs have worn off, the performance level can return to normal, without any intervening training (Hilgard & Bower, 1966).

From the preceding discussion, it seems that traditional learning principles applied to modern training or instructional settings would be effective. Thus, the rest of this chapter should be devoted to a review of the learning principles that have been developed in the last 100 years. However, the assumption is invalid. There is a wide gulf separating learning theories and principles from what is actually needed to improve performance. The transition will not be accomplished easily or quickly, for many reasons.

1. The learning theorist has tended to focus on highly specific laboratory experimentation, which has made generalizations to field

settings extremely difficult. Much research has focused on distinctions that are important in theoretical debates, with little attention to the broader interpretations of data necessary for the training specialist. Thus, the trainer is left with data that do not seem particularly relevant to his needs, and theoretical interpretations, which could provide the link, do not exist (Howell & Goldstein, 1971).

2. Until recently, the learning theorist has ignored the complex areas of human behavior. Thus, there is relatively little information available on problem solving, perceptual motor learning, concept learning, and other topics directly relevant to the needs of the training specialist.

3. The training specialist often demands quick answers and ready solutions to complicated problems (McGehee & Thayer, 1961). When easy solutions are not immediately apparent, the practitioner often assumes that the learning theorist's entire program is irrelevant to his needs. Thus, instead of adding to existing knowledge with what he can glean from the learning field, the practitioner ignores learning theory and contributes little information of his own.

Reactions to this transitional state are varied. McGehee (1958), in an article entitled "Are We Using What We Know about Training?—Learning Theory and Training," suggests that a close examination of what learning theory has given to the training practitioner is important. From such an analysis, he states, it is possible to arrive at a series of generalizations that apply to the training of participants. His generalizations are:

> The learner has a goal or goals; i.e., he wants something.
> The learner makes a response; i.e., he does something to attain what he wants.
> The responses, which he makes initially and continues to make in trying to attain what he wants, are limited by:
> The total of his past responses and his abilities;
> His interpretation of the goal situation.
> There is feedback from his responses—i.e., the consequences of his response. The learner, having achieved his goal (or goal substitute), can make responses that prior to his goal-seeking he could not make.
> He has learned [pp. 5-6].

McGehee has conducted several experiments to demonstrate the potential value of his principles. In one experiment, he notes that foremen refused to cooperate with a training program that consisted of an appreciation course for methods of time study. Time study is a complex technique for analyzing the time and sometimes the motions necessary to perform a job. The course did not enable the foreman to answer questions about the technique or about how changes in job performance might affect pay rates. McGehee's experiment demonstrated that a course that increased knowledge of time-study techniques led to substantial improvements in the handling of time studies. Thus, he synthesized the learning literature in order to produce generalizations about learning variables that might affect the training situation.

Gagné (1962) examined the utility of laboratory learning principles in the performance of a series of tasks. He found that the best-known principles, including feedback, distribution of practice, and meaningfulness, were "strikingly inadequate to handle the job of designing effective training situations" (p. 85). He reached this conclusion after examining data from a variety of different tasks, including tracking and problem solving. Thus, where McGehee has found that learning principles were useful in certain general situations, Gagné's analyses of particular tasks showed that these principles were not helpful at all. While the examination procedures must continue, it is important to be wary of the simple acceptance of learning principles from the laboratory. In Chapter 2, a statement by Gilbert (1961) warned against the use of teaching machines simply because they are available. A modified version of that statement, related to learning principles, is also applicable. If it is uncertain whether knowledge of results (KOR) is appropriate for the behavior and the task for which the training program is being designed, don't assume, without proper investigation, that KOR will work.

INSTRUCTIONAL THEORY

The basic gulf between learning theory and its applications to instructional methodology has led many researchers to believe that an intervening link must be developed between the theorist in the laboratory and the practitioner in the applied setting. As Bruner (1963) states the problem:

> A theory of instruction must concern itself with the relationship between how things are presented and how they are learned. Though I myself have worked hard and long in the vineyard of learning theory, I can do no better than to start by warning the reader away from it. Learning theory is not a theory of instruction. It describes what happened. A theory of instruction is a guide to what to do in order to achieve certain objectives. Unfortunately, we shall have to start pretty nearly at the beginning, for there is very little literature to guide us in this subtle enterprise [p. 524].

Gagné (1962) suggests that it is necessary to organize the total task into a set of distinct components that mediate final task performance. When these component tasks are present in the instructional program, there should be an effective transfer of learning from the instructional setting to the job setting. Thus, the principles of training design would consist of identifying the task components that make up final performance, placing these parts into the instructional program, and arranging the learning of these components in an optimal sequence. This approach suggests a concern with "task analysis, terminal behaviors, component task achievements, the fidelity of training-task components, and sequencing" (J. P. Campbell, 1971, p. 567).

The relationships among tasks, required learned behaviors, appropriate learning principles, and instructional media are complicated. Much of the difficulty centers around the need for a *taxonomy of learning*—that is, a categorization of the behaviors involved (Hilgard & Bower, 1966). While it is agreed that the principles often vary with the type of task, there is substantial controversy over different kinds of learning theories and the classification of tasks in terms of the type of learning necessary (Briggs, 1968). Some effort toward the solution of these problems is being made by researchers associated with instructional activities in educational settings. Unfortunately, many analysts associated with industrial training merely comment about the inadequacies or the usefulness of learning theories.

Later in this section, a few of the approaches developed to examine relationships among tasks, learning behaviors, learning variables, and instructional media will be presented. Before this presentation, it is necessary to examine the basic information obtained from laboratory investigations of learning.

The two basic forms of learning that have been extensively investigated in the laboratory are classical conditioning and instrumental conditioning. The use of both lower animals as subjects and precise laboratory methods has provided rich data about the learning process. The research investigators have described the learning processes and have examined many variables that affect the degree of learning. These data and methods are important basic tools for those who are concerned with understanding the learning that occurs in the training environment. The next several sections describe some of these basic learning processes and variables.

CLASSICAL CONDITIONING

In the 1890s, during his studies of the digestive processes, Pavlov reported a series of observations which introduced the investigations of classical conditioning. He had noticed that dogs salivated at the presentation of stimuli that preceded the appearance of food. Pavlov then discovered that the pairing of a neutral stimulus—for example, a bell—with the presentation of food resulted in the dog's *learning* to salivate at the sound of the bell. The process of learning to respond to a previously neutral stimulus because it is paired with another stimulus that ordinarily elicits the response is called *classical conditioning*. The neutral stimulus (the bell) is called the conditioned stimulus (CS); it elicited the response only because of conditioning. The stimulus (the meat) that consistently elicited the response before the experiment began is known as the unconditioned stimulus (UCS), and the response (the salivation) to the UCS is called the unconditioned response (UCR). The salivation that was elicited to the CS (the bell) is referred to as the conditioned response (CR).

The critical component of classical conditioning is the pairing of the neutral CS and the UCS close together in time. This process can be examined in Table 6-1, which diagrams Pavlov's original experiment.

Table 6-1.   Diagrams of Classical Conditioning

Before Conditioning

Stimuli	Responses
Bell CS	⟶ Head turning
Meat UCS	⟶ Saliva UCR

After Conditioning

Stimuli	Responses
Bell CS	Saliva CR
Meat UCS	Saliva UCR

Note that the CS does elicit a response of head turning, which is unrelated to the eventual salivation effect and typically disappears as conditioning proceeds. Even though the conditioned and unconditioned responses are both salivation, they may differ in various ways. For example, the CR may not elicit as much salivation as the UCR. While many psychologists have suggested that classical conditioning accounts for a small proportion of human learning, there are many behaviors that can be related to classical conditioning. Some researchers believe that the learning of emotional responses (like anxiety) is classically conditioned—for example, the sight of your car eliciting anxiety following an automobile accident (Bourne & Ekstrand, 1973). In this instance, the CS is the sight of the automobile, which did not elicit anxiety before it was paired with the UCS. The UCS is the auto crash and injury, which commonly elicit the UCR—fear. Here, the single pairing of these stimuli leads to a CR so that the sight of the car elicits fearlike reactions of anxiety.

In most cases, the conditioned and unconditioned stimuli must be paired a number of times before a CR occurs. Continual pairing of the two stimuli leads to a stronger conditioned response, which is called acquisition. Extinction refers to a decrease in the strength of a CR, which results when the UCS is no longer paired with the CS; that is, the bell continues to be presented, but it is not paired with the presentation of meat. With each successive trial, the bell by itself elicits less salivation. These processes are illustrated in Figure 6-1. Several other concepts included in the figure are discussed later in this chapter.

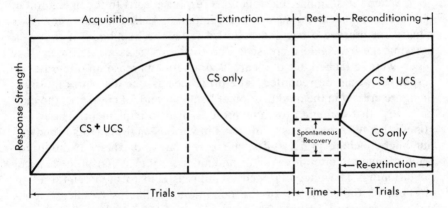

Figure 6-1. Summary of materials on certain basic phenomena in conditioning. From Kimble, Gregory A., & Garmezy, Norman. *Principles of General Psychology.* (3rd ed.) Copyright©1968 by The Ronald Press Company. Reproduced by permission.

INSTRUMENTAL CONDITIONING

B. F. Skinner, the father of programed-instruction techniques, is the person most often associated with instrumental or operant conditioning. In this form of learning, the subject's response is instrumental in gaining a stimulus that reinforces or rewards him. Thus, instrumental conditioning (as compared to classical conditioning) requires an active participant. The learner must produce a response in order to gain reward or avoid punishment; that is, his behavior is instrumental in the learning process. The responses can vary in complexity from a man producing a product at work to a rat pressing a bar, and the rewarding stimuli can vary from praise for the man to a pellet of food for the rat. Operant conditioning is sometimes distinguished from instrumental conditioning in one important respect. In instrumental conditioning, discrete trials are used, and the focus is on the single response; in operant conditioning, the appropriate stimuli necessary for the response (for example, the bar for the rat to press) are present at all times, and attention is directed to a sequence of responses. In either case, the organism must make a response in order to obtain the rewarding stimulus.

REINFORCEMENT

When the stimulus that follows a response leads to the likelihood of that response occurring again, the stimulus is called a reinforcer. If a hungry rat pressed a bar and received food, the likelihood of the rat's pressing the bar again increases. The food serves as a reinforcer. If a timer were attached to the bar, a dramatic increase in the rate of responses would be recorded. The principles associated with reinforcement are critical in the modification of behavior and, of course, in the new behaviors that training programs are designed to implement. The list of stimuli that have served as reinforcers in various environments is endless but might include praise, gifts, money, food, and water. In addition, reinforcement is often invoked as an explanatory mechanism in classical conditioning. The unconditioned stimulus is said to be a reinforcer; it strengthens the tendency of the conditioned stimulus to elicit a conditioned response. Thus, the food following the bell reinforces the response of salivation. Just as the association of the conditioned and unconditioned stimuli leads to the acquisition of learned responses in classical conditioning, the response followed by reinforcement leads to the acquisition of learned responses in instrumental conditioning. If a previously learned instrumental response is no longer followed by reinforcing stimuli, there is an eventual decrease in the strength of the response, known as extinction.

The numerous investigations of reinforcement have led to distinctions that have important implications for those concerned with training. Some of these distinctions include the following.

Primary and secondary reinforcers. Primary reinforcers are considered innate or unlearned reinforcers. Food for a hungry person and water for a thirsty person are considered examples of primary reinforcers that do not have to be learned. Some psychologists believe that secondary reinforcers are established through association with primary reinforcers in a classical-conditioning paradigm. The secondary reinforcer is the conditioned stimulus, while the primary reinforcer serves as the unconditioned stimulus. One example of a secondary reinforcer for man is money. Money, by itself, cannot be eaten and cannot quench thirst, but it has become a learned reinforcer because it buys food and drink. In our society, secondary reinforcers have assumed an important role because most people do not lack the primary reinforcers. Industrial psychologists suggest that secondary reinforcers (like prestige, fame, and attention) are important determinants of behavior.

Timing of reinforcement. Reinforcement should be given immediately following the appropriate response. Any delay might lead to the reinforcement of extraneous, inappropriate behaviors that are emitted after the correct response is made. For example, a parent may reinforce a child's tantrum by ignoring appropriately made requests but immediately attending to the child's screams. Fortunately, human learners can be reinforced by many stimuli. Thus, a trainee may participate in a learning program in order to earn a new job or a higher pay rate. In these cases, he can be rewarded with feedback concerning his progress until he successfully completes the program and earns the new job. The feedback serves to reinforce correct responses and also helps to extinguish incorrect responses while the learner works toward a more ultimate reward.

Partial reinforcement. Experiments in the learning laboratory have also produced results that indicate that it is not necessary to reinforce every correct response for learning to take place. This phenomenon is known as partial reinforcement. Skinner and his associates have examined many schedules on which the learner was not reinforced for every correct response, and they have discovered that learning proceeds in an orderly fashion even with intermittent reinforcement. Data indicate that if the learner is reinforced only after a certain number of correct responses, he will perform vigorously and quickly until the required number of responses is achieved. These data also show that responses learned under conditions of partial reinforcement are much more resistant to extinction than those learned under conditions of complete reinforcement. Behavior at slot machines provides a clear illustration of the effects of partial reinforcement. Even though each response is not rewarded with a payoff, the infrequent jackpots maintain the responses. Unscrupulous gamblers often provide one or two payoffs to a card player early in the game to hook him and then depend on that partial reinforcement to keep the game going even though the payoffs become less and less frequent. In training settings, it is useful to provide continuous reinforcement until the correct response has been learned. At that point, partial reinforcement will maintain the behavior and make the responses more resistant to extinction. Unfortunately, the same principles apply to undesirable behavior, as illustrated by the difficulties that novices have in learning complex motor skills. For example, tennis beginners using inefficient responses every so often hit a good shot, thus being partially reinforced for poor responses. When the learner decides on formal instruction, it is difficult for the instructor to extinguish these partially reinforced responses.

Punishment. Punishment can be conceptualized as stimuli that the learner would like to avoid. A worker might be penalized for unsafe behavior by losing some of his pay or by being criticized by his foreman—both aversive stimuli. The implications of punishment are not as well defined as those associated with positive reinforcement, but it is clear that punishment does not always reduce the likelihood of the same response occurring again. Some of the difficulties with aversive stimuli include the following:

1.   Often the behavior of the respondent is positively reinforced before punishment occurs. The worker may have performed some unsafe behavior, like failing to wear uncomfortable safety equipment, but he may be positively reinforced by being more comfortable. The positive reinforcement has a strong influence because it follows the inappropriate response more immediately than does the aversive stimulus.

2. Punishment tends to become associated with specific stimuli. The worker learns to wear his safety equipment when his foreman is present but quickly discards it when the foreman is not there.

3. There is a tendency to be inconsistent in the application of aversive stimuli. Thus, the parent does not punish the child each time the behavior is inappropriate, and some foremen look the other way to avoid noticing unsafe behavior, because most individuals do not like to administer punishment. There is also a tendency to feel guilty about the use of punishment, which leads the administrator to follow punishment with positive rewards.

4. Laboratory research suggests that the effects of punishment are largely emotional and only suppress, rather than extinguish the inappropriate behavior. Once the emotional effects disappear, the behavior reasserts itself.

5.   Punishment can lead to undesirable side effects. Anxiety associated with punishment can often create an unfavorable environment for learning and hostile attitudes toward the administrator of the punishment as well as the institutions he represents.

One interesting question is whether punishment is necessary. Bass and Vaughan (1966) suggest that it is needed when it is the only way to define the limits of behavior. Even in those situations, however, punishment should be used judiciously to avoid adverse effects.

SHAPING

When the responses to be acquired are difficult to learn, a technique called shaping (or the method of sucessive approximations) is often implemented. Shaping consists of a learning procedure that progresses in graduated steps. The behaviors that represent a step toward the final desired behavior are selectively reinforced until they are learned. Then, the behaviors that represent the next best approximation of the final behavior are reinforced, while the previous steps are extinguished. This process continues until the final behavior is learned. An excellent example of this procedure is the Bourne and Ekstrand (1973) description of a pigeon being trained to peck a key. When the bird is facing the key, the experimenter reinforces the pigeon with food in its tray. After several such trials, the positive reinforcement should lead to an increased probability of the bird's facing the key. However, that is not the final desired behavior, and continual reinforcement of that response will make it difficult to train the bird to do anything but face the key. Thus, the experimenter waits for the next approximation of the desired response, which would be walking toward the key. As in most training situations, this requires a great deal of patience, for the animal may move off in several different directions before advancing toward the key. Eventually, the appropriate response is made, and the animal is reinforced for advancing in the direction of the key. After a number of reinforcements, the pigeon should be in a position directly in front of the key. Now, it is necessary to start reinforcing head movements toward the key until the pigeon eventually pecks at the key.

In some training (for example, learning to fly an airplane), the required responses are difficult to learn without methods similar to successive approximations. The trainee might be given limited aspects of the tasks to perform while the instructor selectively reinforces appropriate responses and extinguishes incorrect responses. As the trainee acquires skill at the rudimentary aspects of the task, more factors can be added until he or she is performing the task as required in the transfer setting. This kind of procedure requires a careful analysis of the task in order to determine appropriate approximations of the final behavior and to control the reinforcement contingencies.

BASIC PHENOMENA IN CONDITIONING

Although the experimental procedures for classical conditioning and instrumental conditioning are different, there are a number of phenomena common to both approaches. The CS followed by the UCS in classical conditioning and the response followed by reinforcement in instrumental conditioning both result in learning. Extinction takes place for classical conditioning when its reinforcer (the UCS) is removed. Similarly, extinction takes place for instrumental conditioning when the instrumental response is emitted without reinforcement. In addition, the following phenomena are recognized in both types of learning.

SPONTANEOUS RECOVERY

The extinction process weakens the learned response until it eventually appears to be eliminated. Thus, the dog's salivation and the pigeon's rate of pecking the key decrease when there is no reinforcement. After a series of extinction trials, the responses stop completely. If the animal is removed from the experimental apparatus for a rest period and then returned, it will respond again for a series of trials, even when its responses are not followed by reinforcing stimuli. Pavlov named this recovery of the strength of the learned response spontaneous recovery. (See Figure 6-1.) If the animal is given another rest period and then replaced in the experimental setting, it will again respond. However, as long as there is no reinforcement, the amount of spontaneous recovery in each series of re-extinction trials will continue to diminish.

Spontaneous recovery makes it difficult to eliminate previously learned responses. We may continually try to eliminate poor responses, such as slicing a golf ball, only to discover that the inappropriate series of responses recurs the very next time we hold a golf club in our hands. Some psychologists (Bourne & Ekstrand, 1973) believe that one way to eliminate spontaneous recovery is to carry out extinction trials long after the response has ceased.

GENERALIZATION

If an animal has been classically conditioned to salivate to a tone of 1200 cycles, it will also salivate to a tone of 1000 cycles, although the strength of the response will be diminished. Similarly, pigeons trained to peck a key with certain illumination characteristics will peck with diminished strength if the color of the light is changed. These are examples of stimulus generalization, in which the organism responds to stimulus characteristics different from those present during the original training. The more similar the stimuli are to those originally used in training, the greater the strength of the response. The change in the strength of the response based on the degree of stimulus similarity is called the *gradient of generalization*. A hypothetical gradient is illustrated in Figure 6-2. While the most common examples of stimulus generalization are based on physical characteristics of stimuli, stimulus generalization can be based on learned similarity. Human subjects classically conditioned to blink their eyes at the word *big* will also blink when the word *large* is substituted. Generalizations that occur because of learned rather than physical characteristics are referred to as *mediated generalizations*.

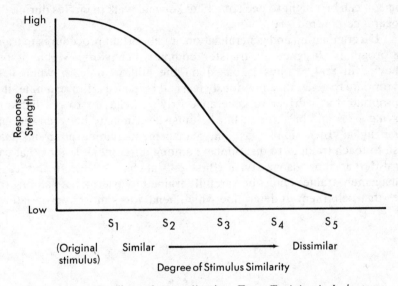

Figure 6–2. Gradient of generalization. From *Training in Industry: The Management of Learning,* by B. M. Bass & J. A. Vaughan. Copyright © 1966 by Wadsworth Publishing Company, Inc. Reproduced by permission of the publisher, Brooks/Cole Publishing Company, Monterey, California.

Stimulus generalization simplifies the environment by permitting a person to respond to similar stimuli without having to acquire a whole new set of responses. After training in a few situations, most humans can respond in a variety of similar settings. We don't have to relearn to drive a car because we switch models, and we can respond to traffic lights in a different city when their size and shades of color are different. But stimulus generalization also has its negative consequences. Undesirable responses are just as likely to generalize to new situations as more appropriate responses. Also, there may be many instances in which the response is appropriate for one setting but undesirable in the similar setting.

DISCRIMINATION

While stimulus-generalization procedures result in organisms' responding in the same way to similar stimuli, stimulus-discrimination procedures train the participant to respond differentially to distinguishable stimuli. Discrimination learning is usually accomplished by reinforcing responses to one stimulus while withholding reinforcement (extinction) for responses to a similar stimulus. Through discrimination training, a pigeon can be taught to peck at a blue key and walk in circles during the appearance of a red key.

Discrimination and generalization are important procedures in training programs designed to transfer complex behaviors. Much of our behavior in real settings is based on the ability to learn when it is appropriate to generalize previously learned responses. For example, it is appropriate for a driver to generalize driving behavior to red lights of varying sizes and brightness, but he must discriminate between red and green lights. In a similar fashion, management-training programs may wish to teach trainees to discriminate among different situations that call for different supervisory styles (Bass & Vaughan, 1966). In this case, management trainees must be carefully trained to discriminate among the cues that help them to determine which behavior is most appropriate.

Chapter Seven

The Conditions for Transfer

Although the previous chapter emphasized basic learning principles and initial learning processes, the question of transfer is paramount, especially for those concerned with instructional programs. Evaluation designs and criteria are chosen to measure performance in the transfer setting as a function of initial learning in the instructional program. Trainees are expected to use the skills, knowledge, and attitudes developed in training in the transfer setting. The main problem is persistence of behavior from the learning setting to another setting.

An experiment by R. C. Atkinson (1972) illustrates the complexities of the transfer task and the necessity for closely examining the characteristics of the training and transfer environment. The task consisted of vocabulary learning, in which large sets of German-English items were to be learned. On each trial, a German word was presented, and the student responded with the English translation. The correct answer was then presented. Three strategies were utilized for the presentation of material. In the first strategy (random-order strategy), the items were randomly selected and presented by the computer. A second strategy (learner-controlled) permitted the student to decide which item was to be studied. A third strategy (response-sensitive strategy) utilized a mathematical model to compute, on a trial-by-trial basis, the individual's state of learning in order to optimize the final level of achievement. All instructions were administered by computer control, with each student being given 336 trials in an instruction session and a delayed test session one week later. Figure 7-1 presents the results of the experiment. During learning, the random-order procedure led to the best performance, followed by learner-controlled and response-sensitive strategies. However, the results on the final test, the transfer setting, were completely reversed. The random-order strategy resulted in good performance in training because it presented many items that had previously been mastered. The learner-controlled strategy allowed the student to concentrate on those items that he had not learned, which resulted in a relatively poor performance in training. The response-sensitive strategy successfully selected those items that had not been mastered by the student, leading to a high error rate in training. However, in the delayed test session, in which the students were examined on all of the material, the

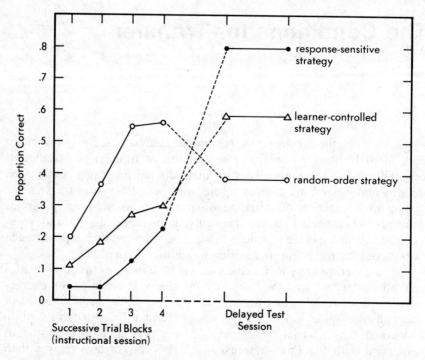

Figure 7-1. Proportion of correct responses in successive trial blocks during the instructional session and on the delayed test administered one week later. From Atkinson, R. C. Ingredients for a theory of instruction. *American Psychologist*, 1972, **27**, 921–931. Copyright 1972 by the American Psychological Association. Reproduced by permission.

response-sensitive strategy produced the best performance, because the training procedure had maximized the amount of time spent on unlearned items.

Atkinson's experiment clearly warns against assumptions about transfer performance that are based only on initial learning scores. (This warning parallels the caution given in the presentation on evaluation against assumptions about training performance that do not consider measures of behavior in the transfer setting.) This experiment illustrates the necessity of carefully designing a training environment that will maximize transfer.

THE BASIC TRANSFER DESIGN

In order to determine transfer effects, we might compare an experimental group that learns one task and then transfers to a second task with a control group that performs only the second task. If the experimental group performs significantly better than the control group on the second task, *positive transfer* has occurred. It can be assumed that the learning that occurred in the first task has transferred and aided performance in the second task. This assumption would be valid only if the experiment were properly executed and if it accounted for the various forms of bias and error discussed in the chapters on criteria and experimental design. If the experimental group performs worse than the control group on the second task, *negative transfer* has occurred. The learning of the first task has resulted in poorer performance on the second task. When there are no differences in performance between the experimental and control groups on the second task, there is *zero transfer*.

While the basic paradigms of transfer of training have been examined for some time, the exact conditions leading to positive or negative transfer are not easily specified, because settings outside the experimental laboratory rarely lend themselves to the type of analysis necessary to accurately specify the degree of transfer. However, it is important to understand the theories that predict varying degrees of transfer, because they provide information about the type of environment necessary to achieve positive transfer. The two major viewpoints that describe the conditions necessary for transfer are the identical-elements and the transfer-through-principle theories.

IDENTICAL ELEMENTS

The theory of identical elements was proposed by E. L. Thorndike and R. S. Woodworth (1901). They predicted that transfer would occur as long as there were identical elements in the two situations. These identical elements included aims, methods, and approaches and were later defined in terms of stimuli and responses. Holding (1965) summarized the work on transfer by detailing the type of transfer expected based on the similarity of the stimuli and responses (see Table 7-1).

Table 7-1. Type of Transfer—Based on Stimulus and Response Similarity

Task stimuli	Response required	Transfer
same	same	high positive
different	different	none
different	same	positive
same	different	negative

Adapted from Holding, D. H. *Principles of Training.* ©1965 by Pergamon Press Ltd. Used by permission.

In the first case, the stimuli and responses are identical. If the tasks are identical in training and transfer, trainees are simply practicing the final task during the training program and there should be high positive transfer. However, it would be unusual for a training program to have the same characteristics as the transfer setting. The purpose of the training program is to provide an environment for learning because the trainee is not capable of performing the task as it exists in the transfer setting. Perhaps he or she requires special modes of feedback or a permissive atmosphere in which to learn new approaches. As instruction proceeds, many programs attempt to develop environments that are as similar as possible to the transfer surroundings. But some differences, however subtle, almost always remain. For example, airline trainees know that a serious pilot error on a well-designed simulator will not have the same disastrous consequences as a similar error in a real airplane.

The second case assumes that the task characteristics, both stimuli and responses, are so different that practice on one task has no relationship to performance on the transfer task. It would be farfetched, although not impossible, to design a training program that is totally unrelated to the transfer situation.

The third case is common to many training programs. The stimuli are somewhat different in training and transfer settings, but the responses are the same. The learner can generalize his training from one environment to another. The person who has learned to drive one type of car usually has little difficulty switching to another (assuming the required responses remain the same), even though minor features may be different (for example, dashboard arrangement).

The fourth case presents the basic paradigm for negative transfer. A certain response to training stimuli is practiced so that the same response is given each time those stimuli appear. If the response becomes inappropriate, negative transfer results. As technology develops, producing continual modifications in control and display equipment without considering the role of man, there are frequent instances of negative transfer. Some airplane accidents provide a clear illustration of this effect (Chapanis, Garner, & Morgan, 1949). In one instance, a pilot attempted to correct for a landing, in which he was about to undershoot the field, by pulling back on the throttle and pushing the stick forward. However, this procedure was exactly opposite to the correct sequence of responses, and the pilot nosed his plane toward the ground. After the accident, the pilot (fortunately) was able to explain that he had been trained with planes in which the throttle was operated with the right hand and the stick with the left hand. In this plane, the positions of these controls were reversed. Thus, he used his left hand on the throttle and his right hand on the stick. When the emergency occurred, the pilot reverted to his old response habits—with disastrous results.

TRANSFER THROUGH PRINCIPLES

Critics of the identical-elements theory have argued that the analysis of transfer need not be limited to those situations in which there are identical elements. Actually, Thorndike and Woodworth did not intend for the identical-elements view to be specific to stimulus and response components (Ellis, 1965). Their elements consisted of items like general principles and attitudes, as well as the more specific components. The principles theory suggests that training should focus on the general principles necessary to learn a task so that the learner may apply them to solve problems in the transfer task. An interesting experiment by Hendrikson and Schroeder (1941) demonstrated the transfer of principles related to the refraction of light. Two groups were given practice shooting at an underwater target until each was able to hit the target consistently. The depth of the target was then changed. One group was taught the principles of refraction of light through water. In the next session of target shooting, this group performed significantly better than the group not taught the principles.

This theory suggests that it is possible to design training environments without too much concern about their similarity to the transfer situation, as long as it is possible to utilize underlying principles. The primary concerns become which environmental design best helps the trainee to learn appropriate principles for application in transfer situations (Bass & Vaughan, 1966) and which design best avoids potential negative-transfer effects.

THE COMPLEXITY OF THE TRANSFER PROBLEM

Equipped with the identical-elements theory and the principles point of view, it should be possible for trainers to construct useful training environments. However, these basic viewpoints, which were developed in laboratory settings, are not easily applied to settings that contain a bewildering display of complexity.

Specification of stimulus and response elements. It is difficult to determine whether the complex stimulus and response elements are similar or different until methods of describing and measuring them are established. The words *same* and *different* are not sufficiently precise to allow accurate prediction of relationships between training and transfer settings—the degree of similarity or difference is not easily specified (Osgood, 1949). For example, research studies show that identical stimuli and very similar responses in training and transfer produce results ranging from slight positive transfer to slight negative transfer, depending on the degree of response similarity.

Determination of relevant characteristics. Most environments do not result in simply negative or positive transfer. There is a complex interaction of components, some of which produce negative transfer and some of which produce positive transfer. For example, when shifting from a mechanical to an electric typewriter, there are some positive effects due to knowledge of the keyboard and some negative effects due to the differing sensitivity of the keys. Thus, each situation must be examined to establish the relevant characteristics of transfer and how they will interact. It would do little good to have high positive transfer on the overall performance of operating an aircraft but negative transfer on one critical element such as altimeter reading (Howell & Goldstein, 1971).

Measurement of transfer. Interpretations of the degree of transfer are hampered by the variety of measuring procedures. Ellis (1965) and Murdock (1957) have shown that differing amounts of transfer are found by using different formulas on the same data. Roscoe (1971) further argued that most formulas are based on percentage transfer, which is insensitive to the amount of prior practice. The basic percentage-transfer formula is:

$$\frac{Yc - Yx}{Yc}$$

where:

Yc = time, trials, or errors required by a control group to reach a performance criterion;

Yx = corresponding measure for the experimental group that has practiced on task 1.

Table 7-2 presents some hypothetical transfer data. An analysis of these data leads to the following:

$$\frac{200 - 100}{200} = \frac{1}{2} = 50\%$$

Thus, each transfer group, as compared to the control group, demonstrated 50 percent transfer, even though Group A spent five hours of prior practice for every hour invested by Group B. Roscoe suggests that designers of training programs would be concerned with such obvious training differences and would be unimpressed by transfer measures that did not reflect these distinctions.

The measurement problem is compounded by considerations of criterion relevance. As with all measurements, it is necessary to determine which criteria are most relevant to the analysis of the task. Flexman, Roscoe, Williams, and Williges (1972) had to develop a large number of criteria to examine transfer on flight simulators, because they found that it

Table 7-2. Hypothetical Transfer Data

Student group	Hours of prior study of German	Hours of tutoring required to pass
Experimental A	500	100
Experimental B	100	100
Control	none	200

Adapted from Roscoe, S. N. Incremental transfer effectiveness. *Human Factors,* 1971, **13,** 561–567. Used by permission of the Human Factors Society.

was difficult to determine whether the differences in transfer on one measure were real differences or spurious effects.

TRAINING FOR TRANSFER

While the preceding issues regarding transfer difficulties are not yet completely resolved, there are guidelines from learning studies that suggest various ways of producing transfer to new learning situations. The following suggestions were adapted from Ellis (1965, pp. 70–72).

1. Maximize the similarity between the teaching and the ultimate testing situation.

2. Provide adequate experience with the original task. Most research shows that adequate practice in training is essential for positive transfer. This is especially true for new skills and concepts for which thorough training must be given early in the learning process.

3. Provide for a variety of stimulus situations so that the student may generalize his knowledge. One way of overcoming the constraints of a training setting is to provide a variety of stimulus situations so that the learner can begin to generalize his concepts to the many situations in which transfer must occur.

4. Label or identify important features of the task. Labeling helps distinguish the significant characteristics of the task. Thus, the learner is able to use the necessary cues to determine when transfer behavior is appropriate or inappropriate.

5. Make sure that general principles are understood. This can be accomplished by presenting a variety of situations and asking the learner to apply the general principle. If the program is based on the learning of principles and the trainee does not thoroughly understand them, he has gained little from the training program that will be useful in the transfer setting.

CONDITIONS OF LEARNING

The previous section on transfer and learning suggests that there are at least two sets of factors affecting the degree of transfer; one set relates to the variables that determine the relationship between the learning and transfer settings, and the other set determines the degree of learning in the training environment. Material concerning this second set of factors is divided into preconditions of learning (trainee readiness and motivation) and conditions of practice (knowledge of results, massed and spaced practice, whole and part learning).

PRECONDITIONS OF LEARNING

Before the learner can benefit from any form of training, he must be ready to learn; that is, he must have the particular background experiences necessary for the training program, and he must be motivated. There is a tendency to believe that some individuals perform poorly in training because they either were ill-prepared to enter the program or did not want to learn. If these reasons are valid and the cause is not an ill-conceived program, the implementer must be certain that the preconditions for learning are satisfied.

TRAINEE READINESS

Trainee readiness refers to both maturational and experiential factors in the background of the learner. Since trainee readiness is critical in the learning process, the instructor must be concerned with the capability of his student to perform certain tasks. Children of a certain age may not have the language development necessary to learn complex concepts. For instance, a child of 7 can learn the meanings of new words, while a child of 4 would experience difficulty. Some psychologists (Gagné, 1970) believe that differences in developmental readiness are primarily due to the number and kind of previously learned intellectual skills. Supporters of this view would argue that many of the abstract rules of calculus could be taught to fourth-graders if they had first attained the skills (for example, algebra concepts) prerequisite to that form of learning. This point has particular significance for instructors responsible for designing instructional programs involving more mature individuals. These programs will fail if the prerequisite skills necessary to perform successfully are not considered. Particular emphasis should be placed on the determination of the incoming trainee characteristics. If the skills necessary to successfully complete the program are not present in the selected group, the program should be designed to establish those skills. It is important to realize that as jobs change in our complex and technologically oriented society, the characteristics necessary to perform the job change. The entrance requirements as well as the training program itself must be responsive to these alterations. The changes in the merchant fleet caused by automation are an illustration of this process. In response to the changing job requirements, the Seafarers International Union, established a basic-training school. As the program increased in complexity, the union discovered that many members of the applicant population could not read at a high school level and thus had difficulty completing the program. Since the union was not likely to experience changes in the applicant population, it solved the problem by establishing a remedial-reading program.

MOTIVATION

Motivation involves behavior that is active, purposive, and goal-directed (Bourne & Ekstrand, 1973). Most researchers agree that motivational level affects performance through an energizing function. Thus, the motivated individual is an active participant, and he will probably work harder as motivational level increases. Industrial psychologists examining the effects of motivational states on performance have directed their attention to two sets of theories. *Process theories* seek an explanation of *how* behavior is energized, directed, sustained, and stopped, and *content theories* consider *what* specific things motivate people. (For a review of these theories and the empirical research, see Campbell et al., 1970, and Miner & Dachler, 1973.) Most of this research is related to performance on the job rather than to learning in the training environment. However, the role of motivation performance on the job can provide important insights into performance in training environments. Also, if the motivational level in the transfer setting is extremely poor, learning in the instructional setting becomes an academic exercise.

Before discussing the implications of the motivational literature for performance in training, it is necessary to consider the relationship between motivation and learning. While psychologists generally agree that proper motivational levels are necessary for performance, there is considerable debate about the necessity for motivation in learning. Most of the data stem from investigations of animal behavior in which subjects are given a task to perform (for example, learning a complex maze) with or without a reward. Subjects given rewards tend to learn the maze faster than the unrewarded subjects. However, when the unrewarded subjects are switched to a reward condition, their performance shows an improvement that usually erases the differences between the two groups. These data suggest to some theorists that the unrewarded subjects were learning without reinforcement but that, as soon as they were given a reward, their performance showed the prior effects of learning. Another interpretation might be that food was not the only possible rewarding agent; that is, the animals might have been learning during the initial trials due to a curiosity drive that was satisfied by exploration. The debate cannot be resolved, because there is always the possibility that something (such as curiosity or exploration) motivated the organism. Similarly, training analysts must recognize that there are a variety of factors that influence motivational levels in human beings and that they might not be the same factors for every individual. It is important to use as many motivational variables as possible to enhance learning. While learning might take place without motivation, instructors should not have to depend on such events.

Although some researchers (Miner & Dachler, 1973) have justifiably criticized the theoretical work for being without sound empirical foundations and the empirical work for being fragmentary, it is important to remember that the entire area of motivational factors in organizational settings is in an early stage of development. The following sections discuss some of the factors that appear important in the establishment of motivational levels in learning settings.

Instrumentality theory and motivation. Vroom (1964) has developed a process theory of motivation related to the question of how behavior is energized and sustained. The theory is based on cognitive expectancies concerning outcomes that are likely to occur as a result of the participant's behavior and on individual preferences among those outcomes. The expectancy can vary, as can the valence, or strength of an individual's preference for an outcome. Vroom states that outcomes have a particular valence value because they are *instrumental* in achieving other outcomes. For instance, money and promotion have potential valence value because they are instrumental in allowing an individual to achieve other outcomes, like an expensive home or a college education for his children. The motivational level is based on a combination of the individual's belief that he can achieve certain outcomes from his acts and the value of those outcomes to him.

Training programs have a valence value for the individual if he believes they will permit him to achieve other outcomes. Thus, training becomes a low-level outcome that permits the achievement of higher-level outcomes (such as a job, a promotion, or a raise), which in turn might lead to other outcomes. The instrumentality theory implies that it will be necessary to show the individual the value of the instructional program in order to properly motivate him. Programs that appear unrelated to future outcomes will probably not meet the desired objectives.

Need theory and motivation. There are a number of content theories that emphasize learned needs as motivators of man's behavior. These theories concentrate on the needs that are to be satisfied and do not attempt to specify the exact processes by which these needs motivate behavior. The theories suggest to the training researcher that his or her programs must meet particular needs in order to have a motivated learner.

One need theory that has been given considerable attention involves the need for achievement motivation (nAch), which is described by Atkinson and Feather (1966) as a behavioral tendency to strive for success. It is assumed to operate when the environment signals that certain acts on the part of the individual will lead to need achievement. An illustration of this approach can be found in the studies of McClelland and Winter (1969), which were designed to instill achievement motivation through training programs. In one study, they found that participants in their training program were successful in later economic ventures. A series of studies (Raynor, 1970; Raynor & Rubin, 1971) combining the approaches of the need and instrumentality theories indicated that persons capable of high achievement don't necessarily perform well unless their behavior is viewed as being instrumental for later success. Thus, students with high achievement motivation received superior grades when they regarded the grades as important for career success.

Maslow (1954) has developed a hierarchy of needs and suggested that needs at lower levels must be satisfied before the higher-level needs can serve as energizers of behavior. Maslow's needs include:

1. Physiological needs: These include the basic needs of the organism, including food, water, and oxygen.
2. Safety needs: These needs refer to an individual's desire for a safe environment, with minimum threats to his existence.
3. Social needs: These needs include friendship and love.
4. Esteem needs: These needs include an individual's desire for self-respect and self-esteem and are based on positive self-evaluations.
5. Self-actualization: Self-actualization involves the need for self-fulfillment, which is based on the achievement of one's life goals.

Maslow's theory is not based on empirical evidence, but it does offer important implications for the training researcher. The theory suggests that it is necessary to consider the individual goals of the learner. An extension of this viewpoint indicates that the attainment of needs does not always involve positive consequences. The individual may be confronted with conflicting goals that have both positive and negative aspects or with two goals, both essentially negative. He may be faced with attending the training program or losing his job, while neither may be very satisfying.

Need theory emphasizes the importance of learning as much as possible about the various needs and viewpoints of trainees. An illustration of such an approach is a study that examines the work goals of engineers and scientists (Ritti, 1968). The author found that the goals of the scientists were largely related to academic achievement (like publication of data and professional autonomy), while the goals of the engineers were related to advancement and decision making. The organization's attempts to increase the professional aspects of the engineering positions were viewed as inconsistent with the goals of the engineer and as not effective motivationally.

Two-factor theory. Herzberg has postulated two sets of work motivators—extrinsic factors and intrinsic factors (Herzberg, Mausner, & Snyderman, 1959). Extrinsic factors (such as pay, job security, supervision, company policy, and working conditions) stem primarily from the organizational environment and are not directly influenced by the individual. Intrinsic factors are based on the individual's relationship to the job and include achievement, recognition, responsibility, and advancement. Herzberg maintains that extrinsic factors can only prevent the onset of job dissatisfaction or the removal of job dissatisfaction, while intrinsic factors do not have any influence on job dissatisfaction but will operate to increase job satisfaction.

Although the evidence regarding this theory is controversial, the hypothesis that the basic conditions surrounding work (extrinsic factors) cannot provide satisfaction has led to increased emphasis on the use of intrinsic factors as motivators of performance. Herzberg feels that an individual receives his reward from his performance of the task. Thus, motivation to work is related to an individual's achievement and his recognition of that achievement.

Since trainers often design the environments that lead to achievement, the use of intrinsic factors may often be built directly into the instructional program. Other writers have reached similar conclusions about the importance of intrinsic interest in a task, without necessarily subscribing to Herzberg's two-factor view of motivation. Gagné and Bolles (1959) have stated that:

> . . . the idea that motivation should be intrinsic rests not so much upon the role motivation plays in learning or in performance during learning; rather, it reflects a concern with the transfer criterion (of efficient training). It seems reasonable to suppose that motives and goals intrinsic to the task are more likely to transfer to the job situation [p. 10].

There can be little disagreement with a view that argues for the design of interesting and meaningful training programs. However, it is a long step from this view to an understanding of how to initially develop interest (McGehee & Thayer, 1961). Suggestions include stressing the future utility or value of the activity, providing feedback that shows the degree of accomplishment attained, relating the material to meaningful activity outside the instructional setting, finding tasks that are interesting because they are challenging, and enlarging the job to make it more interesting and to provide greater degrees of responsibility (which usually means enlarging the training program too!).

Extrinsic factors such as pay scales and company policy are potentially useful; however, they are often not within the direct control of those persons concerned with instructional programs. In those cases in which there is some degree of control, extrinsic factors are potentially useful. Despite Herzberg's theories, there is considerable doubt that extrinsic factors are related only to job dissatisfaction. In addition, some learning tasks display very little potential for the application of intrinsic motivators. The extrinsic motivators with the most general applicability to training settings are those related to gaining rewards and avoiding punishments, usually in the form of praise or reproof but sometimes consisting of financial incentives. In these cases, the recommended technique is to use rewards instead of punishments, because of the many negative aspects associated with punishment.

Goal setting and motivation.   Both Ryan (1970) and Locke (1970) have expressed views of goals and intentions as immediate determinants of behavior. Using a variety of laboratory tasks, Locke (Bryan & Locke, 1967) found that specifically designated goals result in better performance than do goals that are general or nonspecific. If Locke's views are found to generalize to more complex tasks, training models that call for clearly defined objectives will produce increased motivation in the training process. Interestingly, Locke and Bryan (1966) have also found in their analyses of training data that difficult goals lead to correspondingly better performance. They concluded that performance will be satisfying to the extent that important goals are attained. This again suggests that the objectives of training programs must be related to the important aspects of the job and must be conveyed to the trainees.

Campbell et al. (1970) have suggested that setting specific goals could have a cognitive function as well as a motivational function. Goal setting provides direction to the individual that could lead to the same beneficial effects in performance that are sometimes ascribed to motivational outcomes.

Equity theory.   Equity theory is based on the belief that people want to be treated fairly. Thus, individuals compare themselves to other people to see if their treatments are equitable. As stated by Adams (1965), "Inequity exists for a person when he perceives that the ratio of his outcomes to inputs and the ratio of others' outcomes to inputs are unequal" (p. 280). In this definition, outcomes include all factors viewed as having value—for example, pay, status, and fringe benefits. Inputs include all those factors that the person brings with him (such as effort, education, seniority) and perceives as being important for obtaining some benefit (Pritchard, 1969). Inequity is said to create tension that has motivating qualities, requiring the person to reduce or eliminate the discrepancy. This tension is created whether the person compared is perceived as under- or over-rewarded.

While equity theory appears to be especially relevant to the subject of wage factors, it may also have important implications for training. As already noted (Pritchard, 1969), the a priori determination of a variable as input or outcome is not always possible. Training provides such an illustration; that is, instructional programs may be viewed as an input or an output. In the input case, individuals who have acquired the necessary training experiences may view as inequitable other individuals who earn promotions and pay raises without equal educational experiences. In the output case, persons may perceive that they are not given the opportunity to attend advanced training courses. While there has not been any direct utilization of equity theory in such instances, some interview data (Dachler, 1974) suggest that female managers view their opportunities from an equity-theory framework. They feel that, given the same training background as men, they do not have equal opportunities for job advancement or for participation in advanced training. While the results of this situation are difficult to hypothesize, it is interesting to speculate on the behavior expended during the training effort when the trainee perceives that the outcomes are not available. In addition, there are interesting possibilities about the job behavior when the employee perceives that future training and other opportunities are not available.

Task difficulty and motivational level.   While Locke has found that difficult goals produce better performance, the relationship of motivational level to task difficulty indicates that there are other factors that must be considered. The learning literature suggests that increases in motivation beyond some level lead to poorer performance. The colloquial expression used for this lower performance level is that the person is trying too hard. The Yerkes-Dodson law describes the performance curves related to motivational level but adds one more factor, task difficulty. Essentially, the principle states that if the task is an extremely easy one, high motivational levels are extremely desirable. As the task becomes more difficult, intermediate levels of motivation lead to the best performance, with both very high and very low motivational levels leading to correspondingly poorer performance. At the most difficult task levels, the best performance is achieved by those individuals who have lower motivational levels. Thus, the studies relating learning to motivational level and task difficulty indicate that high levels of motivation may not serve the instructional purpose well when the tasks are particularly difficult.

Motivation—A summary. While the theoretical and empirical developments concerning the motivational literature are complex, there are some generalizations that can be made regarding the best hypotheses about the use of motivational factors in instructional settings. The following implications are offered.

1. While some learning theories indicate that learning does occur without explicitly designated rewards, it would be foolhardy for most instructional programs to proceed without a plan of action for the institution of motivational variables.

2. There are a variety of motivational needs that may work in any given setting, but the same incentives are not necessarily rewards for everyone.

3. Some empirical evidence exists to indicate that motivational variables are more effective if they are: (a) viewed as instrumental for future activities; (b) intrinsic; (c) positive rather than aversive stimuli when extrinsic motivators are used; (d) set in terms of clear and concise goals.

4. Learning data indicate that there is a relationship between motivational levels and task difficulty, with correspondingly lower motivational levels resulting in better task performance when the difficulty of the task increases.

CONDITIONS OF PRACTICE

It has been mentioned that the degree of original learning in the instructional setting is an important determinant of the amount of transfer. This section emphasizes those conditions of practice that are likely to increase acquisition. Many variables, like reinforcement, stimulus generalization, and discrimination, have already been established as important factors in the learning process. However, there are additional conditions of practice that are important, although the usefulness of a particular condition is very much dependent on the type of task and behavior being considered. Thus, knowledge of results is an important component of the conditions of practice, even though some researchers (Gagné, 1962) have demonstrated that its use is not a guarantee of learning. The following sections discuss some of the important conditions of practice and their relationship to task and behavior characteristics.

WHOLE VERSUS PART LEARNING

This variable is related to the size of the units practiced during the training session. When whole procedures are employed, the learner practices the task as a single unit. The utilization of part procedures breaks the task into components that are practiced separately. The complexity of the task and the relationship among the components determine the usefulness of whole and part methods (Holding, 1965). Naylor (Naylor, 1962; Blum & Naylor, 1968) suggested that the difficulty of any particular subtask (complexity) and the extent to which the subtasks are inter-related (organization) determine total difficulty. He used the example of a person driving a car to illustrate both the complexity and the organization functions. Driving in rush-hour traffic usually places the greatest strain on forward-velocity control (assuming the driver stays in the same lane), because the operator must continually use his accelerator and brake pedal to maintain varying degrees of speed. When the driver operates his vehicle on a curved section of highway, the steering component becomes the most complex part of the task. Task organization can be illustrated by the inter-relationship of forward-velocity control and steering. When the operator desires to make a turn, the two components must be inter-related in order to properly carry out the turning sequence. Naylor's examination of the part-whole literature since 1930 (see Table 7-3) supports the following basic training principles

Table 7-3.   Percentages of Post-1930 Studies Finding Whole or Part Methods Superior as a Function of Task Complexity and Organization

	Task complexity	Task high	Organization low
Whole	High	100	0
	Medium	50	50
	Low	25	50
Part	High	0	25
	Medium	19	50
	Low	63	50
Inconclusive	High	0	75
	Medium	31	0
	Low	12	0

From *Industrial Psychology: Its Theoretical and Social Foundations*, rev. ed., by Milton L. Blum & James C. Naylor. Copyright ©1968 by Harper & Row, Publishers, Inc. Reproduced by permission.

concerning part and whole methods: When a task has relatively high organization, an increase in task complexity leads to whole methods being more efficient than part methods, and when a task has low organization, an increase in task complexity leads to part methods being more efficient.

The use of part methods suggested by Naylor's analysis does raise some concerns related to the eventual performance of the entire task. Holding's (1965) review of the problem indicated that those tasks that are easily separated can be combined at a later time without difficulty for the learner. The job must be analyzed to discover the important components and to determine the correct sequence for learning the components. During this process, it is necessary to make sure that the student has developed the capabilities necessary to proceed to the next part of the task (Briggs, 1968). If the job is properly analyzed and ordered, a progression method may be used. Here, the learner practices one part at the first session. Then, at the next session, a second part is added, and both parts are practiced together. The addition of parts continues until the whole skill is learned.

MASSED VERSUS SPACED PRACTICE

It is important to determine whether the learner benefits more from as little rest as possible until he has learned his task or from rest intervals within practice sessions. Although the data are not definitive, they suggest that spaced practice for motor skills is typically more effective in acquisition and leads to better retention. DeCecco (1968) presented data obtained by Lorge (1930) that examined massed versus spaced practice on a motor-skill task. The subjects were required to draw a figure from a mirror image. One group, performing the task under massed-practice conditions, was given 20 trials without any rest periods. The other two groups performed the task under spaced conditions. One group was given one-minute rest periods between trials and the other group one-day rest periods between trials. As Figure 7-2 indicates, there were consistent differences between the spaced-practice groups and the massed-practice group, with the spaced-practice group demonstrating better performance. Later research (Digman, 1959) indicated that spaced groups benefited from the opportunity to mentally rehearse the tasks, while massed groups suffered from a buildup of fatigue during the practice sessions. These data show that the massed group, after an evening's rest, often performed better on the first trial of the new session than on the last trial of the previous day's session. This has led some researchers (Holding, 1965) to conclude that massed conditions do not hamper learning; they only depress performance. These views are supported by data showing that

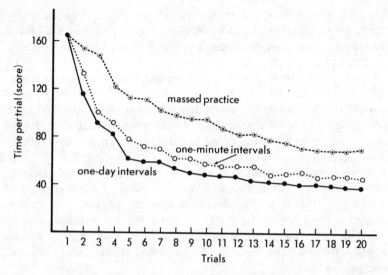

Figure 7-2.   The effect of distribution of practice on mirror drawing. Adapted with permission of the publisher from Irving Lorge, *Influence of Regularly Interpolated Time Intervals upon Subsequent Learning*. (New York: Teachers College Press, copyright 1930 by Teachers College, Columbia University), p. 16.

massed groups perform as well as spaced groups when they are switched to spaced-group conditions or when both groups are given retention tests after a few days have passed (Reynolds & Bilodeau, 1952).

Research exploring the acquisition and retention of verbal skills is not nearly as definitive, although it is still possible to conclude that practice will not be as efficient if the learner has to concentrate for long periods of time without some rest. As most students have discovered, cramming for examinations tends to produce high test scores but rapid forgetting. This example is supported by research (B. J. Underwood, 1964) showing that massed practice is better than spaced practice for acquisition but poorer for retention. Since the retention of learned material is important for the transfer process in training settings, spaced practice is the more useful technique.

Thus, the literature indicates that distributed practice utilizing reasonable rest periods is the favored technique. However, this generalization is not without penalties or exceptions. Massed practice does take less time than spaced practice, which requires learning time plus rest intervals. As DeCecco (1968) has noted, students have ignored warnings against using massed practice just because it takes more time. In situations in which the error tendency is high or the student is likely to forget critical responses, the time between practice periods must be either shortened or eliminated (DeCecco, 1968). This is often the case in problem-solving situations in which the learner must discover the correct answers from a variety of possible solutions. The learner goes through a large number of incorrect solutions before arriving at the correct answer. Here, forgetting the previous inappropriate responses would lead to an increase in learning time. In a more obvious case, it is often more efficient to mass, rather than space, trials when the material to be learned is relatively brief.

OVERLEARNING

Another condition of practice that has implications for both acquisition and transfer is overlearning. Since the criterion of success during training is often arbitrarily set by instructors, the intent of the overlearning concept is to ensure thorough learning of the task (McGehee & Thayer, 1961). The importance of overlearning is based on several factors.

First, the stimuli in the training setting and transfer setting are likely to be slightly different, but, due to stimulus generalization, positive transfer will occur as long as the responses are appropriate and well learned. The overlearning in these situations is especially important when the task is not likely to be practiced often in the transfer setting. Second, Fitts' (1965) review of the research in this area has led him to believe that overlearning is necessary in order to maintain performance during periods of emergency and stress. He has found that improvements in one criterion of the task may asymptote (for example, reduction of errors), but other measures (like response time) might show progressive improvement, implying that learning is still continuing. Improvement in performance might be masked by a failure to examine all the appropriate measures of performance or by artificial limits imposed in the learning setting. This latter case is an example of criterion contamination. The learner may not have the opportunity to demonstrate performance changes that indicate further learning because the equipment won't work at that rate or because social pressure by the group sets artificial limits. The instructor must obtain sensitive criteria of performance to be certain that the learner has gained the degree of competence necessary to transfer his skills.

KNOWLEDGE OF RESULTS

Holding (1965) traced the series of experiments that established the importance of this variable in the learning process. He noted that one of the earliest studies of knowledge of results was provided by E. L. Thorndike (1927), who had two groups of subjects (both blindfolded) draw hundreds of lines measuring 3, 4, 5, or 6 inches over a period of several days. The members of one group were given feedback that indicated whether their response was right or wrong within the established criterion of a quarter-inch of the target area. The members of the second group were not given any feedback. These data indicated that the group that received the knowledge of results improved considerably in its performance, while the other group continued making errors. A later study (Trowbridge & Cason, 1932) repeated this experiment but included a group that received feedback stating the degree of error. The subjects in this group gained even greater accuracy than the group that was just told that the answers were right or wrong. These two studies are examples of the many experiments that have demonstrated the importance of feedback. There is even evidence to indicate that learners often provide their own feedback when other external cues are not available. For example, an analysis of the original Thorndike data by Seashore and Bavelas (1941) showed that the group members who had not received any feedback became more consistent in their performance, even though they continued to make large errors. In this case, the subjects learned to match their previous attempts. Thus, as Holding suggested, learners who are not provided with external standards will often develop their own performance requirements.

Researchers suggest that the reasons why knowledge of results improves performance can be attributed to motivational and informational functions. The feedback in Thorndike's experiment can be viewed as praise or reproof as well as information about performance on the task. In another experiment using the line-drawing tasks (MacPherson, Dees, & Grindley, 1948), subjects were informed in advance that they would not receive feedback on the next block of trials. Their scores dropped immediately, even though feedback was still available, thus leading some researchers (Holding, 1965) to interpret the effect as motivational. Such data have led to conclusions that knowledge of results in all of its various forms serves as a reinforcer for man's behavior and as an incentive that affects his motivation. The research on motivational factors makes it possible to consider the feedback from many points of view, including its instrumentality in achieving later outcomes, positive versus negative reinforcement, information available to set goals, and intrinsic versus extrinsic incentives.

The study by Trowbridge and Cason (1932), which added a group with specific knowledge of results, illustrated the informational function of knowledge of results. Of course, the extra information does not preclude the motivational aspects of the feedback. In most situations, it is difficult to separate the effects caused by the motivational qualities and the informational aspects of knowledge of results. Even the simple feedback of "right" versus "wrong" conveys some information. The important issue regarding the informational nature of knowledge of results involves specificity. Contrary to popular belief, increased specificity does not necessarily lead to improved performance. It can actually lead to performance deficits. While some increases in specificity may be helpful, a saturation point can be reached at which the information is too much for the subject to handle, and which simply leads to confusion. As the subjects become more proficient at a task, they may also be able to learn to integrate more specific feedback. For each task, it is necessary for the trainer to carefully design the feedback to fit that situation and the capabilities of the learner. Additionally, the feedback should be timed so that the information necessary to correct the subject's response is immediately available.

Most training analysts have placed considerable emphasis on the importance of knowledge of results in the learning process. Unfortunately, many of those who emphasize its importance simply assume that any form of feedback with any sort of timing will accomplish the purpose. The preceding discussion indicates that the application of feedback requires real sensitivity for the task and the learner. In addition, there appear to be some tasks, like tracking or trouble shooting, in which the utility of feedback is questionable (Gagné, 1962).

RETENTION

The utilization of previously learned materials in the transfer setting assumes that the learner has been able to retain his recently acquired skills; that is, he has not forgotten. There are a number of variables that determine the degree of retention over a period of time.

The degree of original learning. Any of the variables that affect the degree of original learning also affect the retention of the material. The effects of overlearning are especially important in enabling the learner to retain his information over a long period of time. Other factors that should be examined include the motivational and informational character of the feedback and the distributed-practice methods.

The meaningfulness of the material. There is extensive research to indicate that the more meaningful the material, the more easily it is retained. It is important to properly organize the material and to establish principles to retain information, even if the material appears to be meaningless. Music students are aided in their retention of the musical notes corresponding to the lines and spaces of the staff through the use of coding schemes that organize the information. For example, the lines of the treble staff are the first letters of *every good boy does fine,* and the spaces spell *face.*

The amount of interference. There are two types of interference that hinder the retention of material. In one type, proactive inhibition, previously learned material interferes with the recall of the new material. The other type, retroactive inhibition, pertains to activities that occur after the original learning (during the retention period) that interfere with the recall of the original material. Thus, proactive effects concern interference that results from materials learned before original learning, while retroactive effects relate to interference that occurs after original learning. These two interference problems are diagramed in Figure 7-3.

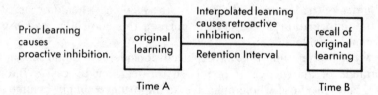

Time A   Time B

Figure 7-3. Interference theory. Material learned at Time A is tested for recall, after a retention interval, at Time B. Material learned prior to Time A (prior learning) produces proactive inhibition; things learned between Times A and B (interpolated learning) produce retroactive inhibition. From *Psychology: Its Principles and Meanings,* by L. E. Bourne, Jr., & B. R. Ekstrand. Copyright © 1973 by The Dryden Press. Reproduced by permission of The Dryden Press.

Interference relationships are often specified in terms of stimulus and response similarity. When the stimuli in the prior-learning and new-learning situations are the same but the responses required are different, strong proactive-interference effects in the recall of the new learning material can be expected. The cases describing stimulus and response interactions that result in interference effects have already been described in the section on transfer of training (see pages 107–109 and Table 7-1).

Motives, perceptions, and retention. There are many instances in which memory is affected by our perception of an event. Freud used the term *repression* to describe the tendency to forget events associated with fear and unpleasantness. Soldiers are sometimes unable to remember particular combat experiences because the events were frightening or because they were ashamed of their performance. Yet, these individuals are able to remember events of ordinary military life with ease. In a more common example, witnesses viewing the same accident give completely different descriptions of the events. In an experimental demonstration of the effects of perceptions on recall (Carmichael, Hogan, & Walter, 1932), subjects were presented with a stimulus figure. Some were told that it was a letter C, while others were told it was a crescent moon. When asked to recall the objects, the subjects drew shapes that resembled the idea they had been given rather than the stimulus object. Thus, one group changed the figure toward a crescent and the other toward the letter C. This occurred for a variety of name pairs, including bottle-stirrup, eyeglasses-dumbbells, and gun-broom.

LEARNING AND TRANSFER—A RECAPITULATION

The design of learning environments requires careful planning. The following are concise steps, adapted from Gagné (1970), that are important in the design of instructional systems. These steps are a good checklist, but those concerned with training should realize that there are many other variables that must be examined in order to design an instructional program.

1. Develop and maintain learner attention. The instructor must work to gain the attention of the learner. Initially, this is often accomplished with verbal instructions, but other techniques, including labels, color, and arrows, might eventually be needed to focus attention on the critical components of the task.

2. Present the expected outcomes to the learner. The learner should be informed of the learning objectives and the terminal performance he will achieve by the end of the instructional sequence.

3. Stimulate the recall of necessary prerequisite capabilities. While the program should be designed so that participants either have the necessary skills or are placed in special programs to obtain them, it is still necessary to spend some learning time stimulating the recall of previously learned intellectual and verbal skills.

4. Present the stimuli underlying the particular learning task. It is necessary to familiarize the learner with the stimulus material necessary for the instructional program. These stimuli vary for different learning situations. Thus, for discrimination learning, it will be necessary for each stimulus to be associated with a different response to avoid confusion. In part learning, the stimulus components must be broken down and properly sequenced.

5. Guide the learner. Through proper shaping techniques, the learner should be guided toward the correct responses until the essential behaviors are learned.

6. Provide knowledge of results. The task should be designed so that the motivational and informational characteristics of feedback can be used to inform the student of his progress.

7. Appraise performance. Assessment procedures should be designed for each component of learning so that it will be possible to determine if the student is meeting the learning objectives.

8. Design the program to achieve transfer. A variety of appropriate stimulus situations should be utilized in order to increase stimulus generalizations and the likelihood of transfer. The instructor should be wary of the dangers of negative transfer.

9. Design the program to achieve retention. The instructional program should be designed so that the newly acquired capabilities can be properly practiced with a minimum of interference effects.

SYSTEMATIC APPROACHES TO THE DESIGN OF LEARNING ENVIRONMENTS

The need for a systematic design of learning environments based on the behaviors to be learned has been discussed previously. This approach requires a careful analysis of the task behaviors, which should lead to the establishment of the most appropriate learning conditions and instructional media for achieving the proper performance. Presently, there are two missing links that have made systematic designs of training programs very difficult. First, there is a requirement for a taxonomy of learning that can be used to group all relevant behaviors into appropriate learning categories. Second, there is a need to establish the relationships between the particular learning categories and the most appropriate instructional media and learning conditions. Research studies of learning variables have attempted to establish such relationships. For example, whole- and part-learning procedures have been related to task complexity and task organization (Naylor, 1962).

J. P. Campbell's (1971) *Annual Review of Psychology* article "Personal Training and Development" described the need for the specification of appropriate learning behaviors based on examinations of the task. He concluded that the studies investigating these issues were ". . . a mere pittance of what they should be" (p. 567). A few studies have analyzed job behaviors so that the specification of training content could directly follow. One study (Glickman & Vallance, 1958) was concerned with the relationship of the subject matter of the Navy's Officer Candidate School (OCS) to the duty requirements of new officers stationed on destroyer-type ships. In an earlier study (Vallance, Glickman, & Vasilas, 1954), the researchers had developed 1073 incidents that provided a description of the significant elements in the duties of the new officers. The technique they employed is called the critical-incident method (Flanagan, 1954). It is designed to determine which critical behaviors lead to successful or unsuccessful performance. The shipboard incidents were sorted into two categories. The first category, labeled *taught*, included the skills, knowledge, and attitudes relevant to the performance of a particular incident that were the result of specific lessons. The second category, called *not taught*, included the material that was not covered. The analysis determined that 62.9 percent of the classified incidents were taught at the school. The researchers found that the incidents covered were, in general, those considered most important. However, they also discovered that there were cases in which 50 or more incidents were covered in only one hour of instruction. This type of analysis could lead to further examinations that might result in an increase in the time spent on the items considered most important. Thus, the Glickman and Vallance study used behavioral incidents to help specify the appropriate content for an existing training program.

Another study (Folley, 1969) utilized a similar approach to specify the important behaviors for retail-sales personnel from the perspective of the customer. Analyses of customers' narratives and checklists resulted in 2000 critical incidents that were grouped into categories of effective and ineffective behaviors. Table 7-4 presents several of the effective and ineffective categories and lists the frequency of each critical behavior. Folley performed the analysis for activity during special sales, when the personnel would have a large number of customers, and for routine activity. An examination of the differences between the two types of activity in the ineffective categories led to some interesting conclusions. It appears that customers were not nearly as concerned with delayed or slow service during a sale as they were with the lack of courteous or exclusive attention in a routine situation.

Table 7-4. Final Effective and Ineffective Categories with Number of Incidents in Each Category

Effective categories		
Category	Normal data	Sale data
I. Volunteered information	188	74
A. Showed how to use or care for item	38	10
B. Wrote down information about merchandise or gave literature	45	5
C. Volunteered information about store procedures or identification of salesperson	47	16
D. Volunteered general information about merchandise	29	30
E. Told about size designations and how to select sizes	29	13

Table 7–4.   Final Effective and Ineffective Categories with Number of Incidents in Each Category (cont.)

Effective categories

Category	Normal data	Sale data
II. Made thorough attempt to get item for customer	209	68
A. Went to the stockroom for item	34	8
B. Looked through extra stock around counter	36	14
C. Told customer where to find item elsewhere	56	21
D. Told customer item would be in at a later date	32	13
E. Offered to obtain or hold item for customer	51	12
III. Gave prompt or quick service	54	26
A. Approached customer promptly	33	9
B. Handled details of transaction quickly	21	17
IV. Gave customer exclusive attention and was courteous	159	49
A. Gave customer exclusive attention	43	17
B. Offered courteous greeting or parting	77	25
C. Offered to help customer in the future	39	7

Ineffective categories

Category*	Normal data	Sale data
I. Did not give sufficient or accurate information	64	10
A.D.E. Gave incorrect or little merchandise information		
C. Did not give requested identifying information		
II. Gave delayed or slow service	94	7
A. Did not approach customer within reasonable time		
III. Did not give customer exclusive attention or was not courteous	67	28
A. Did not give exclusive attention		
B. Did not offer a greeting or parting		

*These area headings are corollaries to the "effective" area headings.

Adapted from Folley, J. D. Determining needs of department store sales personnel. Training and Development Journal, 1969, 23, 24–27. Used by permission of the American Society for Training and Development.

This type of task analysis permits the direct specification of the objectives and the course content of a training program, as well as the types of behaviors that are to be learned in the training program. As previously mentioned, what is missing is a taxonomy that groups the behaviors into appropriate learning categories and then relates these categories to the most appropriate instructional media and learning conditions. There has been little work in this area, but an approach by Gagné (1965, 1967, 1970), based on eight categories of learning, is one systematic attempt to unravel some of the details. Tables 7-5 and 7-6 present the various types of learning, their definitions, and a summary of the learning conditions necessary to produce the required performance. Gagné's system assumes a hierarchy; that is, each higher form of learning assumes the necessity for learning at the previous levels. Thus, problem solving assumes previous rule learning, while rule learning assumes previous classification learning. Gagné and his colleagues (Briggs, Campeau, Gagné, & May, 1967) have further specified the conditions and media necessary for each form of learning. The following are two examples based on multiple discrimination and problem solving (pp. 32–33).

Multiple Discrimination

Instructional Event	*Medium*
1. Presentation of individual stimuli one by one	Actual object or pictures
2. Progressive part practice	Actual object or pictures
3. Confirmation	Actual object or pictures
4. Appraisal	

Problem Solving

Instructional Event	*Medium*
1. Inform learner about performance required.	May require objects or pictures (depending on objectives)
2. Stimulate recall of component concepts.	May be done by oral or printed speech; actual objects or pictures may be desirable (depending on objectives)
3. Verbal guidance	Oral or printed words
4. Appraisal	May require objects or pictures (depending on objectives)[1]

---

[1]From Briggs, L. J., Campeau, P. L., Gagné, R. M., and May, M. A. *Instructional Media: A Procedure for the Design of Multi-Media Instruction, a Critical Review of Research, and Suggestions for Future Research*. Palo Alto, Calif.: American Institutes for Research, 1963. This and all other quotes from the same source are reprinted by permission.

Table 7-5.   Types of Performance That Are Outcomes of Learning, with Definitions, Examples, and Corresponding Inferred Capabilities

Performance type	Definition	Example	Inferred capability
Specific responding*	Making a specific response to a specified stimulus	Child saying "doll" when mother says "doll"	Connection
Chaining: Motor	Exhibiting a chain of responses, each member of which is linked to each subsequent member	Unlocking a door with a key	Chain
Verbal	Exhibiting a chain of verbal responses linked by implicit codes	Giving French equivalents of English words; saying "A stitch in time saves nine"	Verbal association; verbal sequence
Multiple discrimination	Making different (chained) responses to two or more physically different stimuli	Naming a specific set of object colors	Discrimination
Classifying	Assigning objects of different physical appearance to classes of like function	Distinguishing various objects as "plant" or "animal"	Concept
Rule using	Performing an action in conformity with a rule represented by a statement containing terms that are concepts	Placing *i* before *e* except after *c* in spelling various English words	Principle (or rule)
Problem solving	Solving a novel problem by combining rules	Raising an automobile without using a jack	Principles plus "problem-solving ability"

*Also known as *instrumental response*.
Adapted from Gagné, R. M. Instruction and the conditions of learning. Copyright ©1967 by Chandler Publishing Company. From *Instruction: Some Contemporary Viewpoints*, by L. Siegel, by permission of Chandler Publishing Company, an Intext publisher.

Table 7-6. Summary of Conditions Considered Necessary for Seven Kinds of Learning

Performance established by learning	Internal (learner) conditions	External conditions
Specific responding	Certain learned and innate capabilities	Presenting a stimulus under conditions commanding *attention;* occurrence of a response *contiguous* in time; *reinforcement*
Chaining: Motor	Previously learned individual connections	Presenting a *sequence* of external cues, effecting a sequence of specific responses *contiguous* in time; repetition to achieve selection of response-produced stimuli
Verbal	Previously learned individual connections, including implicit "coding" connections	Presenting a *sequence* of external verbal cues, effecting a sequence of verbal responses *contiguous* in time
Multiple discrimination	Previously learned chains, motor or verbal	Practicing to provide *contrast of correct and incorrect stimuli*
Classifying	Previously learned multiple discriminations	Reinstating discriminated response chain contiguously with *a variety of stimuli* differing in appearance but belonging to a single class
Rule using	Previously learned concepts	Using external cues (usually verbal), effecting the recall of previously learned concepts contiguously in a suitable sequence; specific applications of the rule
Problem solving	Previously learned rules	Self-arousing and selecting previously learned rules to effect a novel combination

These authors use this system to specify the behavioral objectives into a type of learning from which they design the instructional events and the media necessary. Thus, the following question would be classified as problem-solving learning: "How could you explain the fact that the bones of a whale have been found in the Sahara Desert?" (p. 87). The specific program must consist of the entire instructional sequence—for example, discrimination, chaining, and concepts necessary to problem solving. Assuming that this sequence has been established, the media program would resemble the following (1963, pp. 88–89):

Instructional Event

1. Inform learner of performance required.

   "Your answer must explain how this fact could come about, in terms of other information that can be substantiated."

2. Stimulate recall of component concepts or principles. (Not all of these prompts should be necessary.)

   "Do whales fly, swim, or walk? Do they live on land or in water? Does a lake, river, or ocean ever dry up? Does the earth's surface change in form and nature over long periods of time? Have whales existed long?"

3. Provide verbal guidance.

   "Can you put all your answers together and give an answer to the question?"

4. Student response.

   "The Sahara Desert could once have been the bed of a sea or ocean."

An analysis of this learning situation indicates that pictures are not required because the student can read or hear verbal statements. However, it is necessary to follow the student's responses to the verbal prompts with feedback. Also, some students will need more prompts than others. Briggs et al. suggest that programed instruction meets these necessary conditions, because it permits the student to record and check his answers. Also, the program can be designed so that students can bypass unneeded prompts. A teacher or a series of slides can provide similar conditions. Thus, older children could use programed instruction, while younger children could use movies and audiotapes. A teacher would be available for individual tutoring.

There is considerable debate over the hierarchies of learning suggested by the Gagné system (Hilgard & Bower, 1966). However, the system is important because it suggests a procedure that organizes behaviors into learning types and then relates the categories to conditions for learning and instructional media.

Another program of research that has systematically attempted to group behaviors into a taxonomy is the work of Fleishman (1972) and his colleagues. These researchers suggest that many of the behavioral categories (for example, discrimination, problem solving, and motor-skill learning) contain a large diversity of functions. Thus, Fleishman has attempted to identify more basic abilities that are related to performance in a wide variety of tasks. The word *ability* refers to the general trait that the trainee utilizes in the learning of a task. The researchers focused on the ability factors common in various tests of performance that describe performance on a variety of tasks. A few of the abilities discovered include the following:

1. reaction time—speed required to respond to a stimulus
2. multilimb coordination—the coordination of the movement of several limbs in the operation of a control
3. gross body equilibrium—the control of balance with nonvisual cues.

Through a variety of studies, Fleishman found that the particular abilities required to perform a task were systematic and subject to change during practice. These changes have important implications for skill training at different stages of learning. For example, Fleishman (1962) analyzed a complex tracking task and found that spatial orientation was important early in the task and multilimb coordination was important later in the task. Fleishman used this information in a training program by first presenting special instructions about orientation and later providing information about coordination requirements. The trained group was found to be superior to several other groups when it was examined on the tracking task. Thus, Fleishman's approach presents an important methodology for the specification of particular abilities and their relationship to the most appropriate instructional technique. Additional systematic attempts like those of Gagné and Fleishman are badly needed.

Part Three

Instructional Approaches

Chapter Eight

A Variety of Instructional Techniques

A complete systematic need-assessment procedure includes a set of learning objectives that determines the type of learning necessary to achieve the goals. The instructional designer is then able to examine the media and techniques available and to choose the method most appropriate for the behaviors being considered. This procedure should be appropriate for all different types of objectives, from motor-skill specifications in pilot training to styles of managerial behavior in various organizations. At a molar level, there is basic knowledge that helps specify the appropriate technique for particular behaviors. For example, machine simulators are used for the development of motor skills, while role playing is designed to acquaint managerial trainees with a variety of interpersonal situations. Unfortunately, there has been no advancement beyond molar generalities. In part, this is due to the difficulties encountered in the development of a comprehensive set of categories to describe the type of learning underlying the behavioral objectives. Another dilemma is the determination of the behaviors that are likely to be modified by the various techniques. J. P. Campbell (1971) expressed this dilemma by noting that it is not possible to organize the empirical research around dependent variables. He believes in examining which kinds of experiences produce particular outcomes and which variables affect the relationship between treatments and outcomes. However, for a variety of reasons, instructional designers have not arrived at that state of knowledge. First (as stated many times before), the empirical research necessary to establish these relationships has been insufficient. Second, most research efforts have emphasized reactions and learning in the training setting rather than performance in the transfer setting. Third, empirical studies have tended to cluster around demonstrations of the value of the technique, rather than the nature of the learning activities for which the method is useful. Thus, this material is organized around instructional approaches, with the hope that future texts on instructional procedures might be able to choose a different format.

Part 3 is titled instructional approaches (rather than media or techniques) because some of the topics are clearly not dependent upon a particular method. Some topics focus on particular groups of trainees, like the hard-core unemployed or individuals searching for second careers, rather than on particular methods. Other approaches, like organizational development, utilize a variety of techniques within the same setting. Also included in this multitreatment category are studies of individual differences in which investigators have attempted to match the abilities of the learner to a variety of different instructional approaches.

Part 3 also includes material devoted to particular methods, like programed instruction, computer-assisted instruction, business games, role-playing, and behavior modification. It is not possible to examine every training technique or the many variations of each technique. The criteria for inclusion are almost as complex and difficult to express as the criteria for most training programs. I have selected techniques that have aroused the interest of the instructional community and that appear likely to be used in the coming decade. I have also favored approaches that elucidate the topics presented in the first seven chapters. For example, organizational development provides an interesting illustration of an approach that focuses on organizational goals and objectives as well as individual trainee needs, while behavior modification represents a technique that is a direct development of the learning literature on operant conditioning. Other approaches are included because they represent attempts to deal with today's serious social problems. Thus, there is a section devoted to training the hard-core unemployed and individuals looking for second careers. In some instances (notably, training for second careers), there is very little information to offer the reader, but the seriousness of the problem demands its exploration.

The tremendous variety of approaches requires a flexible format for the presentation of the techniques. In those cases in which the technique consists of well-defined approaches, such as programed instruction, descriptive background material and specific research examples are included. In those approaches that do not have well-defined characteristics, such as on-the-job instruction, only general descriptions can be included. When enough empirical information was available, there is a general discussion of the evaluation data, with particular emphasis on the problem areas that must be faced by the researcher and the practitioner. Finally, there is a summary of the advantages and limitations of the approach, based on evaluation studies whenever possible.

The order of the techniques in the three chapters in this section is arbitrary. This chapter contains a variety of training techniques, ranging from programed instruction to sensitivity training. Chapter 9 discusses techniques that are all, to a certain degree, simulations, and Chapter 10 presents special issues, including individual differences and treatment interactions, training for those looking for second careers, and training for the hard-core unemployed.

CONTROL PROCEDURES—ON-THE-JOB TRAINING AND THE LECTURE METHOD

Before beginning a discussion of the more specific instructional approaches, it is important to consider the two general procedures that are most frequently used—on-the-job training and the lecture method. Valid information about the utility of these two procedures is not readily available. Everyone uses these methods, but they are rarely investigated, except when they are employed as a control procedure for research exploring another technique. Even in those cases, the discussion of results centers on the "new" technique. This is especially shortsighted since many research investigations have not found any differences in achievement between control techniques and other methods, such as films. The "no differences" results have led many investigators to believe that films and television are at least as good as the more traditional lecture method. Thus, they suggest focusing attention on those situations that are particularly appropriate for films. However, the question could be reversed to determine what lectures and on-the-job training can offer the learner. For example, it could be asked if there are particular learning behaviors that are especially well taught by on-the-job training. Since these control methods are used so often and are relatively inexpensive compared to methods like computer-assisted instruction, some research effort in this direction would appear to be advantageous. It is certainly ironic that the best information available about the two most frequently used techniques is a series of generalizations based mainly on intuition.

ON-THE-JOB TRAINING

Almost all trainees are exposed to some form of on-the-job training. This form of instruction might follow a carefully designed off-the-job instructional program, or it might be the sole source of instruction. There are very few, if any, instructional programs that can provide all the required training in a setting away from the job. At the very least, provisions for transfer to the job setting must be part of the initial learning experience of the actual job environment. Unfortunately, an on-the-job instructional program is usually an informal procedure in which the trainee is simply expected to learn by watching an experienced worker. This informal approach reflects the main argument against the use of on-the-job training as the fundamental instructional system. While there is no reason why a carefully designed on-the-job instructional system should not be as successful as any other approach, the achievement of the program still demands that the objectives and the training environment be carefully prepared for instructional purposes. Given the proper conditions, there are certain advantages to on-the-job training. For example, the transfer problem becomes less difficult, because the individual is being trained in the exact physical and social environment in which he is expected to perform. There is also an opportunity to practice the exact required behaviors. As far as evaluation is concerned, on-the-job instruction could result in the collection of more job-relevant criteria.

Unfortunately, most on-the-job training programs are not planned and, thus, don't work well. Too often, practicality is the main reason that this form of training is chosen. It is cheap and easy to implement without any planning at all. The simple instruction to any employee "Help John learn the job" fully implements the training program. The entire instructional process is placed in the hands of an individual who may or may not be capable of performing the job and who probably considers the entire procedure an imposition on his time. Under these conditions training takes second place to the performance of the job. Even if the "instructor" is capable, it may not be possible to slow down the pace, appraise the responses, and supply feedback to the trainee in a job setting where performance is the criterion for success. Simply put, the job environment may not be a good learning environment. While this point is obvious when very complex behaviors must be learned (for example, flying an airplane), it is too often neglected for other behaviors that appear easy enough to learn on the job.

Many of these difficulties plague on-the-job training programs that have attempted some systematic form of instruction. Apprenticeship systems provide a good example of the difficulties in implementing on-the-job programs. These formal programs are used to teach various skilled trades. Typically, the trainee receives both classroom instruction and supervision from experienced employees on the job. At the end of a specified period of training, the apprentice becomes a journeyman. This system is employed in a wide variety of skilled trades and is commonly accepted as a valid mode of instruction for large numbers of trainees. For example, in 1966, Chrysler Corporation employed 10,600 individuals in the apprenticeable skilled trades (Irwin, 1967). At that time, 2000 of these employees were apprentices. Despite the size and scope of these programs, analyses indicate that the on-the-job portion of the training is not easily adapted into a good learning environment. Strauss (1967) described the problems as follows:

1. While apprenticeship systems are assumed to provide systematic on-the-job training, the sad fact is that they actually provide little systematic guidance by the journeymen or supervisors. Exposure to a broad range of pertinent experiences appears to be mainly a matter of dumb luck.

2. Learning in school systems may be more effective than on-site training simply because learning on the job is secondary to the employer's insistence that the trainee put in a full day's work.
3. On-site training often results in learning sloppy ways of doing things.
4. Many of the newly developed skills, such as electronics, have an intellectual component that is difficult to teach on the job.

However, these difficulties should not lead the reader to conclude that on-the-job training programs cannot produce well-trained employees. A study (Lefkowitz, 1970) of the effects of a training program on the productivity and tenure of sewing-machine operators demonstrated that on-the-job training programs can produce direct benefits. The experimental program integrated off-site simulation training, which was instituted in a room off the assembly line, with on-site training. Some training groups were exposed only to varying lengths of off-site simulation. The group experiencing both off- and on-site training achieved the best balance of productivity and employee retention. Employee retention had been a serious problem before the study, with turnover as high as 68 percent in one year. Lefkowitz noted that the on-the-job phase of the training program provided for job-oriented discussion following the first exposure to the factory. Thus, the trainees were able to discuss various difficulties, like scheduling and job-related tension, and to reach solutions to the problems that led to the high turnover of previous employees. Lefkowitz also noticed that the first-line supervisors paid greater attention to these trainees during their first days of integrated training. He suggested that this occurred because the trainees would be returning to the off-site simulation and reporting their experiences to the trainer.

While on-the-job training can work, as demonstrated by this study, it is not usually successful when it is used to avoid the necessity of designing a training program. As long as programs are designed solely for that purpose, they will face difficulties of incompetent instructors, priority production schedules, and a generally poor learning environment. On-site training must be treated like any other method; the technique should be chosen because it is the most effective way of implementing certain behaviors. Once the training analyst ascertains that on-site training is the most effective technique to teach the pertinent skills, the environment must be designed as carefully as any other instructional environment (Mosel, 1957). This procedure is equally appropriate for on-site training that follows an off-the-job instructional program. Sometimes a trainee completes a carefully designed instructional program, only to be confronted by a bewildering environment on the job. Often, he is not even accorded the benefit of an orientation program that might at least provide an introduction to the individuals with whom he will be working.

LECTURE METHOD

While on-the-job training is the most extensively used procedure in industrial settings, the lecture method enjoys that status in educational environments, from primary school to evening-division programs for employed workers. In addition, the lecture method is the most frequently employed control procedure in the analysis of recently developed techniques, like films, TV, and programed instruction.

Many authors (McGehee & Thayer, 1961; Bass & Vaughan, 1966) question the usefulness of the lecture method as an instructional technique. Their criticisms focus on its one-way communication aspects. Too often, the lecture method results in passive learners who do not have the opportunity to clarify material. In addition, it is difficult for the lecturer to present material that is equally cogent to individuals who have wide differences in ability, attitudes, and interests. By the time a criterion test is employed, some individuals may be hopelessly behind. Many of these difficulties can be overcome by competent lecturers who are able to make the material meaningful and who remain aware of the reactions of their students by effectively promoting discussion and clarification of material.

A large number of studies have compared programed instruction or televised instruction to the lecture technique. The results indicate that these newer techniques do not necessarily lead to superior student achievement, although there is some evidence that the student completes the material faster. Thus, there appears to be little empirical reason for the bias against the lecture procedure. Yet, one survey (Carroll, Paine, & Ivancevich, 1972) found that training directors ranked the lecture method last among nine techniques as a procedure for the effective acquisition of knowledge. The other techniques included case studies, conferences, business games, films, programed instruction, role-playing, sensitivity training, and television. Interestingly, these authors also found that the research does not support the poor opinions of the lecture technique as an instrument in the acquisition of knowledge.

Certainly, the lecture method has shortcomings. It is insensitive to individual differences, and it is limited in providing immediate feedback to the learner. However, considering the low cost of the lecture method, it is important to empirically determine when and how it can be used. There is already evidence that the technique is not appropriate when complex responses (for example, motor skills) are required but may be quite applicable to those situations in which acquisition of knowledge is the goal. There is general uncertainty about the benefits of the lecture method for other behaviors, such as attitude change. Most authors and training directors feel that the lecture method is not useful in promoting attitude change, but, again, there is little empirical evidence to support their view.

Actually, several studies conducted by Miner (1961, 1963) suggested that the lecture was appropriate as an attitude-change technique. One study examined 72 supervisors in the research and development department of a large corporation. These employees had been neglecting their supervisory activities in favor of their scientific interests. Miner developed a course that placed considerable emphasis on scientific theory and research findings relevant to supervisory practices. He found that the experimental group developed more favorable attitudes toward supervisory training as compared to a control group that did not participate in the lecture program. Interestingly, the control group developed negative feelings during the training period because of the threat of department reorganization.

Unfortunately, few studies have examined lecture courses that are specifically designed as part of a training program. Usually, when the lecture method is employed as a control procedure, most of the effort is devoted to the development of the experimental technique. Almost all other techniques have a large number of proponents who excitedly proclaim the validity of their procedure without much, if any, empirical evidence. On the other hand, the lecture technique is viewed with disdain without much empirical evidence. The lecture is still used, however, in a wide variety of settings. It would be interesting to learn which conditions help determine the usefulness of this technique. Is the method of instruction important? Is discussion necessary? What determines the quality of the instructor? Lectures are unlikely to disappear. It would be most appropriate to gain some knowledge concerning their potential.

PROGRAMED INSTRUCTION

Since the mid-1950s, a large number of devices, such as self-instructional materials, automated teaching machines, and programed texts, have been developed. These programed materials systematically present information to the learner while also utilizing the principles of reinforcement (Silverman, 1960). Programed instruction (PI) is dependent not on the physical characteristics of the display (for example, a book, a computer, or a mechanical apparatus) but on the quality of the program.

In 1962, Bass and Vaughan (1966) found that there were 165 commercial programs available. More recent estimates from educational, industrial, and government sources signal an astounding increase in the number and kinds of programs available. For example, a U.S. Civil Service Commission survey (1970) identified over 2300 programs being used in various government installations. Contrary to the original expectations that PI would prove useful only for basic subjects in the school classroom, the topics of these programs included such complex and diverse subjects as air-traffic control, blueprint reading, day-and-night storm signals and their meanings, food-borne disease investigation, magnetic amplifiers, and analyses of tax returns. The number of govern-

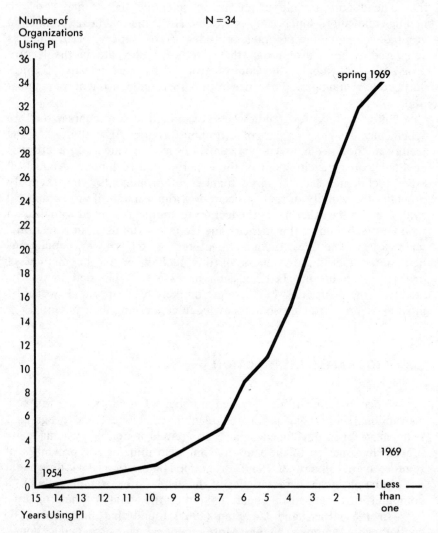

Figure 8-1. Increase in the use of programed instruction (length of time using programed instruction, by organization). From U.S. Civil Service Commission. *Programmed Instruction: A Brief of its Development and Current Status.* Washington, D. C.: U.S. Government Printing Office, 1970.

ment organizations that utilize PI techniques reflects this growing interest. The survey indicates that in 1954 the Air Force became the first unit to employ PI, with the Army, Navy, Forest Service, and Social Security Administration joining in by 1962. Figure 8-1 illustrates the increase in the number of government organizations using these techniques. A survey of educational institutions employing PI would reveal that, even at the university level, there are few students graduating today who have not been exposed to programed devices as teaching aids. Why have these programs been adopted by so many institutions? What is expected from programed learning that is not available from other techniques? In order to answer these questions, it is necessary to examine the historical development and objectives of PI.

APPROACHES TO PROGRAMED INSTRUCTION

Autoinstructional method.   In the early 1900s, Thorndike introduced the *law of effect*. This law states that stimulus-response associations that are followed by a satisfying state of affairs are learned, while those that are followed by unsatisfying states of affairs are weakened and eliminated. In the 1920s, Pressey (1950) applied Thorndike's principles of learning to the classroom environment by utilizing the feedback from examinations. He argued that exams that are scored immediately can provide the feedback necessary to help the student determine his strengths and weaknesses; thus, he developed *autoinstructional* programs to supply immediate feedback. In this system, the student reads a question and chooses the appropriate response from a series of multiple-choice answers. If the student is correct, he is immediately reinforced by a light or a buzzer, which "stamps in" the correct associations. If the response is incorrect, he is not reinforced, thus weakening the incorrect association. He then must respond with one of the remaining alternatives. This process continues until the student picks the correct answer, at which time he is reinforced and proceeds to the next question. Although a number of studies conducted by Pressey indicated that the technique was promising, a movement favoring the use of PI never developed. A variety of reasons have been offered for this lack of interest. Some commentators (Lysaught & Williams, 1963) suggest that the onset of the Depression caused an unfavorable social climate for an "industrial revolution" in the schools. Other educators believe that Pressey's autoinstructional system was really a testing device that did not provide for systematic programing of materials. Thus, they contend that the method had little new to offer.

Linear programing.   Opinions about PI changed radically when B. F. Skinner (1954) published his article "The Science of Learning and the Art of Teaching,'' which applies his models of operant conditioning to the educational process. Skinner argues that a program could successively shape the learner by reinforcing the achievement of small steps in the same way that the pigeon is shaped by the reinforcement of successive approximations to peck a key. Since Skinner believes that positive reinforcement of correct responses is the most efficient way to produce learning, he designed his programs to shape the learner through a series of small steps so that few errors occur. Thus, the learner is expected to continually earn positive reinforcement. If errors are made at a particular point in the program, there is a problem with the program, not the student. The only variability that is permitted among learners is the speed with which they complete the program. Since a student proceeds through each successive step, the technique became known as *linear programing*. Its essential parameters include the following characteristics (Bass & Vaughan, 1966; Fry, 1963):

1. All material is presented in small units called frames. Each frame varies in size from one sentence to several paragraphs, depending on the amount of material necessary to guide the learner.
2. Each frame requires an overt response from the learner. The student reads the frame and then constructs a response by filling in the blank. Thus, he is actively involved in the learning process.
3. The learner immediately receives feedback indicating the correctness of his response. Since the program is constructed for a minimum number of errors, the learner usually receives immediate positive reinforcement.
4. The program is predesigned to provide proper learning sequences. Since the units must be presented in small steps to achieve low error rates, the programer must carefully analyze both the material and the learner's characteristics in order to obtain the most appropriate step size and sequence. This process requires pretesting of the program and revisions based on student responses. If a criterion of approximately 90 percent correct by all trainees is not met, the material must be rewritten.
5. Each trainee proceeds independently through the program at a pace commensurate with his own abilities.

A sample of a program that discusses two of the principles of linear programing, self-pacing and small steps, can be found in Table 8-1.

   Intrinsic or branching programing.   In branching programs, correct responses by the learner lead directly to the next step of the program, while incorrect answers lead to a branch designed to correct the mistake. The branches can vary in complexity from a few short frames to an elaborate subprogram. Intrinsic programs (Crowder, 1960) have had the greatest impact on the development of branching techniques. These programs have relatively long frames followed by a series of multiple-choice answers. If the program is in text form, the learner turns to the page number associated with his answer choice. There, he is presented with another series of frames based on his previous answer. If the chosen answer is correct, his response is simply confirmed, and he is directed to the next frame. If his answer is incorrect, he proceeds to a remedial set of frames designed to correct his previous response. Table 8-2 presents an example of an intrinsic branching program. Branching programs cannot eliminate all errors; however, the student does not proceed until he can

Table 8-1.   Sample of a Linear Program

	1. You are now beginning a lesson on programed instruction. The principle of *self-pacing* as used in programed instructions allows each trainee to work as slowly or as fast as he chooses. Since you can control the amount of time you spend on this lesson, this program is using the principle of self- _____.
pacing	2. People naturally learn at different rates. A program that allows each trainee to control his own rate of learning is using the principle of _____.
self-pacing	3. If a self-pacing program is to be successful, the information step size must be small. A program that is self-pacing would also apply the principle of small _____.
steps	4. The average trainee will usually make correct responses if the correct-size step of information is given. This is utilizing the principle of small _____.
steps	5. A program that provides information in a step size that allows the trainee to be successful is applying the principle of _____.
small steps	6. A trainee knows the material being taught but has to wait for the remainder of the class. What programing principle is being violated? _____.
self-pacing	7. Two principles of programed learning are: (1) _____. (2) _____.
1. *self-pacing* 2. *small steps*	

Note—For practical reasons, the frames are arranged on one page rather than on succeeding pages. The answers should be covered until the preceding frame has been answered.

Adapted from U. S. Civil Service Commission. *Programed Instruction: A Brief of Its Development and Current Status.* Washington, D.C.: U. S. Government Printing Office, 1970.

Table 8-2.   Sample of an Intrinsic Branching Program

Definition of the term "teaching machine"

Page 8

In 1924, Dr. Sidney L. Pressey invented a small machine that would score a multiple-choice examination automatically at the time the answer-button was pushed.

Although he designed it as a testing machine, he perceived that by a simple expedient he could use the machine as a teaching device. All he had to do was design it so that, for each question, the correct answer-button had to be pushed before a subsequent question would appear in the window.

From this simple beginning, the concept of *teaching machines* has grown until now the educator is faced with many types and styles, from the simplest cardboard device costing pennies to incredibly complex electronic wonders costing thousands of dollars.

But don't despair. All teaching machines have three characteristics in common:

1. They present information and require frequent responses by the student.
2. They provide immediate feedback to the student, informing him whether his response is appropriate or not.
3. They allow the student to work individually and to adjust his rate of progress to his own needs and capabilities.

Now, based on the three criteria listed above, is the educational motion picture, as it is normally used, a teaching machine?

YES   *(Turn to page 6.)*
NO   *(Turn to page 4.)*

Page 6

The educational motion picture, as it is normally used, *does* present factual information but does *not* satisfy any of the other conditions set down for a teaching machine; no response is called for, no feedback is given, and the student has no control over his rate of progress.

The standard educational motion picture, then, is similar to a well-prepared lecture but is not a teaching machine.

Please read the conditions on page 8 again, and then select the other alternative.

Page 4

Right! The educational motion picture, as it is normally used, is not a teaching machine.

1. Although the motion picture presents information, it does not require periodic responses from the student in the form of answers, selections, or motor responses.
2. Since it does not ask for responses, it does not indicate whether the responses are appropriate or not.
3. It does not allow the individual class member to adjust his rate of progress to his own needs and capabilities.

Adapted from Cram, D. *Explaining Teaching Machines and Programming.* ©1961 by Fearon Publishers. Used by permission.

demonstrate by his performance on the branching step that he understands the concept that he previously missed. Crowder designed his steps so that they are larger than those that appear in linear programing. The superior student can then proceed through larger steps, while the student experiencing difficulty is directed into branching programs with smaller steps. Crowder believes that this procedure permits the designer to consider the individual differences and backgrounds of the students. The superior student is able to progress through the program without becoming bored, and the slower student is given special attention. Of course, most branching programs have limited flexibility. Only a certain number of branches can be designed for the individual student without the whole project becoming cumbersome. However, computer-assisted instruction (discussed later in this chapter) does offer increased flexibility for branching. Most educators (DeCecco, 1968) agree that there is little empirical justification for a choice between linear or branching techniques. It has become increasingly popular to utilize both techniques within the same program. The particular instructional objectives, entering behavior of the students, and material to be learned should determine the most appropriate procedure at any point in the program.

EVALUATION OF PROGRAMED INSTRUCTION

A large number of programs remain unevaluated; however, as compared with research on most other training methods, the evaluation data available on PI represent a storehouse of knowledge. Holt's studies (Holt, 1963b; Shoemaker & Holt, 1965) provide good examples of and illuminating commentary about the utility of PI as a training technique. In one investigation, he compared the standard lecture-discussion method to a pretested linear PI course in basic electricity for telephone electricians. The main criteria were tests examining facts and concepts given at the completion of training and six months later. The assignment of trainees to treatment conditions was based on when the employees reported for training. The first set of trainees to arrive completed the course using the standard lecture procedure, consisting of 10 days of class work. The next group of trainees was assigned to a PI group that attended only for as many days as were necessary to complete the program. Although this procedure does not utilize random assignments, good sampling is achieved if the variation for individuals assigned to training is not biased across time periods. This assumption is reasonable, but, as a further check, Holt compared the experimental and control groups on a number of factors, including intelligence, knowledge of basic electricity, years of experience, and course work in electricity and math. There were no pretraining differences between groups on these measures. This method provides a good illustration of the procedures that can be employed even when strict randomization cannot be achieved. Holt's study also attempted to control for the Hawthorne effect by treating both groups as part of the experiment. This treatment included informing all trainees of the nature of the experiment as well as instituting similar procedures for both groups regarding pretesting, questionnaires, interviews, and other parameters that were not strictly part of the treatment procedure.

The data analyses indicated that the PI groups achieved superior performance on the immediate post-test and on the six-month retention test. However, on the six-month test, both groups' scores decreased substantially. While this study represents one of the few efforts that examined performance at later time intervals, the retention loss raised some question about the relevance of the training program to job performance. Holt examined the use of PI in a situation in which there was an already existing lecture course. Thus, the need-assessment procedure did not directly precede the development of the PI program. An analysis indicated that the retention loss for both groups occurred because the course itself was not relevant to the technician's job, and, thus, the knowledge gained was not utilized in the transfer setting. A good need assessment could avoid this difficulty by implementing courses that are job relevant and also by helping in the development of job-performance criteria that could establish the utility of the procedure. While there is ample reason to believe that the course was not relevant, there is also the possibility that the criteria were not relevant. There may be many instances in which the six-month retention tests would show a decrease in performance, whereas more job-oriented criteria would not.

Holt's investigations also explore some questions about the time needed to complete the course. In his study, there were no differences between the two groups, but the common finding is that PI groups complete the program more quickly than do traditional groups that are locked into set time intervals. However, Holt noted that the traditional group in his study had materials available for home study, while the PI group did not. Most other investigations do not comment on the availability of other opportunities outside the training setting that could contribute to time differences or changes in achievement scores. So that the outcomes of experiments can be understood, the data must be related to process-oriented criteria that provide information about the procedures employed during training. Otherwise, the interpretation of data remains tenuous.

Since there are a number of studies that have investigated PI, it is possible to ask what generalizations can be gained from this research? Early analyses (Briggs & Angell, 1964; Schramm, 1964) of the literature that compared student achievement in PI and in more traditional methods (for example, the lecture method) found that the majority of studies showed no significant differences between methods. Of the remaining studies, most favored PI. These analyses also tended to indicate that PI groups required less learning time. A more recent review by Nash, Muczyk, and Vettori (1971) examined the relative effectiveness of PI in both academic and industrial settings. The largest proportion of these studies had been performed in academic settings although there was no evidence of differential data due to location. Table 8-3 presents the Nash et al. data for three different criteria, including training time, immediate learning, and retention. These authors included an important additional criterion in their review: in order for the technique to be judged the more

Table 8-3.   Comparisons of Programed Instruction versus Conventional Methods for Each Criterion in Studies That Include Two or More Criteria

	Conventional method superior	*No significant difference between methods*	*Programed instruction superior*
Training time	1	2	29
Immediate learning	3	20	9
Retention[1]	5	16	5

[1]Of the 32 studies that included measures of both training time and immediate learning, only 26 also had a measure of retention.

From Nash, A. N., Muczyk, J. P., & Vettori, F. L. The relative practical effectiveness of programed instruction. *Personnel Psychology,* 1971, **24,** 397–418. Reprinted by permission of Personnel Psychology, Inc.

effective, the statistical test had to be significant and the differences between the techniques had to exceed 10 percent. Nash et al. argued that the development of PI is an expensive endeavor; thus, they felt that new techniques with differences in overall effectiveness of only a few percent would not be worth considering for institutions that had less expensive techniques available. Their analyses of the statistical data (excluding the practicality criterion) supported earlier reviews stating that most studies examining achievement (immediate learning and retention) showed no significant differences, and the remaining studies favored PI. However, when the authors examined those studies in which the statistical differences were significant but the practical effectiveness was not above 10 percent, the trend toward no differences between techniques was even stronger. The analysis of learning-time data supported the established trend, indicating that PI students learn faster (the average reductions often approaching one third). While the data concerning learning time have generally been consistent, they must be interpreted cautiously. The programed-instruction group is self-paced, and the learner may leave the program whenever he has completed the material. However, the more traditional programs have a fixed time limit, and the superior learner cannot leave even if he has learned enough material to achieve the objectives. Of course, that is one of the advantages of programed learning, but it might be interesting to discover what would happen if the learner in the control condition could take his achievement test when he had completed the program to his own satisfaction.

The thoroughness with which Nash and his colleagues performed their review raised one other serious question about the effects of PI on achievement level. These authors divided the studies into effectively and less effectively controlled studies. Effectively controlled studies included the investigations that had (1) experimental and control groups selected by random assignment or a pretest measure used for adjustments when the groups varied on significant variables, and (2) a sample average of 20 subjects, with a minimum of 15 in each group. These, of course, are minimum standards and do not go so far as to require controls for pretest sensitization or a consideration of Hawthorne effects. However, many of the studies that did find that PI resulted in superior achievement levels were "less effectively controlled" studies.

While it is reasonable to conclude that PI does not generally result in higher achievement levels, the evaluation studies are often so poorly designed and executed that it is difficult to reach any definitive conclusions. For example, most studies employ intact sampling rather than random assignment of students. As noted earlier, this preference is often a requirement dictated by systems that do not wish to have their normal groups (such as school classes) broken up. This type of assignment can be analyzed by a quasi-experimental design, but difficulties arise when there is a failure to control the initial differences in prior knowledge that are often found in different classes or groups. If these differences are not determined prior to treatment, it is not possible to establish afterward whether the effectiveness of any method is due to the treatment or to the prior knowledge of the learners. In addition, there is little information about the criterion tests used to determine differences between groups. Some critics (Briggs et al., 1967) question whether the criterion measures are designed carefully enough to detect differences that might exist between methods. Since many of the studies are performed in educational institutions, there is little information about performance on transfer criteria (such as retention of material and on-the-job performance). Certainly, more effort on criteria development and evaluation design is necessary, but, at present, the most valid conclusion is that PI results in faster learning but is not discernibly superior to traditional techniques in the establishment of higher achievement levels.

ADVANTAGES AND LIMITATIONS OF PROGRAMED INSTRUCTION

Advantages

1. Properly designed PI follows the basic steps necessary for an effective training program. Thus, the procedure includes objectives with built-in checks to make sure that the learner understands the material.

2. While there is not much evidence to indicate that trainees learn more using PI techniques, there is sufficient evidence to prove that training time is effectively reduced.

3. Programed materials are easily packaged and can be sent to widely dispersed training centers. In addition, individual students may take the course when it is deemed most appropriate.

4. Many trainers believe that the reinforcement programed learning lead to a more highly motivated learner.

5. The individualization of instruction is an important aspect of PI. The self-pacing provision permits learners to proceed at the rate most comfortable for their ability level. Nash et al. (1971) found a number of studies that show that high- or low-ability trainees, who might be expected to benefit most from self-pacing, perform in a superior manner on immediate learning criteria. Individual modes of instruction will be treated more fully in the discussion of computer-assisted instruction and individual differences.

Limitations

1. The major limitation of PI is the expense and preparation necessary. An examination of the requirements necessary to develop a linear or branching program clearly indicates that it is a time-consuming task involving considerable analyses and pretesting.

2. While there is an increasing variety of programs, the emphasis of PI is still on factual materials; thus, the utility of PI for more subjective material (like manager human-relations training) remains undetermined.

3. Student-reaction data have indicated that PI by itself may not be an acceptable mode of instruction. Several studies (Bushnell, 1963; Patten & Stermer, 1969) have shown that the learner is more satisfied with a combined technique, like a conference or discussion along with the programed material. School systems have often stated that PI has permitted their instructors to spend more time with individual students or small groups of students. It may be equally important for the adult in industry to have similar human interaction. Thus, utilization of PI as the only method for training may not be appropriate.

COMPUTER-ASSISTED INSTRUCTION

One of the most recent innovations in instructional technology is computer-assisted instruction (CAI). The student interacts directly with the computer, which has stored within its systems the information and instructional materials necessary for the program. The degree of computer interaction with the student varies with the individual system. A general model that describes the processes in the design of CAI systems has been presented by Cooley and Glaser (1969). It is interesting to note that many of these steps parallel the instructional model presented in Chapter 2.

1. The goals of learning are specified in terms of observable student behavior and the conditions under which this behavior is to be manifested.
2. When the learner begins a particular course of instruction, his initial capabilities—those relevant to the forthcoming instruction—are assessed.
3. Educational alternatives suited to the student's initial capabilities are presented to him. The student selects or is assigned one of these alternatives.
4. The student's performance is monitored and continuously assessed as he learns.
5. Instruction proceeds as a function of the relationship between measures of student performance, available instructional alternatives, and criteria of competence.

6. As instruction proceeds, data are generated for monitoring and improving the instructional system [pp. 574–575].

STATE OF THE ART

The excitement about the development of CAI is based on the storage and memory capabilities of the computer, which in turn provide the potential for true interaction with the individual student. The proponents of this system believe that this potential provides the ultimate in branching programs. The computer records the individual's previous response, analyzes its characteristics, and determines the next presentation to the student on the basis of the learner's needs. Unfortunately, these developments are more of a promise than a realistic appraisal. While there is significant work being done at several institutions, most of the large number of press releases, research articles, and institutional reports present vague speculations and dwell on hardware development. For example, there are typewriters tied to computer devices, pens that draw curves on cathode-ray tubes, and devices that present auditory material and score student answers. Yet, an examination of the use of these devices rarely presents validation data or cost estimates. Sometimes the sophisticated instrument is simply a PI device that uses electronic presentation instead of textbooks. These misguided efforts should not detract from the tremendous possibilities of computer technology in instructional systems. However, it appears that these developments may be much slower in arriving than originally anticipated. CAI is very expensive, and more than one local school system had faced near bankruptcy because of the adoption of systems that did not meet their glowing expectations in terms of costs and student achievement. The publicity surrounding the development of CAI material has made it difficult for the consumer to prudently choose the best available instructional system. R. C. Atkinson (1968) has participated in a carefully developed system at Stanford University. He suggests that "The problem for someone trying to evaluate developments in the field is to distinguish between those reports that are based on fact and those that are disguised forms of science fiction" (p. 225). Those who are concerned with the developments of useful instructional techniques must be concerned with the distinction between fact and fiction. CAI has tremendous promise, but it can turn into simply a passing fad if valid instructional research does not precede glowing reports.

The following sections describe a few of the better-developed CAI systems. Most of this material is based on research supported by government funds and carried out in educational institutions. Similar activities are beginning in military, government, and industrial organizations.

TYPES OF CAI

The preceding discussion implies that CAI is not a single method but rather a large number of different instructional schemes. Drill and practice, tutorial progams, simulation, and problem solving have all been listed as techniques in CAI instructional programs. The two most well-developed systems are drill and practice and tutorial.

Drill and practice. The simplest of the two systems is drill and practice, which is ordinarily used as a supplement to conventional instruction (Suppes & Jerman, 1970). The program is usually controlled by a teacher, who first introduces the material in class and then specifies the topics that are to be practiced by the students individually at instructional terminals. This CAI system permits the teacher to present creative material in the classroom but also provides immediate feedback to large numbers of students on various sets of problems. The computer can present individualized material to a number of students simultaneously, as well as provide individual feedback to the student and records of progress to the teacher.

The Stanford (Suppes & Morningstar, 1969) drill-and-practice program in mathematics has 20 to 27 concept blocks for each grade level. Each concept block contains a pretest, five days of drill, a post-test, and review drills. This system has provisions for administering the following program: (1) a pretest, which determines the student's entering ability for that concept block; (2) the assignment of a series of lessons (which vary in difficulty) according to the student's ability; (3) a compilation of records on the student's performance on each lesson; (4) the determination of the appropriate lesson as a function of the student's progress on the previous material; (5) a post-test, which assesses the student's progress. Suppes and Morningstar (1969) have reported on a series of research investigations that analyzed the effectiveness of the mathematics program. The data from these studies, which included primary-school students from California and Mississippi, generally favored the CAI group, although there were some criteria on which the traditionally educated students performed better than the CAI students. More interesting was the relative superiority of the experimental group in Mississippi as compared to its control group. An analysis of these data indicated that the differences occurred because the control group in Mississippi was not improving at the same rate as the one in California. This result led the authors to speculate that these programs will have striking benefits in environments that are not socially and educationally affluent. It is in these situations that the student benefits most from the opportunity to learn from effectively designed programs. Considering the difficulties that many industrial institutions have in designing basic instructional material, the opportunity for their employees to work at a terminal that is coordinated with a central instructional system must certainly be appealing. The Stanford project utilized a central computer in California for primary-school students in California, Kentucky, and Mississippi. The usefulness of drill-and-practice programs has also been established at the college level. In another Stanford project, Suppes and Morningstar (1969) reported on a study indicating that CAI students were superior to a traditional class in the first-year Russian program. There were also fewer dropouts in the CAI group, and a greater percentage of the CAl group enrolled in the second year of Russian.

Tutorial. The tutorial program, as compared to drill and practice, assumes the responsibility for most, if not all, of the information incorporated into the program. Most CAI programs are tutorial in nature and may be complete course sequences or special supplementary units. If they are supplementary units, the teacher incorporates the material into his or her course program. Thus, they are especially useful when expertise for a particular unit of subject matter is not readily available. These programs have the capability for real time decisions, with branching contingent upon the student's previous responses or set of responses. The numerous branching patterns often result in students' following diverse paths, with a high probability that no two students will follow the same sequence through an instructional program (R. C. Atkinson, 1968). However, most programs have a set number of responses so that the number of actual alternatives is limited.

Data from a tutorial program are provided by the Stanford CAI program for teaching reading to first-graders. In a series of tests utilizing experimental and control groups, Atkinson (1968) found that the experimental group was superior to the control group on 10 of 11 reading subtests. This study also reversed a trend apparent in most studies of reading behavior. Commonly, girls tend to learn reading more rapidly than boys. Various factors might contribute to this difference, including the predominant number of female teachers in the first grade or the observation that first-grade girls tend to be more physically mature than first-grade boys. Whatever the reason, the differences disappeared in the Atkinson study. Both sexes in the CAI group gained in achievement level, but the boys showed the greatest advancement. Atkinson also presented an effective approach for controlling the Hawthorne effect, a serious problem in these studies because the equipment and computers lead experimental subjects to feel that special attention is given to them. Atkinson had the control group in the reading study work with CAI in the mathematics program. Thus, the traditional and CAI reading groups were both exposed to the instructional environment, but only the CAI group received reading instruction via computer.

EVALUATION OF CAI

CAI research began in the mid-1960s but was hampered by hardware and software difficulties. Most CAI investigations have been little more than demonstrations of technology with an occasional post-test after the treatment. This one-shot case-study approach is useful only for the collection of information preliminary to more thorough investigations. The following section discusses trends and generalizations based on a limited number of well-conceived studies. Due to the scarcity of research, the reader should be wary of attempts to predict future developments. However, it is important to consider the present state of development. In some of these studies the authors have specified particular evaluation problems, related to criterion contamination or experimental design, that have plagued their research. The following tentative statements are offered:

1. A substantial number of studies indicate that CAI requires less time than more traditional methods to teach the same amount of material. For example, studies by the U.S. Army Signal Center and School (U.S. Civil Service Commission, 1971b) found that the CAI course took 11 percent less time than instructor-controlled methods. A revision of this program resulted in further time savings, raising the average savings of all groups to 20 percent.

2. The achievement data appear to parallel programed-instruction analyses. There are a number of studies that have indicated that CAI students perform better than traditionally educated students and a few studies that have shown CAI students to perform poorer, but the largest number of investigations found no significant difference between the two groups.

Most of the studies that were used as a basis for the preceding statements would be included in the Nash et al. (1971) category of effectively controlled studies. Yet, the authors of this research describe a variety of difficulties that hindered the interpretation of their data. One source of difficulty was criterion contamination. The criteria utilized for many of these studies were originally designed for traditional instruction classes. Often, they were national standardized exams constructed years before CAI existed. Some investigators have stated that the behavioral objectives specified in the design process of CAI systems are not appropriately measured by these standardized exams. They believe that the CAI method has unique features that should lead to the specification of new behavioral objectives. For example, CAI tutorial programs might permit students to learn certain concepts that could not be taught by a group lecture; so, the test of these programs should include criterion-referenced measures that adequately reflect the new objectives. Yet, many administrators are unwilling to accept innovations unless the students perform adequately on the traditional normative measures, which may not be a good indicant of the course objectives. One apparent solution to this problem is careful need-assessment procedures that establish the objectives and the criterion measurements before the instructional program begins. A related concern is the appropriate timing of the criterion measurements. Students in traditional methods are given their exams when they complete all of their course material. In many studies, CAI students are also required to take the examination at one specified time, although they may have completed the course material days earlier or may not have even finished it. Thus, the self-pacing procedures of CAI place the student at a disadvantage. The solution to this problem depends on effective testing procedures that are used when the trainee finishes the required material. There is little sense in a system in which students are permitted to self-pace themselves through the entire program only to await mass testing at one designated time.

Threats to external validity resulting from the Hawthorne effect are also a problem in CAI research. While control students remain in their traditional school setting, the CAI students are placed in a unique situation with new equipment, observers, and a general experimental atmosphere. Seltzer (1971) notes that the superior performance of the Mississippi group in the Stanford study occurred in a poor socioeconomic environment where the students tend to be deprived of learning materials. Thus, it is necessary to speculate on the Hawthorne effect generated by the computer terminals and experimental environment. As mentioned earlier, some researchers (such as Atkinson, 1968) have attempted to partially overcome this problem by having the control group in one study participate as CAI students in another subject.

Another concern is the interactive effects of program and teacher quality (Rosenberg, 1972). In most studies, there is little attention paid to the quality of the traditional instructors or to the quality of the program. The interactive effects are especially apparent in the Suppes and Morningstar (1969) Mississippi study. The authors suggest that the superior effect of CAI may have been related not to the program but to poorer teacher preparation or training that adversely affected the traditional group. In order to assess the results of any particular instructional program, it is necessary to examine the quality of the traditional and innovative methods.

ADVANTAGES AND LIMITATIONS OF COMPUTER-ASSISTED INSTRUCTION

Advantages

1. The major advantage of CAI is the individualization of instruction. PI can adapt to the gross characteristics of a specific individual, but

CAI has the potential for responding to detailed characteristics of the trainee and his needs at a precise moment in time (Kopstein & Seidel, 1967). An illustration of this attribute is apparent in the CAI programs called *dialogue systems*. Here student-computer interactions are not restricted by preset response alternatives. Such a system called *Plato*, is being investigated at the University of Illinois (Alpert & Bitzer, 1970). It depends on a set of stored instructions (algorithms), which are used by the computer to construct unique responses to student questions. For example, a student might be asked to draw a particular geometric figure. After he completes the figure, the computer uses a set of algorithms to assess the validity of the answer. Similarly, the student can construct algebraic proofs, and the computer can analyze the responses and indicate errors of arithmetic or logic. When these types of programs become operational, they will provide a real impetus toward the consideration of a large number of individual response parameters. At the present time, CAI programs can attend to individual attributes—that is, demographic information, previous performance, most recent response, and other variables that can be prestored in the computer.

2. The reinforcement provisions of the CAI systems are a real benefit to the learner. As Singer (1968) noted, "the program has infinite patience. It does not have preconceived notions about a student. . . . Mistakes are not penalized by scorn or sarcasm, successes are marked by positive reinforcement" (p. 3).

3. CAI systems present teachers with a new role. The record keeping is performed by machine, and complete analyses of student performance are readily available. This gives the instructor time to spend with individuals or small groups of students. Also, in many programs, the drill work is done by computer, permitting the instructor to spend more time developing important conceptual material.

4. Due to the data-collection provisions, CAI offers the researcher a good opportunity to gain knowledge about learning variables and theories of instruction.

Limitations

1. At the present time, a restraining factor in the use of CAI is the limited state of knowledge. The small number of empirical studies makes generalizations about the utility of CAI extremely hazardous. In addition, as expressed by DeCecco (1968), emphasis on technology is leading instructional efforts astray.

All these facilities and equipment, I must remind you, are much more sophisticated than any theory of teaching we presently have. The temptation in a technological society is to allow our fantastic machines to determine our research problems and our educational practice. It is far more important that we subordinate the machines to the theoretical and practical instructional problems which, undoubtedly, the machines can help us solve [p. 539].

2. The cost of CAI systems is a serious obstacle. Huge outlays of funds are needed for hardware. While few studies attempt to analyze exact costs, Kopstein and Seidel (1968) arrived at a figure of $2.61 per student hour for 10 hours a day for 24-days-per-month use. These same authors feel that CAI cannot be cost effective in primary-school systems but might be substantially cheaper than present methods of instruction in college and higher levels of education. Decreases in cost in the program have been predicted because of decreases in the costs of using the computer. However, Seltzer (1971) suggests that computer systems are going to become more complex and thus more expensive. He doubts that there will be any decrease in costs in the near future. In addition to financial costs, the development of any viable CAI system demands a long-term commitment from a large staff.

Assuming reasonable cost factors, the real issue will probably be related to what unique contributions CAI offers society rather than to cost. However, the development costs of CAI programs make it unlikely for smaller organizations to participate until the system is fully developed. This may tend to result in the development of prepackaged programs that do not consider the particular needs of the organization. Of course, this is a danger with all packaged materials that are simply sold off the shelf without any consideration of each buyer's uniqueness.

3. One remaining question concerns the effects of a machine-oriented learning environment on satisfaction, motivation, and development. As noted in the discussion of programed instruction, there have been several studies suggesting that adult learners do not prefer to be taught exclusively by machine. Bundy (1968) notes that most students like CAI instruction, but they also feel the need for short sessions with student-teacher interaction and discussion. At the present time, students spend very little of their time in a CAI environment. However, if the technique becomes widespread, it will become necessary to ask if a rich enough stimulus environment is being provided. Systems like CAI cannot be evaluated just in terms of learner achievement. CAI leads to new environments that must be investigated in relation to attitudes and the socialization process.

TELEVISION AND FILMS—MOVING PICTURES

Both television and films extend the range of stimuli that are normally brought into the training environment; they display events and sequences of events rather than simply present objects. The major differences between the two techniques relate to the administrative adaptation of the material. Television often does not have the flexibility of options regarding time of showing, but it is available over a large geographical area and is more likely to be revised and up-to-date. Since these two techniques are similar from the standpoint of research findings (Chu & Schramm, 1967) and instructional functioning, for the purposes of this discussion, they will be treated as a single instructional technique and called *moving pictures*, a term adapted by Gagné (1970).

VARIETY AND SCOPE OF MOVING PICTURES

The implementation of this instructional technique is extensive in scope, with a variety of topics covered and studies performed. Topics covered include such subjects as customer engineering, dentistry, driver education, and literacy training, which partially demonstrate the range of versatility. It is not unusual to find reviews that report on several hundred studies (for example, Schramm, 1962) or investigations that have samples of several hundred thousand students. The following examples are chosen from a number of settings to illustrate the considerable variety of approaches to moving pictures.

Chu and Schramm (1967) reported on a study in American Samoa designed to implement a modern educational program from a traditional rote-learning system through the use of television. Almost all of the teachers were trained under the traditional system, and the educational administrators realized that it would take a century to proceed through the normal evolutionary process. Thus, they consolidated their one-room schoolhouses, installed a six-channel television system, and brought in expert teachers to train new instructors and to help the established instructors adapt to the innovations. Similar developments are being implemented in other countries where teachers are not available to instruct the hundreds of thousands of children who are presently without any educational facilities.

Another illustration comes from the *Sesame Street* TV program (Ball & Bogatz, 1970), which showed that preschool children could be taught a variety of linguistic and cognitive skills through the use of television. Studies indicated that: (1) the children who watched the program learned more than those who didn't; (2) those skills that were emphasized on the program were learned best; and (3) disadvantaged children as compared with middle-class children began the program with lower achievement scores on the topics being emphasized, but their performance surpassed middle-class children who watched the program infrequently. Viewers who were not part of the experimental design often did not realize that this creative and entertaining program was an experiment designed to achieve specific behavioral objectives. These objectives were carefully determined in a series of workshops attended by representatives of all the pertinent personnel, including psychologists, sociologists, teachers, film-makers, writers, advertising personnel, and evaluators. They established objectives related to symbolic representation, cognitive processes, and physical and social environments. For example, behavioral objectives for symbolic representation might include: "Given a set of symbols, either all letters or all numbers, the child knows whether those symbols are used in reading or counting" or "Given a series of words presented orally, all beginning with the same letter, the child can make up another word or pick another word starting with the same letter" (Ball & Bogatz, 1970).

The evaluation design and criteria for *Sesame Street* were developed as part of the entire instructional program. The measures included outcome criteria, such as degree of learning, as well as process measures, which assessed what occurred during instruction. The process measures included the number of hours that the child viewed the program and the child's reactions while viewing. These measures also permitted the investigator to relate the number of hours of viewing to other criteria like learning. The pretests indicated that older children performed better than younger children. However, after viewing the program, the younger children who watched regularly often scored higher than older children who were infrequent viewers. This program is a fine example of the information that can be gained by the utilization of a variety of criteria developed from carefully defined goals and objectives. An especially encouraging note is that the objectives call for future analyses of transfer behavior. Thus, the students will be followed to determine if the gains are maintained and if they influence school performance. This program has been criticized by some commentators who feel that low priority has been given to the development of children's imagination and exploration of ideas (Cook & Mack, 1971). Essentially, these critics are accepting the evidence indicating that learning did take place, but they are questioning the original objectives of the program. These criticisms can result from changing values or from a failure to consider all aspects of the instructional need, but they are not discouraging, since they are simply a part of the evaluative information that feeds back into the assessment of instructional need. In this way, instructional programs are continually modified and responsive to the information provided by the evaluative process.

Program directors in industrial training support the belief that the extensive early implementation of moving pictures simply foreshadows future events. Davis (1973), general manager of the Association for Continuing Education, stated that "Industry needs a better delivery system for its education and training program if companies are going to update or retrain employees fast enough to keep pace with rapid changes in the business environment" (p. 3). The form suggested by Davis is represented by a closed-circuit TV system operated by Stanford University, which has as participants a large number of companies, including GTE-Sylvania, Hewlett-Packard, IBM, Philco-Ford, and Standard Oil of California. The programs include technical, professional, and business subjects, ranging from human relations to modern secretarial skills. The centralized system has a feedback provision so that the student with a question can press a button and receive immediate attention from the central facility. The proponents of this system note that it permits the use of a top-flight instructor who could not ordinarily be present at each student location. The federal government has also started television instruction in a variety of fields, including secretarial practices and income-tax law. One preliminary study (Mathewson, 1969) investigated a specially designed TV course for secretaries entitled "From Nine to Five." It showed that the course led to a 59 percent reduction in the need for training as determined by supervisors' ratings. The course was particularly effective for entry-level secretaries who are most unfamiliar with basic secretarial practices. While it is difficult at this juncture to predict the eventual outcome of the use of moving pictures, we can gain some insight by examining previous evaluation research.

EVALUATION OF MOVING PICTURES

While most evaluation studies compare moving-picture techniques to conventional lecture-type instruction, there are a surprising number of studies that compare moving-picture techniques to control groups that receive no instruction at all. The investigators are asking whether the student or trainee learns anything from media like television and films. As reported by Chu and Schramm (1967), these studies showed that the moving-picture groups systematically improved their performance over that of control groups. Several of these studies compared the experimental groups' scores to national scores on standardized tests, with the moving-picture groups again performing in a superior manner.

The results of the studies that compare moving pictures to other techniques are consistent. Two major reviews that analyzed 393 comparisons (Schramm, 1962) and 421 comparisons (Chu & Schramm, 1967) showed few significant differences in achievement, with those differences present favoring moving pictures. From another perspective, Schramm (1962) notes that in well over 80 percent of the cases, the moving-picture technique was as good as or better than the conventional technique. Thus, the majority of "no significant difference" cases should not lead to a rejection of the technique but rather to a determination of where and how it can be effectively utilized. For example, moving pictures are extremely useful when good teaching is not immediately available or where courses or materials cannot be presented in the traditional instructional mode. The identification of other effective ways to utilize moving pictures will undoubtedly contribute to the implementation of the technique. For example, several studies have found that moving pictures are more effective if the learner is active rather than passive. In one study (Lumsdaine, May, & Hadsell, 1958), the participants' performance was improved by splicing questions about the material into the film. In summary, most studies indicate that the effective use of television is dependent on the basic qualities of good teaching. Chu and Schramm (1967) feel that the important qualities are " . . . simplicity, good organization, motivation, practice, knowledge of results, rest pauses at appropriate points, cues that direct the pupil to the essential things he is to learn . . . " (p. 100).

Unfortunately, many of the studies have not provided useful information for reasons similar to those affecting PI and CAI. The research efforts for these media have been especially victimized by sampling procedures in the selection of subjects, by the Hawthorne effect, and by inadequate criteria. However, there is one interesting factor that should be mentioned because of its implications for all training procedures. Chu and Schramm (1967) discovered that almost all of the investigations compared instructional groups taught completely by television to those taught completely by conventional methods. However, they contend that this is not a realistic comparison "because almost nowhere in the world is television being used in classrooms without being built into a learning context managed by the teacher" (p. 6). Thus, the technique should be examined in the context of how it can fit into the total learning environment as part of the instructional process. In the previous discussion of external threats to validity, it was indicated that it is difficult to generalize from multiple-treatment environments to environments where a single treatment is used in isolation. The opposite problem is present in this discussion. It is difficult to generalize from the application of a single treatment to situations in which the media are combined with other treatments. The only solution is to begin investigations that examine combinations of treatments.

ADVANTAGES AND LIMITATIONS OF MOVING PICTURES

Advantages

1. The results of a large number of experiments indicate that moving-picture techniques can be effectively utilized for a wide variety of subjects when one-way communication is an acceptable instructional mode.

2. Moving-picture techniques are especially useful for those situations in which competent instructors are not immediately available or in which travel costs make instruction prohibitive. In one instructional program developed by the Association for Continuing Education (Davis, 1973), the 400 students enrolled saved approximately 1000 hours a week in travel time.

3. Moving pictures are uniquely qualified to present dynamic events that unfold over time. Thus, it is possible to demonstrate the terminal performance expected in a complex motor sequence (Gagné, 1970). Pictures used in learning sequences can also provide effective feedback to the participant. This medium can also be utilized to control time, by speeding up or slowing down particularly important aspects of behavior and by instant replay.

4. This particular medium is useful for presenting events that cannot be recreated in the traditional classroom. For example, films of simulated accidents can vividly demonstrate what happens to individuals who are not wearing a seat belt.

Limitations

1. The technique is essentially a one-way communication device. There have been attempts to introduce procedures to enable the participant to communicate during the presentation, but moving-picture techniques are limited in providing feedback or active participation. Thus, it is necessary to use teachers or monitors at the conclusion of the presentation to overcome these difficulties (Chu & Schramm, 1967). Also, moving pictures are not adaptable to those situations in which there are wide differences in the ability levels or interests of the participants. Programed instruction or CAI is more effective in such cases.

2. Moving pictures can be difficult to fit into the learning environment. Television presentations ordinarily come at a designated time from a central studio many miles from the instructional setting. This makes the implementation of this material difficult for the instructor, especially if the medium is being utilized because the instructor does not have the prerequisite capabilities for presenting the material; he cannot easily call on the central facility to provide answers to students' questions that are beyond his capabilities.

3. As with CAI, the implementation of elaborate moving-picture techniques is expensive, requires considerable time and preparation, and, ideally, includes teacher training. This limitation applies more to specially prepared sequences of instruction that serve as an adjunct to the teaching process than to occasional films that demonstrate specific objectives. However, even in the latter case, the effective use of the technique demands careful planning and preparation by the instructor.

LABORATORY TRAINING

Laboratory training refers to a variety of techniques, such as T-group training, encounter groups, L- (for learning) groups, and action groups. This approach originated in an intergroup community-relations workshop held in Connecticut in 1946. The learning results of this group-interaction meeting stimulated the participants into organizing the first formal sensitivity-training session in Bethel, Maine, during the summer of 1947. From this session, a group known as the National Training Laboratories (NTL) was formed to promote and investigate sensitivity training. This group is still active today presenting programs, which vary in length from a few days to several weeks, on topics such as power in organizations, supervisory relationships, and personnel development for executives and managers. In addition to NTL, there are hundreds of other organizations sponsoring similar laboratory training. The large number of laboratory techniques vary not only in length but in focus (from personal growth to the building of teams), qualifications of the trainer (from individuals trained at NTL to self-designated leaders), and type of participants (strangers, members of the same firm, married couples) (Buchanan, 1971).

CHARACTERISTICS AND OBJECTIVES OF LABORATORY TRAINING

Buchanan (1964) describes the basic characteristics of laboratory groups as follows:
1. The approach utilizes a face-to-face unstructured group as the format for the learning experience.
2. The activities consist of interaction among individuals or groups.
3. There is frequent feedback and analysis regarding the here-and-now events that occur during the group interactions.
4. Problems that cannot be solved by the old forms of behavior are emphasized.

5. There is emphasis on generalizations from concepts and values that develop from the direct experience in the laboratory exercise.

Argyris (1964) adds that the group is designed to discuss the here and now rather than past personal history. While there is a leader present, he does not assume a guiding role but, rather, permits a power vacuum to develop so that the members are free to discuss any topic. The setting is designed to foster psychological safety where members are away from their organizations and free to voice their opinions. Some of the remarks may cause hard feelings, but Argyris feels that any pain caused must be viewed from the perspective of personal growth. In order to be effective, the experience should be gut-level and emotional. Anxiety is viewed as useful in creating an atmosphere in which individuals examine interpersonal and group problems in order to gain a deeper understanding of their own reactions toward colleagues and supervisors (Burke & Bennis, 1961).

As an example of the processes that occur during a laboratory session, we can examine Argyris' (1967) sample of a group experience. The president and nine vice-presidents of a large corporation attended a retreat for a week to discuss their problems. The seminar leader defined the objectives of the educational experience and prompted the group to begin. There was a long period of silence that was eventually broken by various individuals who asked what was going on and who was in charge of this meeting. Then one participant began:

> "You know, there's something funny going on here."
> "What's funny about it?"
> "Well, up until a few minutes ago we trusted this man enough that all of us were willing to leave the company for a week. Now we dislike him. Why? He hasn't done anything."
> "That's right.... He's the leader and he ought to lead."
> "... I honestly feel uncomfortable and somewhat fearful...."
> "That's interesting that you mention fear, because I think that we run the company by fear."
> The president turned slightly red and became annoyed: "I don't think that we run this company by fear, and I don't think you should have said that."
> A loud silence followed. The vice-president thought... and said "I still think we run this company by fear, and I agree with you. I should not have said it."
> The group laughed, and the tension was broken [p. 66].

At this point, the president apologized for his remarks and indicated a desire to achieve an open and trusting relationship. He went on to say that he always had an open door and that it wasn't easy to hear his company described as being run by fear. The group members discussed how they judged the openness of a person and how they had all inhibited one another.

These types of educational experiences are designed to achieve a variety of different goals. The following, summarized by Campbell et al. (1970), lists most of the objectives:

1. To give the trainee an understanding of how and why he acts toward other people as he does and of the way in which he affects them.
2. To provide some insights into why other people act the way they do.
3. To teach the participants how to "listen"—that is, to actually hear what other people are saying rather than concentrating on a reply.
4. To provide insights concerning how groups operate and what processes groups go through under certain conditions.
5. To foster an increased tolerance and understanding of the behavior of others.
6. To provide a setting in which an individual can try out new ways of interacting with people and receive feedback as to how these new ways affect them [p. 239].

THE CONTROVERSY OVER LABORATORY TRAINING

It is clear that laboratory training often utilizes anxiety-provoking situations as stimulants for learning experience. Many observers (for example, House, 1967; Odiorne, 1963) feel that these experiences are disruptive to the health of some of the participants. Critics also feel that it is one matter to express true feelings in the psychological safety of the laboratory but quite another to face the participants back on the job. These views are buttressed by reports that some individuals are hurt by the emotional buffeting experienced during the session and that more than one person has left the group feeling disturbed. For example, Klaw (1965) reports that some people return from these sessions liking themselves less and not sure what to do about it. His survey of 100 graduates from Western Training Laboratories revealed that one in ten graduates felt that way. The views of these critics are expressed by Kirchner (1965):

> Do we really want to rip off the "executive mask," which hides from the individual his true feelings, desires, and knowledge of self? Most people have taken many years to build up this "mask" or to build up their psychological defenses. While it can be very enlightening to find out that nobody loves you and that some people think that you have undesirable traits, this can also be a very shocking experience to individuals and not necessarily a beneficial one [p. 212].

These concerns are heightened by serious questions regarding the credentials of T-group leaders. Some critics feel that the give and take of laboratory sessions demands a qualified professional as a leader. House (1967) notes that many training directors and business consultants are ducting laboratory sessions, and, because these leaders are not trained psychology, the individual who has suffered emotional disturbances because of the sessions does not have the therapeutic aid normally available to a person undergoing therapy.

There are also ethical questions concerning the voluntary nature of laboratory participation. House (1967) suggests that as long as there are questions regarding the safety of trainees, participation should be entirely voluntary. Thus, a manager should not be able to order an employee into laboratory training, and company-wide laboratory training should be avoided so an individual will not participate only to conform to the group. Ethics should also require that employees be thoroughly informed about the potential benefits and dangers of the training. It is important to note that these suggestions result in some evaluation difficulties. If the participants are all volunteers, there will be limited generalizability because of the threat to external validity resulting from possible interactions of the selection of subjects and the experimental treatment. However, until the effects of laboratory training are more certain, it is safer to accept limited generalizability and to perhaps initiate studies toward understanding the volunteer effect in this situation by comparing the characteristics of persons who do or do not volunteer to participate in laboratory-training exercises.

Some observers believe that the controversy about the use of laboratory training is related to the lack of evaluative studies. This is not true. While there are serious questions regarding methodology and doubts about what is transferred to the job, there are more studies of laboratory training than of any other managerial-development technique. Yet other training procedures have not suffered the criticism leveled at laboratory training. The controversy is really related to the psychological safety of the individual who participates in T-group experiences.

EVALUATION OF LABORATORY TRAINING

Due to the ethical issues and concern for individual participants, critics (like Dunnette & Campbell, 1968) of laboratory-training methods are correctly insistent in their demand for studies designed according to scientific standards. The standards include pre- and postmeasurement, a control group, and some procedures to control for interaction between the pretest and behavior in the training program. This latter point is often referred to as the reactive effect of pretesting, which is a procedure to control for increased sensitivity to the training program caused by exposure to the pretest. This effect is a special concern in human-relations-type training in which the participants' expected changes do not concern complex motor skills but rather attitudes and social skills. Several techniques can be used to provide some estimate of the presensitization effect. For example, a group can be given a pretest with feedback and then a post-test after an intervening period that does not include training. Any changes in the scores provide an estimate of the sensitization effect, although there is also the possible contaminant resulting from specific events that occur between pre- and post-testing. A second procedure can have one group undergo training and the post-test without even taking the pretest. Then, it is possible to compare those scores to scores of the group that participated in the pretest, training, and post-test. These control procedures are not especially demanding, but, as we have already noted in our discussion of other training techniques, they are not often adopted.

The studies that utilize criterion measures collected during laboratory training have investigated changes in interpersonal sensitivity, self-awareness, personality, and various types of attitude change. Few studies report systematic changes, and those that report some effect are often without any control comparisons, which renders interpretations difficult at best. However, there are a few indications that well-conceived laboratory training can produce positive changes in behavior. One such study was reported by Rubin (1967), who hypothesized that T-group experiences should increase participants' level of self-acceptance. He further hypothesized that persons high in self-acceptance should have lower levels of ethnic prejudice. Two weeks before the program began, Rubin obtained questionnaires by mail to measure self-acceptance and ethnic prejudice for 14 of 50 participants. The entire group of 50 participants completed questionnaires upon their arrival (before training) and again at the end of the two-week training session. Thus, Rubin obtained pre- and postmeasures for an experimental and control group. The control group consisted of the 14 individuals who were pretested by mail and then tested again before undergoing training. The results of his study indicated that the control group had not changed during the two-week period before laboratory training but that the group of 50 showed substantial change toward increased self-acceptance and lower ethnic prejudice after the laboratory-training exercise.

Another set of studies has examined criteria that include behavior changes on the job. Most of these investigations have concentrated on measures of perceived change. In the typical study, the laboratory-training participant chooses an on-the-job associate who fills out a questionnaire describing specific perceived changes in the participant's behavior. The questionnaire is usually completed several months after the conclusion of laboratory training. Several of these studies have control groups, but they are usually chosen by the participants, who are instructed to nominate people similar to themselves. These procedures result in several evaluation problems. First, it is difficult to determine what type of person is chosen as a control. Dunnette and Campbell (1968) suggest that participants might choose individuals who have a history of interpersonal relationships less effective than their own. The biases are simply unknown, and, certainly, the choice is not random. A second difficulty is the choice of observers. It is possible, and some might even say likely, that the participant will choose observers who are friendly co-workers likely to have more favorable reactions. Basically, these factors affect the results in an unknown fashion, making interpretations of the effects of the treatment variable difficult.

One of the better investigations of behavior changes on the job was performed by Underwood (1965). In this study, the control subjects were matched by several relevant variables (department, supervisory level, age, and sex) instead of chosen by the participant. Also, although the observers were chosen by the participants and control subjects, they were kept uninformed about the training or any other part of the study. Underwood's investigation is also one of the few studies that evaluated the consequences of the perceived changes on job performance. The experimental group consisted of 15 supervisors in an engineering and manufacturing plant who volunteered to attend a two-hour session each week for 15 weeks. The observers were instructed to report any changes in the subjects' (both experimental and control) characteristic behavior patterns. For each incident, the observer was instructed to report the change, give a case example, and present a value judgment as to whether the change led to more or less effective supervisory behavior. There were 25 change incidents for the experimental group as compared to 11 for the control group, a ratio of 2.3 to 1. For the experimental group, 15 of the incidents were said to increase supervisory effectiveness, 7 to decrease it, and 3 involved no change; for the control group, 8 incidents were in the increase category, 2 in the decrease category, and 1 involved no change. Thus, there were more changes for the experimental group, but not all incidents were considered to be effective. Underwood reported that an analysis of the decreased-effectiveness changes revealed a heavy emotional loading. He speculated that "these subjects were venting emotion to a greater degree than usual, and to the observers, operating in a culture which devalues such expression, this behavior yielded a negative evaluation" (p. 40). Whether such changes are acceptable is dependent on the organization's objectives. At the present stage of development, it appears that laboratory training has the potential to modify the behavior of at least some of the participants. It would be very interesting to learn if there are particular characteristics of individuals that make them more amenable to change, but that is a research issue that remains to be explored. In any case, each organization and each individual must explore the potential changes that could occur due to the implementation of a T-group program. Then, they must make a decision whether to participate based on their own personal and organizational objectives.

BEHAVIOR MODIFICATION

Behavior modification is a direct application of the principles of reinforcement developed by B. F. Skinner in his operant-conditioning studies. Originally, behavior modification was utilized in clinical settings as a change technique for maladaptive behavior. Recently, some training analysts (Nord, 1970; Feeney, 1972) have suggested that the principles of behavior modification might be effectively utilized in the design of training programs. The basic procedures suggested by this approach can be summarized in the following way.

1. An assessment is performed to specify where problems exist and to help in the determination of precise behaviors that require elimination, modification, or development.

2. Reinforcers, appropriate to the situation and to the individual, are selected.

3. The implementation of the actual program consists of a variety of different operant-conditioning procedures dependent on the behavior of the trainees. For example, extinction is implemented when undesirable responses must be eliminated, and shaping is included when the responses to be learned are not in the behavioral repertoire.

4. Desired responses are immediately and continuously reinforced. Once the behavior is established, intermittent programs of reinforcement are instituted.

5. Evaluation procedures are employed to determine the degree of change.

At the present time, the actual implementation of behavior modification in training environments is quite limited. Most efforts consist of a reinterpretation of previous work into a reinforcement framework to demonstrate the potential value of the system. For example, Nord (1970) describes a program instituted by a retail firm to reduce tardiness and absenteeism. The absenteeism problem affected secretaries and sales and stock personnel at the firm's stores, warehouses, and offices. The firm instituted a program whereby monthly drawings were held for prizes, which were appliances worth approximately $25.00. There was one prize for each 25 employees. In order to be eligible, the employee had to have a perfect attendance and punctuality record for the preceding month. Similar drawings for a major prize (such as a color TV) were based on performance over a six-month period. After one year, absenteeism and tardiness were reduced to about one-fourth the level prior to the program. Sick-leave payments were reduced approximately 62 percent. Nord concludes that the lottery system served as a stimulus to reinforce punctuality and attendance at work.

Particular responses and associate contingencies represent the core of the behavior-modification system. Proponents of the system, like Feeney (1972), criticize other training efforts for emphasizing the teaching of processes like general management skills with the hope that the knowledge gained will solve a problem. Instead, Feeney suggests a performance audit to define a particular difficulty, followed by the reinforcement of the appropriate responses necessary to overcome the problem. These principles were demonstrated by Feeney in a project conducted at Emery Air Freight. A performance audit indicated that the employees believed that, nine out of ten times, they were responding to customer inquiries within 90 minutes. Emery Air Freight was also committed to combining small packages into large containers. The employees believed that they were effectively using containerized shipments 90 percent of the time. Feeney's data showed that the responses to customer inquiries were occurring within 90 minutes only 30 percent of the time and that the use rate on shipments was actually 45 percent. Focusing on these particular problems, Feeney instituted a program based on the principles of positive reinforcement. He talked with employees and found out their needs. Then, he used positive reinforcers to reward early approximations of the desired terminal responses. He focused on frequent reinforcement at the onset of the program and later switched to more intermittent programs. In all cases, the reinforcement was directly related to the performance. This emphasis on performance and feedback is illustrated by one aspect of the program, called the feedback system. The key elements are:

1. Find out what people think they should be doing.
2. Find out what they are doing—not by asking but by getting the raw data and comparing that with their perceptions.
3. Be sure feedback is measurable and that it gives comparisons to performance in previous similar periods.
4. Ensure that feedback gets to the proper unit in the organization—to the people who need it, as well as to their supervisors and intermediate management levels.
5. Make certain the feedback is timely—provided as soon after the performance as possible. The best procedure is to have the worker measure his own performance. That way, feedback is immediate; the employee is more likely to accept it and more likely to react favorably to it.
6. Design feedback in positive terms; even if there is no performance improvement, at least the employee can be complimented on his honesty in reporting accomplishments [p. 8].

Feeney estimates that Emery Air Freight saved several million dollars in a three-year period because of the changes in performance resulting from the application of reinforcement principles.

At this stage of development, it is possible only to suggest that this method has potential as a behavior-change technique. The demonstrations and reinterpretations of previous programs do not permit any powerful statements about the accomplishments of the program or about the important parameters of the technique. When a program is introduced, there are many variations in the environment that could be responsible for changes in behavior. Unfortunately, the lack of scientific procedures (for example, a control group) makes it difficult to ascertain why changes occurred. It has already been mentioned that on-the-job training is often employed to avoid the development of training programs and generally indicates a lack of commitment by the organization. Perhaps the use of any method, including behavior modification, with appropriate fanfare and commitment by management could result in changes similar to those achieved by Emery Air Freight. Any real gains in understanding await the employment of procedures beyond case studies or pre/post designs without control procedures.

Certain aspects of behavior modification promise that careful attention will be paid to some of the most important determinants of program success. First, the emphasis on program audits before and after the implementation of the technique suggests that the proponents of behavior modification will look at the accomplishments of their program rather than assume that success will follow automatically. Also, the concern with particular performance problems and associated behaviors requires careful need-assessment procedures before the design of the program. If this technique follows a path that includes need assessment and evaluation, there is reason for an optimistic outlook. On the other hand, the identification of positive reinforcers in complex organizations represents a serious obstacle.

In any particular job, it will be necessary to determine which stimuli serve as reinforcing agents. These reinforcers may be attention, status, privileges, promotion, and recognition, as well as the more obvious reinforcers such as bonuses, pay raises, and vacation time. McIntire (1973) cautions us that the determination of reinforcers for adult behavior is a complex task. For example, he suggests that it is difficult to modify safety practices in certain high-accident industries (for example, coal mining) by having contests and awarding lapel pins, because these stimuli are typically not viewed as positive reinforcers. More likely, peer approval and the social reinforcers controlled by experienced workers would be effective. These reinforcements can be established by having respected and experienced workers serve as models to demonstrate the safe approach or by pairing a new trainee with an individual who uses correct procedures, thereby providing peer approval of the safe approach. The various views on motivation and learning (see Chapter 7) suggest that the reinforcing stimuli will be viewed differently by different individuals. In these cases, the treatment of individual differences results in additional complications for behavior modification. If different reinforcers are needed for different responses for different learners, the implementation of this technique in an on-the-job setting or in a training environment will present a real challenge.

One criticism often made about behavior modification in clinical settings (and likely to be repeated in training environments) is related to the manipulation of human behavior by reward systems. Actually, any training technique is designed to modify human behavior, and it is unreasonable to single out behavior modification if the method succeeds in changing behavior. The key issue should be the careful determination of individual and organizational goals. Where conflict exists, the issues must be resolved before training begins. A sure way to fail, no matter what the technique, is to proceed with a training program when there is wide-scale disagreement about the goals and objectives. If behavior modification requires the organization to face these problems, it has a definite advantage.

ORGANIZATIONAL DEVELOPMENT

Organizational development (OD) is an educational strategy designed to produce organizational change. Beckhard (1969) describes OD as a planned organizational procedure directed by top management to improve organizational effectiveness through intervention based on behavioral-science methods. The procedures incorporate many different types of educational and training strategies, but, in each case, the accent is on organizational modification. Beckhard suggests that traditional programs fail to provide a link between the program and the changes that should follow the training effort. Thus, the training program often becomes an end in itself rather than a basis for a systematic attempt to alter the organization.

The basic characteristics of this approach are presented by Bennis (1969) and Beckhard (1969). They include the following:

1. There is a planned educational strategy for the entire organization based on a firm commitment from top management. The strategies can vary widely, from sensitivity training to feedback of information based on questionnaires and group discussions.

2. The planned organizational changes are focused on the problems facing the organization, including growth in size, more complex technologies unexpected shifts in markets, communication difficulties, and changes in the social-class structure and in job roles.

3. Organizational development is dependent on experience-based learning activities. Various methods (for example, group discussions) are utilized to provide data and experiences from which the changes in attitudes and behavior may result.

4. Change agents are employed to examine the problems and to help devise solutions. Bennis feels that change agents should be outsiders, who are more likely to view the issues objectively and thus avoid the internal conflicts that could consume an internal change agent.

5. OD is dependent on a collaborative relationship between the change agent and the clients. This relationship involves mutual trust and joint decisions on goals and means.

6. OD operates at the group level. It typically involves large cross sections of the organization representing different levels and departments.

7. The change agents share a common social philosophy that shapes their strategies. They believe that their changes may lead to more humane and democratic systems. They reject the values (such as authority-obedience relationships, delegated and divided responsibility, and centralized decision making) that OD proponents believe dominate most modern organizations. OD proponents believe that these values lead to impersonal and task-oriented behavior that causes poor and mistrustful relationships. In place of these values, OD stresses interpersonal competence, concern with human feelings, and development of increased understanding, trust, confidence, and shared responsibility among and within groups.

While it is not possible to examine all the different procedures employed in OD research, a study by Blake, Mouton, Barnes, and Greiner (1964) involves many of the basic characteristics. This investigation focused on team goal-setting and involved all 800 managers in a 4000-member unit. The research was prompted by difficulties related to a recent merger, strained relationships among departments, and a concern for fitting people and productivity together. The focal instrument utilized in this investigation was the Managerial Grid ® (Blake & Mouton, 1964), which identifies two major variables that are considered relevant to most organizations. As presented in Figure 8-2, the first variable represents a concern for productivity or output, and the second represents a concern for people. The scale for each of these units ranges from a value of 1, reflecting minimal concern, to a value of 9, for maximal concern. The Grid program works toward the achievement of a 9,9 climate.

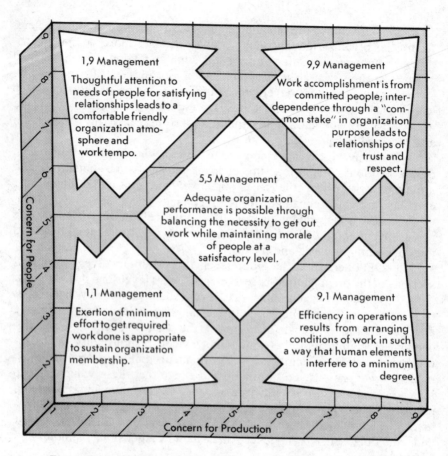

Figure 8-2. The Managerial Grid.® From Blake, R.R., Mouton, J.S., Barnes, L.E., and Greiner, L.E. Breakthrough in organization development. *Harvard Business Review,* 1964, **42,** 133–155. Reprinted by permission.

The research program was divided into the following six phases:

1. Laboratory-Seminar Training. During this phase, conferences and seminars were held to introduce the Grid approach. There were also programs in problem solving, self-evaluation, and team evaluation to help implement the Managerial Grid style of behavior. Groups were designed to include a diagonal slice of the organization so that many levels and departments were represented in each group.

2. Team Development. During this stage, the general concepts of 9,9 development were extended to on-the-job situations. Initially, this phase began with the top-level executives and immediate subordinates, who explored their managerial styles and operating practices.

3. Intergroup Development. Here, the discussion of 9,9 ground rules was extended from tensions within a single group to tensions that existed among groups. The authors stated that the goal of this phase was to move from the win/lose patterns of group conflict to joint problem-solving activity.

4. Organization Goals. At this stage, the focus was on issues of major importance, including union-management relations, safety, and promotion policies.

5. Organizational Attainment. As the problems were identified, teams were organized to gather information and to work toward agreement on the key dimensions of the problems. The corrective actions were based on the 9,9 approach.

6. Stabilization. This final phase assessed the changes and focused on the implementation of procedures to withstand pressures that could cause a reversion to old procedures.

The researchers collected data on a large number of criteria related to productivity and profits, practices and behavior, and perceptions, attitudes, and values. The data indicated that during the year of the development program, there was a considerable rise in profits and a decrease in costs. In these analyses, Blake and Mouton attempted to control for factors like fluctuating market prices, availability of raw materials, and changes in the size of the labor force. By utilizing multiple criteria and process criteria, the authors were also able to determine that there were more frequent meetings and that measures of management appraisal were changed. Also, there was increased mobility, as evidenced by an increase in transfers within the plant and to other branches of the organization. The attitude analyses showed a definite shift toward 9,9 values.

There were many difficulties in the analyses of these data, which the authors have suggested in their report. Most important were the criterion-contamination factors, such as price fluctuations and size of the work force, which were extremely difficult to isolate. In on-the-job settings, these factors can never be completely controlled. Thus, the investigators examined many factors and treated each finding as only a piece of the puzzle. They feel that the consistency and direction of the many different pieces of data support the value of their program. Unfortunately, the lack of control procedures makes it difficult to distinguish the real source of the effect. Thus, it is difficult to localize the effects of the specific aspects of the Grid program as compared to the group participation and team spirit that characterize most organizational-development studies (Campbell et al., 1970). Future decisions that determine which parts of the program are to be emphasized and supported depend on research designed to specify the sources of the effects. If the changes are a result of the excitement generated by initial participation in the implementation of the program, future training groups may not show similar effects. Conversely, the Grid approach and the interactions necessary to utilize the system may be the major source of the changes. In this case, future training groups are more likely to benefit from the program. In any case, the present study is important because of the insights offered about the difficulties and potential solutions to organizational research. More studies using multiple criteria as well as process and outcome measures are sorely needed.

One final question to consider is whether OD offers anything new or whether it is simply a more explicit statement about the necessity of examining organizational goals as a function of educational experiences. Certainly, most training analysts agree that criteria of on-the-job behavior and organizational results are necessary in addition to training-performance data. If this method offers little new except a demand that all effects be examined, it will still be a major contribution to the field. However, a careful analysis of OD suggests other important considerations that may arise from this approach. For example, there is relatively little information about the ways to implement training programs into organizational settings. OD suggests particular relationships between the change agent and the client as well as hypotheses regarding the most effective way to implement training programs across and within departments. Any research that stems from an exploration of these types of issues would be extremely valuable. Unfortunately, there has been little work related to these subjects in the few years since the emergence of OD. Most reports are simply anecdotal case studies that don't consider measurement problems, criteria, or various evaluation designs. If this is symbolic of future developments, OD will have little new to offer.

Chapter Nine

Simulation

Training simulators are designed to replicate the essential characteristics of the real world that are necessary to produce learning and transfer. These efforts can vary from flight simulators, which have a substantial degree of *physical fidelity* (that is, representation of the real world of operational equipment), to role-playing methods, in which the degree of physical simulation is minimal. In any case, the purpose of the simulation is to produce *psychological fidelity*—that is, to reproduce in the training tasks those behavioral processes that are necessary to perform the job. There are a variety of simulators that have been designed for specific training purposes, including skills development, decision making, and problem solving. Before examining these specific efforts, it is instrumental to discuss the reasons for simulation.

REASONS FOR SIMULATION

CONTROLLED REPRODUCIBILITY

Simulations permit the environment to be reproduced under the control of the training analyst. They represent a training laboratory outside the real-world setting, where uncontrolled parameters make it difficult to produce the desired learning environment. By careful design and planning, environments can be created that supply variation in the essential characteristics of the real situation. In addition, simulation permits the trainer to expand, compress, or repeat time, depending on the needs of the trainees. A business game designed to simulate market and supply conditions can present six weeks of essential financial operations in six hours, and an airline simulator can present months of aircraft-landing experience in several hours.

SAFETY CONSIDERATIONS

In many cases, the required terminal behavior is too complex to be safely handled by a trainee. The simulator permits the learner to be slowly introduced to the essential task characteristics, without any danger to himself, his fellow workers, or the expensive equipment. While many observers recognize the validity of carefully planned introductions to complex tasks, like flying an airplane, they fail to realize that many jobs, like assembly-line operations, also require considerable pretraining. Some industrial firms solve this problem by a *vestibule* training program, which consists of a simulation, off the production line, of the equipment and materials utilized on the job. Simulations also permit the trainee to practice emergency techniques before being exposed to hazardous situations in real settings. The focus of safety should not be narrowed to skills development. It is also reasonable to consider the psychological safety of a manager required to face the problems of racial strife on the job. Role-playing several solutions to that situation in the comparative safety of the training environment could have some benefits.

UTILIZATION OF LEARNING CONSIDERATIONS

Most simulations permit the effective utilization of learning principles. Since the environment is carefully controlled by the trainer, he can easily: (1) introduce feedback, (2) arrange for practice, (3) use part or whole and massed or spaced methods, and (4) design the environment according to the best-known principles of transfer. Thus, careful design of simulations can produce an environment conducive to positive transfer.

COST

The acquisition of skills requires practice, and if practice is not feasible in the real world, simulation provides a viable alternative. While most simulation efforts are expensive, they are often an economical alternative to using high-priced, on-the-job equipment. For example, Americans being trained to assume vital roles in overseas environments are being exposed to simulated training settings because trial-and-error performance in foreign countries is too expensive. And, quite probably, the behavior of a beginning trainee handling a multimillion-dollar jet might quickly convince passengers to make donations to simulation training programs.

TECHNIQUES OF SIMULATION

With this background, we can examine some of the major types of simulation efforts and the particular issues affecting each technique.

MACHINE SIMULATIONS FOR SKILLS DEVELOPMENT

All of the previously mentioned reasons for simulation have prompted the development of skill simulators. These simulators are utilized when the required skills are quite explicit and the behavior can be measured objectively. Frequently, these simulations have extensive physical fidelity and can represent a large number of potential environmental situations. For example, the advanced-training simulator for the Boeing 747 was designed to produce aborted takeoff, normal takeoff, approach to stall, steep turn, emergency descent, instrument-landing approaches, and two-engine approaches (Stein, 1968). A good description of a complex flight simulator is provided by J. A. Adams (1961).

> Most commonly, the term "flight simulator" refers to a complex electronic device designed to reproduce with considerable fidelity, for one or more aircrew stations, the location and physical features of controls and instruments, the aerodynamic response of instruments and controls under various conditions of flight and operator response, switches, warning lights, radio and navigational aids, and sometimes auditory stimuli. If a combat aircraft is simulated, there usually will be armament controls, radar controls and displays (if required), and target stimuli for combat problems [p. 88].

The design of simulators need not be limited to expensive large-scale operations. Many efforts are *part-simulations*, which replicate a critical or difficult portion of the task without attempting to provide the complete environment that is present in whole-simulators. An interesting study of part-simulators was reported by Rubinsky and Smith (1973). They examined simulated accident occurrence in the use of a grinding wheel. Traditionally, teaching the operation of power tools relies on written or verbal instructions, with an occasional demonstration. These authors devised a task that exposed operators (college students) to a simulated accident (a jet of water). The "accident" was designed to occur when the operator stood in front of the grinding wheel during the starting operation—that is, the time when there is the greatest danger of the wheel exploding. The investigators found that those subjects who experienced a simulated accident as part of their training program were less likely to repeat the hazardous behavior than those who were given written instructions or demonstrations of safe procedures. The results were maintained over a series of retention tests. The authors suggest that simulated accidents might be effective in reducing power-tool accidents. Certainly, this procedure provides an interesting form of feedback for incorrect responses.

Due to their task complexity, machine simulators often require the coordinated performance of several individuals. Thus, they are some-times utilized to investigate *team training*, with a team being defined as a group working together to achieve a common goal (Blum & Naylor, 1968). Of course, the term *team training* could apply equally well to other group instructional efforts, like organizational development and business games. Interestingly, most training efforts have not considered whether teams require special considerations beyond the principles utilized in the train-ing of individuals or whether there are significant interactions among teams. The intricacies of the team situation are exemplified by the com-plexities in providing feedback. Glanzer (1965) noted that errors caused by members of a team were especially burdensome because it was not always possible to determine who caused the error. Even if the source was discovered, considerable delay had occurred before feedback could be given. In addition to these difficulties, there is the question of what type of feedback should be presented—team, individual, or both. If given individual feedback, the team member might concentrate more on his own, rather than his team's, performance. However, team feedback does not provide direct information about an individual's performance. Per-haps the best solution is a combination of both types of feedback, but the empirical literature has little to offer in the way of advice.

In addition to feedback, another important issue is the determina-tion of the most appropriate instructional procedure for team training. Should the trainees be instructed individually or as team members? While logic might dictate that team training is the most appropriate procedure, Blum and Naylor (1968) note that the research is scanty and ambiguous. They suggest, however, that the literature on whole and part learning might offer some hypotheses. Naylor (1962) found that for tasks of high organization, whole training was best; for tasks of low organization, whole training was best for low complexity, and part training was best for high complexity. Thus, a potential analog to team training might state that highly organized tasks require cooperation and communication that would best be learned through team training. With tasks requiring limited amounts of cooperation, team training is effective if the tasks are simple, and individual training is effective if the tasks are complex (Blum & Naylor, 1968). The empirical evidence is limited, but a few studies (for example, Naylor & Briggs, 1965) do support these hypotheses. Certainly, team training is important, because more and more working activities consist of necessary interactions with other individuals. Research that provides information on this topic is likely to have ramifications for a variety of different instructional procedures.

Another example of the innovative procedures stemming from simulation development is *adaptive training* (Kelly, 1969; McGrath & Harris, 1971). In this system, the stimuli presented to the student are varied as a function of his immediate past performance. The task is made easier if the learner performs poorly or harder as he becomes skilled. Kelly suggests that this is a machine implementation of immediate feedback on an individual basis, which an instructor is usually unable to perform. Indeed, with a few exceptions, like computer-assisted instruction, the instructional mode does not permit much attention to individual differences. The proponents of this technique feel that the procedure is efficient for many different skill levels, because it always provides a task at the appropriate learning level rather than one that is too simple or too difficult. One interesting ramification of this procedure is the need for additional feedback systems. Since the task is continually modified to adapt to the individual's performance level, he does not improve in terms of error or accuracy. Thus, for the learner to be aware of his progress, a supplemental form of feedback must be introduced. As with all new forms of training systems, the viability of adaptive training remains to be determined.

There are a number of important design issues that have plagued the training analyst, such as the questions of fidelity and realism. Most researchers (for example, J. A. Adams, 1961) maintain that simulation efforts must have psychological fidelity (that is, the representation of the essential behavioral processes necessary to perform the job) as their chief objective. However, the question of how much physical representation is necessary in order to achieve psychological fidelity remains. The entire task is never produced in a simulation. In some cases, it is simply too expensive or dangerous, while, in other instances, certain factors are judged as not important to the learning of the task (for example, opening or closing the door to the aircraft). However, the choice is not always clear. For example, it is still not certain whether the simulation of motion is a necessary aspect of pilot training (Williges, Roscoe, & Williges, 1972). In these types of situations, there is no solution except careful design based on task analyses, empirical tests, and retests. There is little gained in the production of expensive simulators in which tasks that are critical for positive transfer are being excluded. Another aspect of the fidelity issue is the development of part-simulators designed to reflect the critical components of the task. The importance of part-simulators is emphasized by those who maintain that the expense of whole-simulators cannot be assumed by most training programs. Of course, the development of effective part-training programs is dependent on the identification of the components to be included and the effective integration of the part-simulation with the training media used to implement the remaining features of the instructional program.

As mentioned earlier, the development of simulation efforts has contributed to the basic learning literature on transfer of training. Yet, despite accomplishments in the literature and laboratories, the degree of understanding that might be expected has not been achieved. In part, the limitations are a result of inadequate evaluation efforts. For example, Blaiwes and Regan (1970) suggest that evaluation efforts must consider three criteria: (1) original learning efficiency, (2) transfer of learning to the new task, and (3) retention of learning. Yet, in the area of flight simulation (the most advanced simulation effort to date), the emphasis has been on the most immediate criterion—original learning efficiency. Even these original-learning studies have been plagued by serious problems. Williges et al. (1972) note that there is little agreement on what constitutes ideal pilot performance, since the reliability of most pilot-performance grading systems has been disappointing. Thus, the studies are difficult to evaluate because there is little agreement on what constitutes terminal performance. Studies investigating the transfer of skills from simulation to on-the-job efforts are less frequent and suffer from serious design flaws, usually caused by the lack of a control group. Studies concerning retention measures are virtually nonexistent. Thus, there is little information on whether skills obtained through simulation efforts are maintained over a period of time or whether certain learning variables (for example, massed versus spaced practice or amount of original learning) make any difference in long-term retention. Williges et al. (1972) describe the research difficulties in the following manner:

> Measurement of retention is hindered by such problems as variations in the original training of subjects, difficulty of controlling the amount of flying experience each individual receives during the retention period, and unavailability of subjects after a sufficiently long retention period. The lack of simulator studies using a retention measure reflects the general insufficiency of information relating to retention of pilot skills or, for that matter, retention of any complex motor skill [p. 13].

Simulator training for complex skills, motor or otherwise, offers a real opportunity for research that will contribute to an understanding of the learning process. Most sponsors prefer to have their trainees learn skills on simulated instruments rather than on original equipment. Thus, the research opportunities are there; it is not necessary to sell anyone on the need for training. Rather, it is necessary to produce the carefully designed research that contributes to understanding and knowledge.

BUSINESS GAMES

Business games are a direct outgrowth of the war games that are used to train military officers in combat tactics. One military war game developed in 1798 used a map with 3600 squares, each representing a distinctive topographical feature, on which pieces representing troops and cavalry were moved (Raser, 1969). After visiting the Naval War College in 1956, members of the American Management Association developed the first business game. It is estimated that over 30,000 executives participated in the large number of games that were developed in the following five years (Stewart, 1962). A general description of business games is given by Dill, Jackson, and Sweeney (1961):

> A business game is a contrived situation which imbeds players in a simulated business environment where they must make management-type decisions from time to time, and their choices at one time generally affect the environmental conditions under which subsequent decisions must be made. Further, the interaction between decisions and environment is determined by a refereeing process which is not open to argument from the players [pp. 7–8].

Most business games include the following steps (Greenlaw, Herron, & Rawdon, 1962; Moore, 1967):

1. The participants are first oriented to the simulated game by instructions describing the business objectives, decisions required, and rules of the game.

2. The competing teams then organize themselves and become cognizant of background information on the operations of the business. Then, the first series of decisions are made. Depending on the simulation, the decision may be based on one day or several months of operations.

3. After the first period is completed, the decisions for the competing teams are given to the game administrators.

4. The results are tabulated, manually or by computer, and are returned to the team participants along with other information that describes changes in their operating environment.

5. The cycle is repeated a number of times. Usually, at the completion of the game, the results are analyzed in a critique session. While this description is appropriate for most business games, there are many variations. For example, the complexity of the games in terms of days played and variables implemented as part of the gaming process varies greatly. The following description comes from one of the most complex games, known as the Carnegie Tech Management Game (Cohen, Cyert, Dill, Kuehn, Miller, Van Wormer, & Winters, 1962).

> The packaged detergent industry has served as a general model for the industry of the game. The selection of this industry for our model was primarily one of convenience. Its advantages included the existence of a national market, a small number of firms, and a set of differentiated products. . . . There are three companies in the game. The players have the role of executives in the three competing companies. Each firm consists of one factory, located in one of the four geographical territories that comprise

the total detergent market. At this factory, there are the following facilities: (1) a raw-materials warehouse, (2) production facilities that can be used to produce different mixes of product, (3) a factory warehouse for the storage of finished product, and (4) offices and facilities for new-product research and development [pp. 105–106].

The players receive realistic and copious data in almost all areas of operations, including finance, sales, production, and marketing. They are expected to make realistic decisions based on this information. The computer processing of players' decisions, based on a programed economic model, results in a new supply of data, and the cycle repeats.

Experience is necessary to develop real skills in decision making. Yet, most firms cannot afford the trial-and-error learning period necessary for the development of such skills. Business games are seen as the solution to this problem. The game provides practice in decision making, interaction among various components of the firm, and interaction among participants. Similar to machine simulations, business games permit control over time. Thus, numerous samples can be presented in a short period of time. Furthermore, most games place a premium on planning that requires the participants to consider objectives, long-term plans, and overall point of view. The feedback provisions and dynamic quality of the play are seen as being intrinsically motivating to the participant.

Others (for example, Bass & Vaughan, 1966) suggest that this dynamic quality can result in an environment that is not effective as a teaching tool. The participants may become so involved in the excitement and the competitive aspects of the game that they lose sight of the principles and evaluation of consequences that are its most important functions. Instead, the participants tend to become more concerned with beating the system and one another. Perhaps, the careful use of critique sessions could circumvent this problem. Another problem relates to the fidelity of simulation. Most business games are not based on a real business enterprise, but (hopefully) they are based on psychological fidelity. However, there is the danger that particular solutions, rather than basic principles and concepts, are carried away from the game and inappropriately applied in the real-business setting. Most of these issues are empirical questions that can be answered by an analysis of the transfer of learning from the game to the job setting. Thus, by scrutinizing evaluative research, valuable information can be gained about the utility of the technique.

Shortly after business games had first become popular, McGehee and Thayer (1961) stated that there was no research on the relative effectiveness of games as compared to other techniques. There were also no data on the utility of various approaches, like competition or no competition and complex or simple games. These authors concluded: "For all we know, at this time, there may be a negative or zero relationship between the kinds of behavior developed by business game training and the kinds of behavior required to operate a business success-fully" (p. 223). Since these authors stated their opinion, other inves-tigators have expressed concern about the cost of gaming (for example, Raia, 1966) and the continued lack of descriptive and statistical informa-tion. In 1971, J. P. Campbell concluded in his *Annual Review* article "Personnel Training and Development": "There have been almost no recent attempts to study the development of problem-solving and decision-making skills, even though a number of strategies exist for developing these skills" (p. 585). Except for a few isolated investigations, business games remain unexplored. A study by Raia (1966) provides an illustration of the types of research that can be performed. He compared the effects of two forms of business games and a control condition on the ability of business-administration seniors to solve analytic case studies. The game groups submitted a series of decisions over a two-month period on sales, production, and finance. One group manufactured and produced a single product. The other game group manufactured and sold three products. In addition, they had a complex set of rules governing the relationship of raw materials to the production of finished goods. All groups covered the same instructional material in the regular course sessions (essentially a case-study method), although the control group was given additional outside reading material and required to review and critique each assignment. The criteria were a test on case problems, a final exam, and an attitude questionnaire. The case problems were administered in a pre- and post-test design. Basically, there were no statistical differences in interest among the groups, although the author felt that the trends indicated higher interest and motivation for the game groups. Both game groups were significantly superior to the control on case problems and final exams. However, there were no differences between the two game groups. Thus, the more complex game did not result in any additional benefits.

Since there are not many other investigations of business games, the efficacy of the technique is based on the proponents' hard-sell verbal approach. The investigations of other media like PI and moving pictures have not always produced definitive results. However, the empirical research already accomplished on PI, CAI, and moving pictures has resulted in an appreciation for their advantages and limitations that does not exist for business games. In 1961, Haldi and Wagner suggested a series of substantive research issues. They include:

1. How can it be determined whether the time a student spends in a business game is as useful as time spent on some other classical educational approach?
2. What criteria should be used to determine whether students learn more from a business game or from an alternative approach?
3. If we decide that business games are worthwhile, how can we introduce them into a curriculum?
4. Can business games be used successfully by groups that have not participated in their design and development?
5. To what degree should a business game be realistic?
6. Do business games bolster the basic business principles that are thought to be valid, or do they contradict such principles?
7. Do business games have a significantly different impact on under-graduates, graduates, and businessmen?

At the present time, evaluators have not begun the systematic efforts necessary to answer these questions.

IN-BASKET TECHNIQUE

The *in-basket* technique is a business game that is a simulation of several aspects of a manager's job. The participant is presented with information regarding his role in the company. Then, he is given an in-basket consisting of letters, memoranda, notes of incoming telephone calls, and other materials related to the job. The trainee is told that he is the new employee, and, rather than play a role, he is to act out the job as if it were his own. Thus, the participant does not indicate what he would like to do. Instead, he writes letters and memos, prepares meeting agendas, and generally performs as if he were on the job. Once the participant completes the task, the simulation is concluded. Often, a group critique follows the session. However, as compared to a business game, the feedback is not followed by another set of responses.

In a study of this technique, Frederiksen (1962) established several behavioral dimensions: (1) preparation for action—Those who score high on this dimension defer final decisions and spend their time in prepara-tion for decision making; (2) amount of work—A high score on this dimension means that the participant has high work output; (3) guidance —Those who score high on this dimension ask for the advice of others.

The utility of the technique for managerial training remains unde-termined. There is no information on the psychological fidelity, and no one has determined if the participant transfers any skills to his job. As compared to most business games, the in-basket technique is inexpensive and easy to use with large groups of participants, who can also participate in the critique session. The critique, which provides the feedback to the participants, appears to be a key element of this procedure. This is also true of business games, role-playing, and case studies. Unfortunately, there is no empirical information to establish the important parameters of the critique session.

CASE STUDY

The conditions of an organization are sometimes simulated by a case study. The trainee receives a written report that describes an organizational problem. Then, he is expected to analyze the problem and offer solutions based on a number of factors, including people, environment, rules, and physical parameters. The trainee usually studies the case individually and prepares his solutions. Then, he meets with a group that discusses the various solutions and tries to identify the basic principles underlining the case. The group procedure is designed to promote feedback and allow the individual to learn by observing others developing their respective solutions. It is generally recognized that there is no correct solution; thus, the trainees are encouraged to be flexible.

Critics of this approach feel that the method is not useful for learning general principles and that the lack of guided instruction that generally characterizes the group processes is detrimental. The proponents of this technique feel that the self-discovery occurring during these sessions is likely to lead to longer retention of the principles generated by the trainees. (For a discussion of these views, see Campbell et al., 1970.) As discussed earlier, Raia (1966) found that business games, as compared to the case-study method, led to superior performance on several criterion measures, including standardized case studies and the final exam. Moore (1967) also examined business games and case studies. Essentially, he found no differences between the two groups on a series of criterion measures. However, he suggests that one disadvantage of business games was the preoccupation of the participants with beating one another instead of learning the basic concepts. Thus, he suggests that the case study, with the more static setting, provides an atmosphere more conducive to the examination of general principles and issues.

The validity of Moore's point depends on the ability of the participants or the leader (if he is included) to evaluate and reinforce one another. Participants in the case-study technique can become entangled in the large amount of information presented and never find the basic issue; the technique cannot work unless the group focuses on the issues. Also, the principles learned from the case study should be applied to everyday situations on the job to avoid the danger of the trainee's becoming so engrossed in the case study that he never sees the relevance of the principles to everyday life. Finally, Byers (1970) suggests that groups involved in case studies should meet for several hours a week over an extended period of time to become acquainted so that they can communicate freely.

ROLE-PLAYING

In this technique, trainees act out simulated roles. Role-playing is used primarily for analyses of interpersonal problems and attitude change and development of human-relations skills (Bass & Vaughan, 1966). This technique gives the trainees an opportunity to experience and explore solutions to a variety of on-the-job problems. The success of the method depends on the participants' willingness to actually adopt the roles and to react as if they were really in the work environment (Campbell et al., 1970). There are many different role-playing techniques. In one variation, trainees who disagree are asked to *reverse roles* (Speroff, 1954). This procedure is intended to make a person more aware of the other's feelings and attitudes. In another variation, called *multiple role-playing* (Maier & Zerfoss, 1952), a large number of participants are actively involved in the role-playing process. The entire group is divided into teams that each role-play the situation. At the end of a specified period of time, the participants reunite and discuss the various results achieved by each separate group.

One of the more recent and unique uses of role-playing is called self-confrontation. In this procedure, the trainee is shown a videotape replay of his entire visual and audio performance. During the viewing of the tape, he is given a verbal critique of his performance by the trainer. One set of studies exploring this technique was prompted by the image of American advisers and officers overseas (King, 1966). Researchers feel that a lecture on how to behave in a foreign country is equivalent to a lecture on how to fly an airplane. With the self-confrontation technique, the trainee is first given information about the culture and the desired general behavior. Then, he plays the role of an adviser in a foreign country. Typically, the trainee interacts with a person from the foreign country who is a confederate of the trainer. After the role-playing, the trainee views the tape and is given a verbal critique of his performance by the trainer. Several studies have indicated that the videotape and feedback session does result in changes in behavior. In one study (King, 1966), the subjects played the role of a United States Air Force captain who was required to report to his foreign counterpart. They were required to reprimand the counterpart on one aspect of his behavior and to commend him for another aspect. This conversation was to take place in a highly prescribed way, consistent with the culture and containing 57 different behaviors, ranging from gross motor movements to subtle voice cues. The results of this study indicated that trainees who participated in self-confrontation performed consistently better than another group of subjects who had spent an equivalent amount of time studying the behavioral requirements outlined in the training manual. Retention tests given two weeks later indicated that the self-confrontation group maintained their skills. While self-confrontation techniques can be applied as a feedback supplement for a variety of training techniques, a number of studies (Haines & Eachus, 1965; Eachus & King, 1966) have demonstrated that it is especially useful with interaction procedures like role-playing. It has already been mentioned that the key to techniques like role-playing and business games is the feedback and critique session. The self-confrontation method provides accurate and detailed feedback, and, when it is combined with sensitive analyses of performance, it appears to be a very useful procedure.

Besides the recent analyses of self-confrontation techniques, there are relatively little evaluation data available on role-playing. Some observers warn us that role-playing has several limitations that are a result of the acting role assumed by the participants. There is some concern that participants might find the role-playing childish (Liveright, 1951) and that they might have a tendency to put more emphasis on acting than on problem solving (Bass & Vaughan, 1966). If the emphasis is on the acting of roles, there is a possibility that participants will behave in a manner that is socially acceptable to other members of the group but not reflective of their actual feelings. In this case, the role-playing may not lead to any behavioral changes outside the role-playing environment (Ingersoll, 1973). In the traditional format, the feedback is controlled by the participants in the role-playing setting. If the feedback focuses more on the acting ability of the participant than on the solution to problems, the entire learning process can be circumvented. Again, the leader becomes the key element to a successful training session.

Chapter Ten

Special Approaches to Training Issues

This chapter focuses on general approaches to training problems rather than on analyses of specific techniques. The first topic is an examination of individual differences and their relationship to learning and training, with emphasis on selecting techniques that fit the individual characteristics of different learners. The second topic concentrates on instructional programs for the hard-core unemployed. In this type of program, training in the traditional sense will not work because of the diverse values and attitudes of individuals raised in different cultural environments. These programs must consider many aspects of a complex system, including the support services (for example, counseling and job placement) necessary for individuals who have never been employed. It is also clear that training programs are only part of an answer to a complex problem. The final topic in this chapter is retraining for second careers. Some of the individuals in these groups have been placed out of work by technological changes, while others have decided that they are no longer interested in their first career. As an additional barrier, these potential employees face the hurdle of age discrimination. The hard-core unemployed and the second-career groups present a complex social problem that cannot be resolved by narrowly examining specific techniques of training.

INDIVIDUAL DIFFERENCES

The current emphasis placed on the examination of individual-difference parameters in learning and training represents a merging between two separate camps that had rarely recognized each other's existence. Until recently psychologists concerned with learning and training examined the effects of their treatments and considered individual differences an annoyance that made the establishment of general laws of behavior difficult. Differential psychologists ignored treatment effects and busied themselves with the study of individual variability. For example, applied psychologists concerned with selection used measures of individual variability to predict future performance on various measures of success.

The reason for the current interest in individual differences and learning behavior is difficult to ascertain. Melching (1969) feels that it is related to a desire for education for the masses without mass education. He suggests that our society does not approve of lock-step educational procedures in which all students are treated as having equal ability and the same learning needs. While some commentators might argue that societal pressure prompted the development of instructional technology, there is also little doubt that the hardward developments stimulated the instructional community to be responsive to individual differences. Thus, CAI has storage capabilities that permit consideration of many demographic variables, and PI and CAI have branching and self-pacing options. For whatever reason, a growing group of educators and psychologists are espousing the viewpoint that the design of instructional programs for the average participant is not the most efficient learning procedure. This view is especially well expressed by Lawrence (1954).

> ... studies on training methods concerned with spaced versus massed practice, motivational level, and the like are primarily directed at modifying the average rate of learning. Normally, however, a standardized procedure for the spacing of practice and like factors is adopted for all individuals of the group. It is doubtful if this produces the optimum effect for each individual. The optimum value for one individual might well differ considerably from the optimum value for other individuals in the group, depending upon the variability in levels of performance at any given time, the rates of learning, and other characteristics of the individuals involved [p. 374].

There are several different approaches that can be utilized in the treatment of individual differences (Cronbach, 1967). The following presentation discusses these approaches as applied to instructional programs.

FIXED-PROGRAM APPROACH

One method for treating individual differences is to design a single program with fixed objectives and to require the trainee to continue in the program until the criteria are achieved. Essentially, this procedure permits the individual learner rate to vary but requires that each participant eventually meet the criteria. This type of program is very much in evidence in primary-school systems in which children are not promoted until they learn to read. Similarly, the linear-programing approach to PI is designed to allow the individual to proceed through the material at his own pace until he completes the program. There are several problems in the employment of this method. One administrative concern is that many types of training programs are likely to be prohibitively expensive and unwieldy if it is necessary to extend the instructional time for many trainees beyond minimal limits. Another problem is whether the attainment of certain skills can be accomplished by manipulating the learning time. While this is an empirical issue that cannot be resolved at the present time, some investigators (for example, Cronbach, 1967) feel that psychologists will achieve more by altering the technique than by just extending the duration.

ADAPTING-GOALS APPROACH

This method utilizes separate programs to achieve the differential goals of the learner. Cronbach notes that this approach can be traced to the time when high schools stopped viewing the dropout problem as a way of reducing an undesirable population that was not interested in an academic education. Thus, different types of programs (for example, vocational instruction) were introduced based on decisions regarding the hypothesized role that the student might have as an adult. There is some recognition of this approach in industrial selection and placement programs. On the basis of employment tests and interviews, the applicant may be assigned to an instructional program that matches his needs. However, in most instances, the recognition of individual differences is more apparent in decisions that specify who should undergo training than in decisions that indicate which form of training is best (Howard, 1971). Thus, laboratory education is not recommended for individuals who have weak egos or who have a history of emotional disturbances. Unfortunately, when a laboratory-education program is instituted for managerial personnel, alternatives are not likely to be offered to those who are poor candidates.

ERASING-INDIVIDUAL-DIFFERENCES APPROACH

In this approach, the instructional system is designed to minimize individual differences by offering remedial branches. For example, PI branching programs are based on a diagnosis of the type of learner errors that occur in the instructional sequence. In industrial training programs, this approach is illustrated by the design of remedial sequences for those trainees who are not prepared for the fixed instructional programs—for example, remedial reading instruction for the hard-core unemployed.

All the preceding approaches are potentially useful in the treatment of individual differences. Future developments in instructional media, such as PI and CAI, are likely to contribute information about the most effective procedures in the implementation of these approaches. However, the most intriguing approach is the determination of instructional programs on the basis of individual characteristics.

ALTERING-INSTRUCTIONAL-METHODS APPROACH

The goal of this approach is to match alternate modes of instruction to the different characteristics of the individual so that each person utilizes the most appropriate learning procedure. This approach is often called *Aptitude-Treatment Interaction* (ATI). Figures 10-1 and 10-2 illustrate two types of ATI relationships. Figure 10-1 shows that all persons, regardless of aptitude level, improve with treatment A. In that case, there is no reason to use treatment B; thus, all individuals should be presented with treatment A. Figure 10-2 illustrates an interaction called the *disordinal aptitude-treatment interaction*. In this case, individuals to the right of the cutoff line (those with higher aptitude levels) perform best

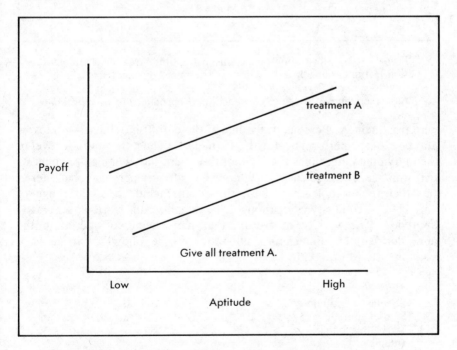

Figure 10-1. Illustration of no aptitude-treatment interaction. From Cronbach, L. J. The two disciplines of scientific psychology. *American Psychologist,* 1957, **12,** 671–684. Copyright 1957 by the American Psychological Association. Reproduced by permission.

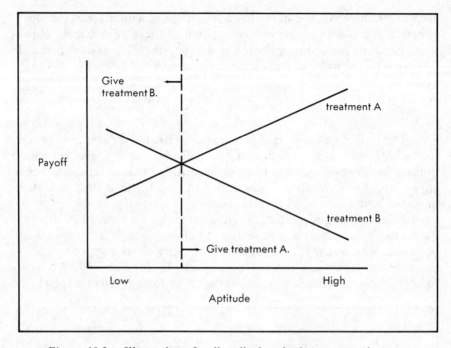

Figure 10-2.   Illustration of a disordinal aptitude-treatment interaction. From Cronbach, L. J. The two disciplines of scientific psychology. *American Psychologist,* 1957, **12,** 671–684. Copyright 1957 by the American Psychological Association. Reproduced by permission.

with treatment A. Persons to the left of the cutoff line (those with lower aptitude levels) perform best with treatment B. Thus, the aptitude level of the individual determines the form of treatment that will lead to superior performance. In these cases, *aptitude* refers to any personal characteristics that relate to learning and, thus, can include a broad range of variables, such as styles of thought, personality, and various scholastic aptitudes. The variety of factors that have been considered in the aptitude-treatment dimension is illustrated by the following partial list of variables (Howard, 1971).

Aptitude

Scholastic aptitude
Spatial aptitude
Verbal reasoning
Intelligence
Deductive/inductive reasoning
Cognitive style (analytic/nonanalytic)
Mathematics ability
Interests

Ascendancy, dominance
Introversion/extroversion
Need for achievement
Motive to avoid failure
Anxiety
Overachievement/underachievement
Sociability
Attitudes to instruction or subject
Need for autonomy
Miscellaneous personality characteristics

Treatment

Visual presentations
Verbal presentations
PI difficulty or complexity
Multiple-choice versus constructed PI responses
Classroom social change
PI—knowledge of results
PI—overt/covert responding
PI—immediate feedback
Verbal-figural material
Inductive/deductive method
Step size
Praise/blame as reinforcement
Lecture/PI text/teaching machine
Bypassing versus linear programing
PI sequencing (standard/random order)
Rote versus conceptual instruction

As an illustration of this type of research, we can consider a study of Navy technical training made by Edgerton (1958) and reanalyzed by Cronbach and Snow (1969) for ATI effects. Two methods of instruction were utilized in a course for aviation mechanics. In one method, which was essentially rote learning, the trainees were told to memorize the material and reproduce it on examinations. In the second method, the instructor presented explanations and stimulated students to ask questions. This procedure was dubbed the "why" method. The test predictors taken by the 150 trainees in each group were the Tests of Primary Mental Abilities. The interaction analyses showed that those individuals who scored highly on the verbal-abilities tests were more likely to perform well under the rote treatment. However, a similar relationship was not found for the "why" group. Cronbach and Snow suggest that the explanations in the "why" condition overcame some of the potential learning difficulties for those trainees who scored poorly on the test. Another interesting interaction was established between scores on an interest test and performance in the course. Those individuals who performed best in the rote treatment had previously expressed interest in the kind of content being taught. There was no relationship between interests and performance in the "why" treatment. In this instance, the more meaningful treatment in the "why" condition may have compensated for whatever handicaps were established by the lack of interest.

Unfortunately, the results of the Edgerton study are atypical. An analysis by Cronbach and Snow (1969) and a review by Bracht (1970) found little evidence of ATI. Bracht's review examined over 100 individual-difference treatments and found evidence of interactions in only five cases. However, Cronbach and Snow note that few of these studies planned for analyses of ATI effects and that the control conditions and the choice of variables were not consistent with well-planned ATI studies. At this stage of development, these remarks are justified. Unless a long history of trial-and-error empirical studies is involved, it is necessary to examine the processes in the various forms of learning. Then, the choice of aptitude variables can proceed from an analysis of strategies utilized in each form of learning rather than from which measures of aptitudes happen to be available. Thus, it is possible to ask which learning processes are utilized in problem solving and which aptitude variables are likely to interact with those processes.

If this research does begin to produce consistent interaction data, there is another problem that has serious implications for training research. Cronbach and Snow (1967) warn us that particular training conditions that result in poor performance in one type of short-term treatment should be examined further. It must be determined how that particular problem (for example, inability to cope with a discussion method) can be rectified, because it is likely to limit the individual in other types of social and work situations. Thus, the problem for the trainer will be to design an instructional program that will allow the learner to profit from group discussions so that he will not suffer from that inadequacy in a job setting. In this way, interaction research may eventually offer another important tool by identifying problem areas that require further training. It is clear that individual-difference research needs development before it can offer useful information for instructional technology, but the potential utility of the information should make the effort worthwhile.

TRAINING FOR THE HARD-CORE UNEMPLOYED

The civil disorders of the 1960s prompted a reconsideration of our poverty-ridden communities. In the cities alone, there were 500,000 unemployed persons (Report of the National Advisory Commission on Civil Disorders, 1968). Many of the members of these communities are hard-core unemployed (HCU); that is, they are not regular members of the work force, and, in many cases, they have been without employment for more than six months. The HCU are usually young, members of a minority group, and lacking a high school education. In addition, they are below the poverty level specified by the Department of Labor (Goodman, Salipante, & Paransky, 1973). Recent estimates support the fact that the HCU represent a serious problem. For example, the national unemployment average for 1972 was approximately 5.6 percent. Yet, the jobless rate for black teenagers seeking employment was 33.5 percent (Manpower Report of the President, 1973).

Solutions to the problems of the HCU focus on training programs in remedial education, specific job skills, and motivational or attitudinal factors. Although some programs emphasize only one of these areas, most programs combine them. For example, remedial education and specific job skills are interwoven because many investigators have found that the HCU are limited by their educational background in programs that stress only skill proficiency. The need for sensitivity in designing programs is illustrated by the semantic differences that disrupt communication between trainees and employers. "Words that sound the same have different meanings. Sentence structure is different. Business and technical terms comprise another language. Thinking that they (minority-group trainees) understand, they often find that they really don't know what is wanted" (Van Brunt, 1971, p. 2). Also, many of the HCU have speech dialects that are not readily understood outside their own culture. When the basic literacy scores of the HCU are examined, the scope of these difficulties is apparent. In one study of 1500 Chicago trainees, the achievement-test scores showed an average ability to read and figure at the sixth-grade level, despite an average background of ten years of education (Seiler, 1969). An auxiliary benefit for the HCU from combined programs is increased interest in remedial work, resulting from the opportunity to utilize the knowledge on job-related tasks. Programs that include motivational and attitudinal considerations are few; however, research indicates that programs that do not consider such factors are often doomed. This point will be explored later in this section.

It is important to note that training analysts have attempted to modify traditional techniques by applying their hypotheses about the characteristics of their trainee population. For example, one program revised the characteristics of the traditional role-playing exercise for members of a group of HCU (Kennedy, 1970) in an effort to develop their interpersonal skills in dealing with customers and other personnel in the retail industry. In this program, the trainee is given a situation like "Your manager is impatient with you and won't give you an even break." He then role-plays that situation while a videotape records his performance.

Kennedy suggests that the replay of the videotape for the trainee reduces the threat of feedback that is ordinarily provided by other observers. In this situation, the trainee has an opportunity for self-criticism during the replay. Also, the videotape permits the trainee to view certain cues that can result in interpersonal difficulties, such as a loud voice or a facial sneer.

Another example of the adaptation of training techniques is the use of simulations to provide work samples for the HCU. Here, the simulation is designed not to teach job skills but to acquaint trainees with various aspects of the job. Thus, the individual is given information to help him decide which types of employment might serve his interests and aptitudes. One study of this program (Seiler, 1969) reported that trainees provided with initial orientation through work samples are less likely to switch or drop out of training programs.

The dangers in using any instructional technique without considering the characteristics of the trainees are particularly obvious in a study that utilized PI materials as part of an instructional program for automobile mechanics and general machine operators. The program for each job was 225 hours long and was designed to prepare youths for job entry. During the PI program, the trainees continually checked one another's work to see who was proceeding fastest. Also, there was persistent peer pressure to work as quickly as possible; thus, the self-pacing aspect of PI was nonexistent. The speed pressure led to a tendency to cheat by looking at the next page of the programed text for the answer. In spite of these difficulties, the trainers judged the program a success because 80 percent of the PI group, as compared to 60 percent of the earlier traditional group, completed the program. Also, considerably more PI trainees were placed on the job. How much of this success was due to the student-modified PI section of the training curriculum is hard to ascertain.

It is possible to describe a vast number of techniques that have been applied to the problems of the HCU. However, if we concentrate on studies that emphasize only remedial programs or job skills, there are few programs that have any demonstrable utility. This is partially due to the now-familiar lament that there are many reports of programs but few reports of research studies focusing on results. However, another basic consideration is that programs that concentrate just on job skills, whether they be auto mechanics or retail selling, don't seem to work very well. This is evident in a study (Miller & Zeller, 1967) that followed 418 trainees who had graduated from a training program for highway-construction-machinery operators. The authors were able to obtain information from 279 graduates. Of these graduates, 61 percent were employed and 39 percent were unemployed at the time of the interview. In addition, more than half of the total group said they were without jobs more than 60 percent of the time. Some of the reasons for the unemployment situation related to inadequacies in training, which included limited task practice and insufficient training time. One trainee noted that "The contractors laughed when I showed them my training diploma and said 'Come back after you get some schooling, buddy' " (pp. 32–33). However, the inadequacies of the training program were only one of the problems faced by the potential employees. Miller and Zeller state the problem this way: "It might have been helpful to have included, within the training experience itself, practice in job hunting, assistance in contacting employers before the end of training, follow-up counseling, and job-placement help" (p. 31).

Job placement and counseling are two indicants of a common theme in HCU research; that is, training systems must be examined from a much broader perspective than just the trainee, the trainer, and the necessary job skills. A program that considers job training as only one aspect of the instructional program was developed at the Pittsburgh Technical Institute (Nester, 1971). The lengths to which this program goes to gain the trust of the trainee are extraordinary. The trainers not only call the trainee if he does not report by 9:00 A.M., but they also arrange for special tutoring, baby sitters, and a variety of incentives to motivate the trainee. Most interesting is the approach taken by the staff to ensure the success of the trainee on the high school equivalency exam. In addition to tutoring the students, they arrange for a special testing, pay for the exam, provide transportation, and have two staff members present so that the student who looks up sees a familiar and friendly face. Another aspect of the total approach is a counseling program. Nester notes that some of the students have deep-rooted personal problems that make it difficult to learn or to keep a job. Therefore, it is necessary to have counselors available from the beginning of the program to gain insights into the causes of the problems and to suggest éffective ways of coping. At the time of the author's report, the training program in drafting had resulted in 40 of 52 trainees being successfully placed, with 8 possibilities pending. The commitment toward job placement is apparent from the 135 interviews that were arranged for the trainees.

The same themes of job placement, counseling, and attention appear in most programs that have evidence of success. In some cases, the attention is manifested in health care for individuals who were not able to attend training previously because of their ills. In other cases, the attention is focused on careful transportation directions to aid the trainees in finding their way to the training or job site. These factors make careful organizational analysis and need assessment mandatory. For example, conflicts among government sponsors, employers, and training institutions can completely disrupt a program (Goodman, 1969). Many of these conflicts are based on differing goals and expectations. For example, the community training organizations are concerned with introducing people into the world of work, while the employer is concerned with obtaining and retraining people at a minimum cost. When these clashes remain unresolved, there is a situation with conflicting goals and objectives that eventually undermine the potential success for the HCU.

While training analysts are still struggling with the factors that determine the success of HCU instructional programs, the emerging emphasis on the nonskill variables suggests that the original analyses of the trainee population were not very astute. The important issue of motivation was rarely considered. One framework that can be utilized to examine this issue is the instrumentality theory of motivation (Goodman et al., 1973). This view states that the HCU expectancies about reward contingencies and attractiveness of these rewards determine whether the trainee will remain in the instructional program and on the job. From this framework, Goodman and his colleagues have interpreted some of the results of HCU research. They note that older workers are more likely to be successful than younger workers. This suggests that younger workers are more distrustful of the system and therefore perceive lower expectancies, while older workers have higher expectancies and greater desires for rewards. This particular hypothesis receives additional support from data indicating that male HCUs who have family responsibilities are also less likely to drop out. Proponents of behavior modification would probably say that, for these conditions, salary operates as a positive reinforcer. Regardless of the theoretical framework, the point is that a multitude of factors determine the success of the HCU, including the treatment that they receive from other employees and supervisors on the job. Thus, supportive behavior by the supervisor (Friedlander & Greenberg, 1971) relates to more effective HCU performance. "An important inference is that programs geared primarily toward adapting the HCU's work attitudes to the predominant social structure in the organization are far less potent than those that also incorporate the adaptation of the organizational climate" (p. 287). All these variables strongly suggest that training programs cannot operate in isolation. Training analysts should not decide that training programs designed for remedial work or job skills don't work. Instead, they must realize that training programs need to include a number of factors, like job placement, counseling, health needs, and the training of supervisors. Future gains in this area of training are dependent on the careful specification of these variables, including those motivational factors that are important to the younger trainee and to the person without family responsibilities.

TRAINING FOR SECOND CAREERS

Another serious employment problem that has drawn considerable attention in recent years concerns individuals who had previously been employed but for a variety of reasons find themselves seeking retraining for new jobs or careers. For example, 43 percent of the 4.8 million jobless in 1972 had lost their last job. Since 1969, the number of job losers has risen dramatically, as has the number of workers (chiefly women) who wish to re-enter the job market (Manpower Report of the President, 1973). Most of the publicity concerning these groups has focused on the changes in national priorities that have resulted in layoffs for workers in defense and space-related industries, for Ph.D.s as well as blue-collar workers. However, these changes represent only one recent illustration of a growing problem. There are a number of personal, societal, and work-system characteristics that have resulted in a search for second careers. They include the following (Haug & Sussman, 1970):

1. A major reason for job shifts is the incumbent's inability to continue in his chosen field. In some instances this is a result of the formal or informal age limits imposed by the occupation (for example, airline pilots or athletes) or of a variety of individual characteristics, such as physical handicaps.

2. Another reason is the recognition that the first career is at a dead end; that is, there can be no further advancement. Thus, military men who recognize that future opportunities are limited retire at the first chance. Also, housewives who find that their child-rearing career is finished explore new interests.

3. In many cases, rapid technological changes, including automation in offices and factories, eliminate the employee's original job or occupation.

4. In other instances, the individual's desire for change results in a shift from a career that is no longer perceived to be stimulating or adequate in pay, status, or security. While the causes are difficult to specify, representatives of state employment offices (Fait, 1970) describe experiences with lawyers, teachers, ministers, and managers who have discovered at the age of 40 that they are no longer interested in their first careers.

As might be expected, the characteristics of these individuals vary considerably from those of the HCU. In general, they tend to be older, with higher salary demands and considerable financial responsibility. However, it would be a mistake to suggest that second-career seekers have homogeneous characteristics. Persons who lost their jobs during the defense-plant layoffs include workers with few basic technical skills as well as highly skilled workers with graduate degrees. One interesting study (Haug & Sussman, 1970) that focuses on these characteristics examined 326 students who graduated in the spring of 1965 from 38 training programs in rehabilitation counseling. Of these students, 112 represented a second-career group that had previously worked in such fields as nursing, teaching, and business. Basically, the second-career group was older (average age of 37 as compared to 27) and economically more affluent, as measured by funds available and home ownership. Most interesting is the fact that a third of the second-career group were disabled, with the most frequent afflictions being blindness and neuromuscular disorders. While it would be foolhardy to generalize from this study to other samples, it is important to recognize that second-career groups have their own set of descriptive characteristics that are likely to differentiate them from most other training populations.

There is one common problem that affects a large part of this group—that is, age discrimination. The antidiscrimination laws have eliminated overt forms of discrimination but have not necessarily provided increased opportunities. Most of this discrimination is based on the belief that older workers cannot perform as well on the job and cannot easily acquire new skills. The few studies treating this issue present a mixed bag of results. Foremen in Britain (Chown & Heron, 1965) noticed that older workers slowed down on skill jobs but believed the change in pace was offset by increased conscientiousness. Other studies have shown that older workers had difficulties in accuracy and detail (Murrell & Tucker, 1960), but there are also data to indicate that older workers have fewer accidents (Chown & Heron, 1965). Basically, the data are scanty and derived over so many different types of jobs and workers that it is unreasonable to try to establish conclusions. In addition, the research has the following serious limitations (Sheppard, 1970):

1. It fails to differentiate various aspects of the work situation, including physical, psychomotor, sensory, and social characteristics.

2. Most of the emphasis is on average performance, with little, if any, attention to the substantial number of individual differences.

3. There is a blind faith in straight-line trend extrapolations. If 30- to 40-year-old workers have lower morale than 20- to 30-year-olds, it is simply assumed that 40- to 50-year-olds will have even lower morale.

These limitations emphasize the ignorance about the characteristics of our second-career population and about the relationship of particular methods to various required behaviors. As long as all behaviors, individuals, and jobs are treated as part of one large package, the picture will remain ambiguous. However, one point is emerging. The age-discrimination picture is not based simply on the ability of older workers. When skilled workers are displaced, the older among them are the ones who have difficulty finding re-employment. One study indicated that all the younger skilled workers of a displaced group obtained jobs, while 38 percent of the older workers stayed unemployed (Sheppard, 1970). In addition, the older workers who found jobs were usually paid less than they had previously earned. In this study, the older worker was defined as anyone over 38!

Besides contributing to biases, the lack of knowledge about appropriate training techniques and support variables makes it difficult to properly design training programs. However, there is some research that permits speculation on future developments of training programs.

Several studies in the learning literature indicate that methods stressing activity rather than conscious memorization or rote learning are especially helpful for older learners (Belbin, 1958). These types of studies have led to the development of a technique called the *discovery method*. It is described by Belbin (1970) as follows:

> The art of applying the Discovery Method lies in devising tasks which are not beyond the unaided accomplishments of the trainee at each stage in the learning process, even if he starts by knowing virtually nothing about a subject. The trainee may be helped to discover the right response by reducing the complexity of the task as it appears in the real situation; for example, by introducing cues such as the use of a colour to indicate which controls have to be operated on a complex machine and so leaving the trainee free to concentrate on other problems confronting him. . . . In other words, the physical changes are designed to increase the prospects that the trainee will be able to discover something for himself [p. 57].

This method encourages the trainee to progress at his own pace, with a minimum of verbal instruction and physical demonstration. If mistakes occur, an instructor is available to immediately help the trainee onto the correct path. Essentially, the discovery method adapts shaping (the method of successive approximations) to older workers. While it is too early to judge the success of this approach, several studies (Barkin, 1970) suggest that the method was successful in teaching basic electricity to older workers who were being retrained from steam-locomotive to diesel-electric trains.

While the development of media appropriate to the characteristics of these trainees is an important step, experiences with the HCU and several developments in the study of second careers suggest that it is not good to emphasize only job skills and remedial education. Although the characteristics of the HCU and of those training for second careers are quite different, many of the attitudinal and motivational variables are remarkably similar. For example, there is evidence that the assurance of job placement and payments for training-program participation are important determinants of the individual's willingness to continue in a training program (Barkin, 1970). The needs for counseling are equally apparent. Many employees faced with losing their jobs refuse to enter training programs designed to create similar employment. One study (Rosen, Williams, & Foltman, 1965) found that older workers were not likely to volunteer for training programs because they had little confidence in their learning ability. The interaction between age and education was even more striking. Younger workers with a poor educational background were likely to volunteer for retraining, even though they were satisfied with the prospects for promotion and were unsure about their ability to learn. However, older workers with poor educational backgrounds were not willing to volunteer. Thus, it appears that older workers wait until they find themselves out in the street with what has now been termed "job-interview anxiety" (Sheppard, 1970), either afraid to enter programs or frozen by anxiety in those programs in which they are placed. In addition, many are unable to adjust to the thought of changing fields or lowering their salary demands to begin anew in another career, even though either activity might lead to retraining and a new job (Sobel & Folk, 1965). Obviously, the problems of retraining for second careers are very complex. At this point, little is understood except that it will be necessary to deal with many attitudinal and motivational variables besides job skills and remedial training.

Epilog

Instructional Programs: A Recapitulation

The instructional model presented in this book (see Figure 2-1, page 18) suggests that the success of instructional programs is dependent on an approach that considers a number of interacting components. Behavioral and organizational objectives, as well as multiple criteria and rigorous designs, are necessary. The literature presents only a few programs that offer more than lip-service consideration of the factors that determine successful development and evaluation of instructional programs. Instead, there is a whirlpool of actions and reactions that utilizes immediate testimonials in support of a favorite approach. Unfortunately, the resulting effort has usually led to the consideration of a favorite medium rather than to the examination of the capabilities of different approaches for various learning behaviors. As long as the focus remains on each passing fad, the body of knowledge required to make intelligent choices will never be developed.

With the present emphasis on individual techniques, a data base has hopefully been developed that permits a new perspective on the utility and the critical parameters of each approach. Actually, the degree of progress depends on the particular approach involved. Despite the pronouncements of ardent supporters, many techniques (for example, business games) remain virtually unexamined. Other procedures, like CAI and behavior modification, are still in their infancy. However, the number of announcements and descriptions of programs, as compared to research investigations, creates a question about the objectives of those individuals involved with the techniques' futures. On the other hand, some approaches (for example, laboratory training, moving pictures, and PI) have been analyzed in many research studies. Unfortunately, many of these studies have been marred by the quality of the effort. It is especially sad to see the number of investigations that could have been made more productive by careful planning sessions. However, there is a developing literature that deserves careful examination by anyone who intends to plan instructional programs based on these approaches. Laboratory-training research is prompted by a healthy debate about the proper procedures and variables that must be examined in order to determine the efficacy of the technique. Probably, this debate is a result of ethical concerns about the psychological safety of the participants. Other techniques should be scrutinized even without such concerns. The magnitude of the effort of PI and moving pictures gives some reason for optimism. Researchers in these areas have started to question the relevance of their procedures for different behaviors and environmental settings. In addition, they are attempting to determine which specific parameters of their technique determine its utility.

The following suggestions are offered as directions for future research activity:

1. It is imperative to establish programs that systematically utilize empirical measurement techniques to determine whether the objectives specified by the need-assessment analyses have been achieved. It is interesting to note that behavior modification is a new technique that emphasizes many aspects of the systematic approach. Behavior modification includes carefully specified objectives and a learning environment that stresses careful shaping of the sequences of behavior toward the final terminal behaviors. Thus, the proper development of this technique may offer a model for other instructional approaches. However, the dangers that might lead enthusiastic supporters to ignore the careful need-assessment procedures necessary to establish the organizational and individual objectives must be avoided. In addition, the measurement of empirical changes will not be established simply by using behavior-modification techniques. For example, the dangers of criterion contamination are potent, irrespective of the method employed. Hopefully, the advocates of this approach will not turn it into the next fad applicable to all forms of behavior but will instead help to determine which learning behaviors are amenable to change.

2. Investigations should not focus entirely on the consideration of single treatments. There are several implications to this suggestion. First, there are the difficulties associated with investigating a single method when it would not ordinarily be employed in isolation. For example, Chu and Schramm (1967) note that most studies have compared programs taught completely by television to those taught completely by conventional instruction. Yet, television is unlikely to be used in a program without being a part of a learning environment that employs many other procedures. Investigations of moving pictures in a total learning environment might even provide information about the interaction between the quality of the trainer and the instructional program. Also, approaches that examine combined techniques might provide some information on the utility of different methods for changing different learning behaviors. There may be difficulties in determining the effectiveness of particular media because one technique is not completely amenable to the various

forms of learning that are required to achieve different terminal behaviors. Hopefully, this suggestion will also lead to further investigations of aptitude-treatment interactions, which require the examination of different instructional methods in conjunction with individual differences among learners. However, any gains in determining aptitude-treatment interactions are dependent on systematic analyses of learner and media characteristics that go far beyond the typical approach of using the most convenient measures of individual differences paired with a random choice of media.

3. Evaluation must be treated as an information-gathering process that cannot possibly result in decisions that categorize programs as all good or all poor. These evaluation attitudes will be established only if it is clear that instructional programs are never complete but, instead, are designed to be revised on the basis of information obtained from evaluations that examine relevant multiple criteria. Chu and Schramm (1967) reported on a series of moving-picture investigations showing that when the programs were tested, revised, and tested again, there was a marked improvement in learning. Unfortunately, the feedback process that could result from effectively designed evaluations has been likely to lead to emotional reactions rather than to decisions to use the information to improve the program. Evaluation is only one part of a long-term systematic approach; therefore, it is necessary to pay particular attention to developing relevant criteria of learning and transfer performance. It is difficult to understand how instructional designers can accept training measures without any consideration of the transfer criteria that their programs have been designed to achieve. The importance of result criteria has been established but it should be noted that, aside from one analysis of PI literature (Nash et al., 1971), there is virtually no mention of practical significance.

There are few studies that employ the most rigorous design possible within the limitations imposed by the environment. In many instances, the authors of research articles apologize in advance for poor designs, which obviously could have been strengthened by some initial effort. The potential rewards of carefully designed evaluation are expressed by Lumsdaine and May (1965).

> Progressively better definitions of variables and analysis of their interaction should in the long run permit us to reduce considerably the amount of trial and error in empirical tryout and revision, by providing dependable generalizations which can be communicated and taught as programming principles. While this long-range goal is being progressively approximated, increased reliance on empirically-demonstrable performance characteristics of particular programs, as a basis for their improvement, selection, and use, may be the best way to attain substantial and demonstrable improvements in the effectiveness of instructional media [p. 513].

While there are many knowledge gaps, training analysts are far from ignorant about the procedures that should be employed. The challenges of many important societal problems (for example, training for the HCU and for second careers) await our constructive suggestions. I hope that the information provided in this book will prove to be a stimulus for some of that necessary work.

References

Abelson, P.H. The fourth revolution. *Science,* 1972, **177,** 121.

Adams, J.A. Some considerations in the design and use of dynamic flight simulators. In H.W. Sinaiko (Ed.), *Selected papers on human factors in the design and use of control systems.* New York: Dover, 1961.

Adams, J.S. Injustice in social exchange. In L. Berkowitz (Ed.), *Advances in experimental social psychology.* Vol. 2. New York: Academic Press, 1965.

Alpert, D., & Bitzer, D.L. Advances in computer-based education. *Science,* 1970, **167,** 1582–1590.

Argyris, C. T-groups for organizational effectiveness. *Harvard Business Review,* 1964, **42,** 60–74.

Argyris, C. We must make work worthwhile. *Life,* 1967, **62**(18), 56–68.

Argyris, C. Issues in evaluating laboratory education. *Industrial Relations,* 1968, **8,** 28–40, 45.

Atkinson, J.W., & Feather, N.T. *A theory of achievement motivation.* New York: Wiley, 1966.

Atkinson, R.C. Computerized instruction and the learning process. *American Psychologist,* 1968, **23,** 225–239.

Atkinson, R.C. Ingredients for a theory of instruction. *American Psychologist,* 1972, **27,** 921–931.

Ball, S., & Bogatz, G.A. *The first year of Sesame Street: An evaluation.* Princeton, N.J.: Educational Testing Service, 1970.

Barkin, S. Retraining and job redesign: Positive approaches to the continued employment of older persons. In H.L. Sheppard (Ed.), *Towards an industrial gerontology.* Cambridge, Mass.: Schenkman, 1970.

Bartlett, C. J. Personal Communication, 1973.

Bass, B.M., & Vaughan, J.A. *Training in industry: The management of learning.* Belmont, Calif.: Wadsworth, 1966.

Becker, S.W. The parable of the pill. *Administrative Science Quarterly,* 1970, **15,** 94–96.

Beckhard, R. *Organizational development: Strategies and models.* Reading, Mass.: Addison-Wesley, 1969.

Belbin, E. Methods for training older workers. *Ergonomics,* 1958, **1,** 207–221.

Belbin, R.M. The discovery method in training older workers. In H.L. Sheppard (Ed.), *Towards an industrial gerontology.* Cambridge, Mass.: Schenkman, 1970.

Bellows, R.M. Procedures for evaluating vocational criteria. *Journal of Applied Psychology,* 1941, **25,** 499–513.

Bennis, W.G. *Organizational development: Its nature, origins, and prospects.* Reading, Mass.: Addison-Wesley, 1969.

Berlak, H. Values, goals, public policy, and educational evaluation. *Review of Educational Research,* 1970, **40,** 261–278.

Blaiwes, A.S., & Regan, J.J. *An integrated approach to the study of learning, retention, and transfer—a key issue in training device research and development.* (NAVTRADEVCEN-1H-178) Orlando, Fla.: Naval Training Device Center, 1970.

Blake, R.R., & Mouton, J.S. *The managerial grid.* Houston, Tex.: Gulf, 1964.

Blake, R.R., Mouton, J.S., Barnes, L.B., & Greiner, L.E. Breakthrough in organization development. *Harvard Business Review,* 1964, **42,** 133–155.

Blum, M.L., & Naylor, J.C. *Industrial psychology.* New York: Harper & Row, 1968.

Borg, W.R. *Educational Research.* New York: David McKay, 1963, 1971.

Bourne, L.E., & Ekstrand, B.R. *Psychology: Its principles and meanings.* Hinsdale, Ill.: Dryden, 1973.

Bracht, G.H. Experimental factors related to aptitude-treatment interactions. *Review of Educational Research,* 1970, **40,** 627–645.

Briggs, L.J. *Sequencing of instruction in relation to hierarchies of competence.* Palo Alto, Calif.: American Institutes for Research, 1968.

Briggs, L.J., & Angell, D. Programmed instruction in science and mathematics. *Review of Educational Research,* 1964, **34,** 354–373.

Briggs, L.J., Campeau, P.L., Gagné, R.M., & May, M.A. *Instructional media: A procedure for the design of multi-media instruction, a critical review of research, and suggestions for future research.* Palo Alto, Calif.: American Institutes for Research, 1967.

Bruner, J.S. Needed: A theory of instruction. *Educational Leadership,* 1963, **20,** 523–532.

Bryan, J.F., & Locke, E.A. Goal setting as a means of increasing motivation. *Journal of Applied Psychology,* 1967, **51,** 274–277.

Buchanan, P.C. Innovative organizations—a study in organizational development. In *Applying behavioral science research in industry.* New York: Industrial Relations Counselors Report No. 23, 1964.

Buchanan, P.C. Sensitivity, or laboratory, training in industry. *Sociological Inquiry,* 1971, **41,** 217–225.

Bundy, R.F. Computer-assisted instruction—where are we? *Phi Delta Kappan,* 1968, **49,** 424–429.

Burke, H.L., & Bennis, W.G. Changes in perception of self and others during human relations training. *Human Relations,* 1961, **14,** 165–182.

Bushnell, D.S. *Technological change and the journeyman electrician: An experimental study in continuing education.* Menlo Park, Calif.: Stanford Research Institute, 1963.

Byers, K.T. (Ed.) *Employee training and development in the public service.* Chicago: Public Personnel Association, 1970.

Campbell, D.T. Reforms as experiments. *American Psychologist,* 1969, **24,** 409–429.

Campbell, D.T., & Stanley, J.C. *Experimental and quasi-experimental designs for research.* Chicago: Rand McNally, 1963.

Campbell, J.P. Personnel training and development. In *Annual Review of Psychology.* Palo Alto, Calif.: Annual Reviews, 1971.

Campbell, J.P., Dunnette, M.D., Lawler, E.E. III, & Weick, K.E., Jr. *Managerial behavior, performance, and effectiveness.* New York: McGraw-Hill, 1970.

Canter, R.R., Jr. A human relations training program. *Journal of Applied Psychology,* 1951, **35,** 38–45.

Carmichael, L., Hogan, H.P., & Walter, A.A. An experimental study of the effect of language on the reproduction of visually perceived form. *Journal of Experimental Psychology,* 1932, **15**, 73–86.

Carroll, S.J., Jr., Paine, F.T., & Ivancevich, J.J. The relative effectiveness of training methods—expert opinion and research. *Personnel Psychology,* 1972, **25**, 495–510.

Castle, P.F.C. Evaluation of human relations training for supervisors. *Occupational Psychology,* 1952, **26**, 191–205.

Catalanello, R.F., & Kirkpatrick, D.L. Evaluating training programs—the state of the art. *Training and Development Journal,* 1968, **22**, 2–9.

Chapanis, A., Garner, W.R., & Morgan, C.T. *Applied experimental psychology: Human factors in engineering design.* New York: Wiley, 1949.

Chown, S.M., & Heron, A. Psychological aspects of aging in man. *Annual Review of Psychology.* Palo Alto, Calif.: Annual Reviews, 1965.

Chu, G.C., & Schramm, W. *Learning from television: What the research says.* Washington, D.C.: National Association of Educational Broadcasters, 1967.

Cicero, J.P. Behavioral objectives for technical training systems. *Training and Development Journal,* 1973, **28**, 14–17.

Cogan, E.A. Systems analysis and the introduction of educational technology in school. *HumRRO professional paper 14–71.* Alexandria, Va.: Human Resources Research Organization, 1971.

Cohen, D.K. Politics and research: Evaluation of social action programs in education. *Review of Educational Research,* 1970, **40**, 213–238.

Cohen, K.J., Cyert, R.M., Dill, W.R., Kuehn, A.A., Miller, M.H., Van Wormer, T.A., & Winters, P.R. The Carnegie Tech management game. In H. Guetzkow (Ed.), *Simulation in social science: Readings.* Englewood Cliffs, N.J.: Prentice-Hall, 1962.

Cook, E.M. The in-basket exercise: For secretarial training? *Training and Development Journal,* 1973, **27**, 26–27.

Cook A., & Mack, H. The discovery center hustle. *Education Digest,* 1971, **36**, 50–53.

Cooley, W.W., & Glaser, R. The computer and individualized instruction. *Science,* 1969, **166**, 574–582.

Cram, D. *Explaining teaching machines and programming.* San Francisco: Fearon, 1961.

Cronbach, L.J. The two disciplines of scientific psychology. *American Psychologist,* 1957, **12**, 671–684.

Cronbach, L.J. Evaluation for course improvement. *Teachers College Record,* 1963, **64**, 672–683.

Cronbach, L.J. How can instruction be adapted to individual differences? In k.M. Gagné (Ed.), *Learning and individual differences.* Columbus, Ohio: Charles E. Merrill, 1967.

Cronbach, L.J., & Snow, R.E. *Individual differences in learning ability as a function of instructional variables.* Final report, School of Education, Stanford University (Contract No. OEC–4-6061269-1217), U.S. Office of Education, 1969.

Crowder, N.A. Automatic tutoring by means of intrinsic programming. In A.A. Lumsdaine & R. Glaser (Eds.), *Teaching machines and programmed learning.* Washington, D.C.: National Education Association, 1960.

Dachler, H.P. Personal Communication, 1974.

Davis, C.M. TV delivery of continuing education programs. *Training and Development Journal,* 1973, **27,** 3–7.

Dawson, R.E. Simulation in the social sciences. In E. Guetzkow (Ed.), *Simulation in social science: Readings.* Englewood Cliffs, N.J.: Prentice-Hall, 1962.

DeCecco, J.P. *The psychology of learning and instruction: Educational psychology.* Englewood Cliffs, N.J.: Prentice-Hall, 1968.

DePhillips, F.A., Berliner, W.M., & Cribbin, J.J. *Management of training programs.* Homewood, Ill.: Irwin, 1960.

Digman, J.M. Growth of a motor skill as a function of distribution of practice. *Journal of Experimental Psychology,* 1959, **57,** 310–316.

Dill, W.R., Jackson, J.R., & Sweeney, J.W. (Eds.) *Proceedings of the conference on business games as teaching devices.* School of Business Administration, Tulane University, April 26–28, 1961.

Dorcus, R.M. Methods of evaluating the efficiency of door-to-door salesmen of bakery products. *Journal of Applied Psychology,* 1940, **24,** 587–594.

Dunnette, M.D., & Campbell, J.P. Laboratory education: Impact on people and organizations. *Industrial Relations,* 1968, **8,** 1–27, 41–44.

Eachus, H.T., & King, P.H. *Acquisition and retention of cross-cultural interaction skills through self-confrontation.* (AMRL-TR-66-8) Wright-Patterson Air Force Base, Ohio, Aerospace Medical Research Laboratories, 1966.

Edgerton, H.A. *The relationship of method of instruction to trainee aptitude pattern.* (Technical Report, Contract Nonr 1042 [00] New York: Richardson, Bellows, Henry, & Co., 1958.

Ellis, H.C. *The transfer of learning.* New York: Macmillan, 1965.

Fait, E. Research needs in industrial gerontology from viewpoint of a state employment service. In H.L. Sheppard (Ed.), *Towards an industrial gerontology.* Cambridge, Mass.: Schenkman, 1970.

Feeney, E.J. Performance audit, feedback, and positive reinforcement. *Training and Development Journal,* 1972, **26,** 8–13.

Feifer, I. Training on the train: By Art Buchwald. *Training and Development Journal,* 1970, **25,** 43.

Fitts, P.M. Factors in complex skill training. In R. Glaser (Ed.), *Training research and education.* New York: Wiley, 1965.

Fitzpatrick, R. The selection of measures for evaluating programs. In *Evaluative research: Strategies and methods.* Pittsburgh: American Institutes for Research, 1970.

Flanagan, J.C. The critical incident technique. *Psychological Bulletin,* 1954, **51,** 327–358.

Fleishman, E.A. The description and prediction of perceptual-motor skill learning. In R. Glaser (Ed.), *Training research and education.* New York: Wiley, 1965.

Fleishman, E.A. On the relationship between abilities, learning, and human performance. *American Psychologist,* 1972, **27,** 1017–1032.

Fleishman, E.A., Harris, E.F., & Burtt, H.E. Leadership and supervision in industry. *Bureau of Educational Research, Report No. 33,* The Ohio State University, 1955.

Flexman, R.E., Roscoe, S.N., Williams, A.C., Jr., & Williges, B.H. Studies in pilot training: The anatomy of transfer. *Aviation Research Monographs,* 1972, **2,** 1–87.

Folley, J.D., Jr. Determining training needs of department store sales personnel. *Training and Development Journal,* 1969, **23,** 24–27.

Frederiksen, N. Factors in in-basket performance. *Psychological Monographs,* 1962, **76,** (22, Whole No. 541).

French, S.H. Measuring progress toward industrial relations objectives. *Personnel,* 1953, **30,** 338–347.

Friedlander, F., & Greenberg, S. Effect of job attitudes, training, and organizational climate on performance of the hard-core unemployed. *Journal of Applied Psychology,* 1971, **55,** 287–295.

Fry, E.B. *Teaching machines and programmed instruction.* New York: McGraw-Hill, 1963.

Gagné, R.M. Military training and principles of learning. *American Psychologist,* 1962, **17,** 83–91.

Gagné, R.M. *The conditions for learning.* New York: Holt, Rinehart & Winston, 1965, 1970.

Gagné, R.M. Instruction and the conditions of learning. In L. Siegel (Ed.), *Instruction: Some contemporary viewpoints.* San Francisco: Chandler, 1967.

Gagné, R.M., & Bolles, R.C. A review of factors in learning efficiency. In E. Galanter (Ed.), *Automatic teaching: The state of the art.* New York: Wiley, 1959.

Ghiselli, E.E. The placement of workers: Concepts and problems. *Personnel Psychology,* 1956, **9,** 1–16.

Gibson, J.J. (Ed.) *Motion picture testing and research.* Army Air Force Aviation Psychological Program Research Report No. 7. Washington, D.C.: U.S. Government Printing Office, 1947.

Gilbert, T.F. On the relevance of laboratory investigation of learning to self-instructional programming. In A.A. Lumsdaine & R. Glaser (Eds.), *Teaching machines and programmed instruction.* Washington, D.C.: National Education Association, 1960.

Glanzer, M. Experimental study of team training and team functioning. In R. Glaser (Ed.), *Training research and education.* New York: Wiley, 1965.

Glickman, A.S., & Vallance, T.R. Curriculum assessment with critical incidents. *Journal of Applied Psychology,* 1958, **42,** 329–335.

Golembiewski, R.T., & Carrigan, S.B. Planned change in organization style based on the laboratory approach. *Administrative Science Quarterly,* 1970, **15,** 79–93.

Goodacre, D.M. Experimental evaluation of training. *Journal of Personnel Administration and Industrial Relations,* 1955, **2,** 143–149.

Goodman, P.S. Hiring and training the hard-core unemployed: A problem in system definition. *Human Organization,* 1969, **28,** 259–269.

Goodman, P.S., Salipante, P., & Paransky, H. Hiring, training, and retraining the hard-core unemployed: A selected review. *Journal of Applied Psychology,* 1973, **58,** 23–33.

Grayson, L.P. Costs, benefits, effectiveness: Challenge to educational technology. *Science,* 1972, **175,** 1216–1222.

Greenlaw, P.S., Herron, L.W., & Rawdon, R.H. *Business simulation in industrial and university education.* Englewood Cliffs, N.J.: Prentice-Hall, 1962.

Guba, E.G. The failure of educational evaluation. *Educational Technology,* 1969, **9,** 29–38.

Guion, R.M. Criterion measurement and personnel judgments. *Personnel Psychology,* 1961, **14,** 141–149.

Guion, R.M. *Personnel testing.* New York: McGraw-Hill, 1965.

Haines, D.B., & Eachus, H.T. *A preliminary study of acquiring cross-cultural interaction skills through self-confrontation.* (AMRL-TR–65-137) Wright-Patterson Air Force Base, Ohio: Aerospace Medical Research Laboratories, 1965.

Haldi, J., & Wagner, H.M. Games to teach principles of economics. In W.R. Dill, J.R. Jackson, & J.W. Sweeney (Eds.), *Proceedings of the conference on business games as teaching devices.* School of Business Administration, Tulane University, April 26-28, 1961.

Harmon, P. A classification of performance objective behaviors in job training programs. *Educational Technology,* 1968, **8,** 11–16.

Haug, M.R., & Sussman, M.B. The second-career variant of a sociological concept. In H.L. Sheppard (Ed), *Towards an industrial gerontology.* Cambridge, Mass.: Schenkman, 1970.

Hendrickson, G., & Schroeder, W. Transfer of training in learning to hit a submerged target. *Journal of Educational Psychology,* 1941, **32,** 206–213.

Herzberg, F., Mausner, B., & Snyderman, B. *The motivation to work.* (2nd ed.) New York: Wiley, 1959.

Hilgard, E.R., & Bower, G.H. *Theories of learning.* (3rd ed.) New York: Appleton-Century-Crofts, 1966.

Holding, D.H. *Principles of training.* London: Pergamon, 1965.

Holt, H.O. An exploratory study of the use of a self-selection instruction program in basic electricity. In J.L Hughes (Ed.), *Programmed learning: a critical evaluation.* Chicago: Educational Methods, 1963, (a)

Holt, H.O. Programmed instruction. *Bell Telephone Magazine,* **Spring,** 1963. (b)

House, R.J. T-group education and leadership effectiveness: A review of the empiric literature and a critical evaluation. *Personnel Psychology,* 1967, **20,** 1–32.

Howard, A. Training for individuals and individual differences. Unpublished paper, University of Maryland, 1971.

Howell, W.C., & Goldstein, I.L. *Engineering psychology: Current perspectives in research.* New York: Appleton-Century-Crofts, 1971.

Ingersoll, V.H. Role playing, attitude change, and behavior. *Organizational Behavior and Human Performance,* 1973, **10,** 157–174.

Irwin, D. The Chrysler Corporation, Detroit. In *Research in apprenticeship training.* The University of Wisconsin, Center for Studies in Vocational and Technical Education, 1967.

Isaac, S., & Michael, W.B. *Handbook in research and evaluation.* San Diego: Knapp, 1971.

Jaffee, C.L., & Friar, L. Use of simulation in training disadvantaged employees for secretarial positions. *Training and Development Journal,* 1969, **23,** 30–34.

Jenness, J.S. Change for the future. *Training and Development Journal,* 1972, **26,** 2–4.

Kelly, C.R. What is adaptive training? *Human Factors,* 1969, **11,** 547–556.

Kennedy, J.B. Use of audio-visual techniques in training the hard-core. *Training and Development Journal,* 1970, **24,** 30–33.

Kimble, G.A., & Garmezy, N. *Principles of general psychology*. (3rd ed.) New York: Ronald Press, 1968.

King, P.H. *A summary of research in training for advisory roles in other cultures by the behavioral sciences laboratory*. (AMRL-TR–66-131) Wright-Patterson Air Force Base, Ohio: Aerospace Medical Research Laboratories, 1966.

Kirchner, W.K. Book review of A.J. Marrow's *Behind the executive mask*. *Personnel Psychology*, 1965, **18**, 211–212.

Kirkpatrick, D.L. Techniques for evaluating training programs. *Journal of the American Society of Training Directors*, 1959, **13**, 3–9, 21–26; 1960, **14**, 13–18, 28–32.

Klaw, S. Inside a T-group. *Think*, 1965, **31**, 26–30.

Kopstein, F.F., & Seidel, R.J. *Computer-administered instruction versus traditionally administered instruction: Economics*. (HumRRO professional paper 31–67) Alexandria, Va., Human Resources Research Organization, 1967.

Kozoll, C.E. The air left the "bag"—a training program that failed. *Training and Development Journal*, 1971, **25**, 22–25.

Lawrence, D.H. The evaluation of training and transfer programs in terms of efficiency measures. *Journal of Psychology*, 1954, **38**, 367–382.

Lefkowitz, J. Effect of training on the productivity and tenure of sewing machine operators. *Journal of Applied Psychology*, 1970, **54**, 81–86.

Lindahl, L.G. Movement analysis as an industrial training method. *Journal of Applied Psychology*, 1945, **29**, 420–436.

Lindbom, T.R., & Osterberg, W. Evaluating the results of supervisory training. *Personnel*, 1954, **31**, 224–228.

Liveright, A.A. Role playing in leadership training. *Personnel Journal*, 1951, **29**, 412–416.

Locke, E.A. Job satisfaction and job performance: A theoretical analysis. *Organizational Behavior and Human Performance*, 1970, **5**, 484–500.

Locke, E.A., & Bryan, J.F. Cognitive aspects of psychomotor performance: The effect of performance goals on level of performance. *Journal of Applied Psychology*, 1966, **50**, 286–291.

Lorge, I. *Influence of regularly interpolated time intervals upon subsequent learning*. Teachers College Contributions to Education, No. 438. New York: Teachers College Press, Columbia University, 1930.

Lumsdaine, A.A., & May, M.A. Mass communication and educational media. In *Annual Review of Psychology*. Palo Alto, Cal.: Annual Reviews, 1965.

Lumsdaine, A.A., May, M.A., & Hadsell, R.S. Questions spliced into a film for motivation and pupil participation. In M.A. May & A.A. Lumsdaine (Eds.), *Learning from films*. New Haven, Conn.: Yale University Press, 1958.

Lynton, R.P., & Pareek, U. *Training for development*. Homewood, Ill.: Irwin, 1967.

Lysaught, J.P., & Williams, C.M. *A guide to programmed instruction*. New York: Wiley, 1963.

MacKinney, A.C. Progressive levels in the evaluation of training programs. *Personnel*, 1957, **34**, 72–77.

MacPherson, S.J., Dees, V., & Grindley, G.C. The effect of knowledge of results on performance: II. Some characteristics of very simple skills.

Quarterly Journal of Experimental Psychology, 1948, **1**, 68–78.

Mager, R.F. *Preparing instructional objectives.* Belmont, Calif.: Fearon, 1962.

Mager, R.F., & Beach, K.M., Jr. *Developing vocational instruction.* Belmont, Calif.: Fearon, 1967.

Maier, N.R.F., & Zerfoss, L.R. MRP: A technique for training large groups of supervisors and its potential use in social research. *Human Relations,* 1952, **5**, 177–186.

Maslow, A.H. *Motivation and personality.* New York: Harper & Row, 1954.

Mathewson, F.W. *From nine to five* (evaluation report). United States Government Memorandum, U.S. Civil Service Commission, 1969.

Mayo, G.D., & DuBois, P.H. Measurement of gain in leadership training. *Educational and Psychological Measurement,* 1963, **23**, 23–31.

McClelland, D.C., & Winter, D.G. *Motivating economic achievement.* New York: Free Press, 1969.

McGehee, W. Are we using what we know about training?—learning theory and training. *Personnel Psychology,* 1958, **11**, 1–12.

McGehee, W., & Thayer, P.W. *Training in business and industry.* New York: Wiley, 1961.

McGrath, J.J., & Harris, D.H. Adaptive training. *Aviation Research Monograph,* 1971, **1**, 1–130.

McIntire, R.W. Behavior modification guidelines. In T.C. Tuttle, C.B. Grether, & W.T. Liggett (Eds.), *Psychological behavioral strategy for accident control: Development of behavioral safety guidelines.* Final report for National Institute for Occupational Safety and Health (Contract No. HSM-99-72-27) Columbia, Md.: Westinghouse Behavioral Safety Center, 1973.

Melching, W.H. Behavioral objectives and individualization of instruction. *HumRRO professional paper 18-69,* Alexandria, Va.: Human Resources Research Organization, 1969.

Miller, R.W., & Zeller, F.A. *Social psychological factors association with responses to retraining.* Final Report, Office of Research and Development, Appalachian Center, West Virginia University (Research Grant No. 91-52-66-56), U. S. Department of Labor, 1967.

Mindak, W.A., & Anderson, R.E. Can we quantify an act of faith? *Training and Development Journal,* 1971, **25**, 2–10.

Miner, J.B. Management development and attitude change. *Personnel Administration,* 1961, **24**, 21–26.

Miner, J.B. Evidence regarding the value of a management course based on behavioral science subject matter. *The Journal of Business of the University of Chicago,* 1963, **36**, 325–335.

Miner, J.B., & Dachler, H.P. Personnel attitudes and motivation. In *Annual Review of Psychology.* Palo Alto, Calif.: Annual Reviews, 1973.

Moore, L.F. Business games vs. cases as tools of learning. *Training and Development Journal,* 1967, **21** 13–23.

Morsh, J.E. Job analysis in the United States Air Force. *Personnel Psychology,* 1964, **17**, 7–17.

Mosel, J.N. Why training programs fail to carry over. *Personnel,* 1957, **34**, 56–64.

Murdock, B.B., Jr. Transfer designs and formulas. *Psychological Bulletin,* 1957, **54,** 313–326.

Murrell, K.F.H., & Tucker, W.A. A pilot job study of age-related causes of difficulty in light engineering. *Ergonomics,* 1960, **3,** 74–79.

Nagle, B.F. Criterion development. *Personnel Psychology,* 1953, **6,** 271–288.

Nash, A.N., Muczyk, J.P., & Vettori, F.L. The relative practical effectiveness of programmed instruction. *Personnel Psychology,* 1971, **24,** 397–418.

Naylor, J. C. *Parameters affecting the relative efficiency of part and whole practice methods: A review of the literature.* United States Naval Training Devices Center (Technical Report No. 950-1), February 1962.

Naylor, J.C., & Briggs, G.E. Team training effectiveness under various conditions. *Journal of Applied Psychology,* 1965, **49,** 223–229.

Nester, O.W. Training the hard core: One experience. Pittsburgh Technical Institute Report, undated. Review of work also appearing in *Training and Development Journal,* 1971, **25,** 16–19.

Nord, W. Improving attendance through rewards. *Personnel Administration,* 1970, **33,** 37–41.

Odiorne, G.S. The trouble with sensitivity training. *Journal of the American Society of Training Directors,* 1963, **17,** 9–20.

Ohmann, O.A. A report of research on the selection of salesmen at the Tremco Manufacturing Company. *Journal of Applied Psychology,* 1941, **25,** 18–29.

O'Leary, V.E. The Hawthorne effect in reverse: Effects of training and practice on individual and group performance. *Journal of Applied Psychology,* 1972, **56,** 491–494.

Osgood, C.E. The similarity paradox in human learning: A resolution. *Psychological Review,* 1949, **56,** 132–143.

Patten, T.H., Jr., & Stermer, E.P. Training foremen in work standards. *Training and Development Journal,* 1969, **23,** 25–37.

Povenmire, H.K., & Roscoe, S.N. An evaluation of ground-based flight trainers in routine primary flight training. *Human factors,* 1971, **13,** 109–116.

Pressey, S.L. Development and appraisal of devices providing immediate automatic scoring of objective tests and concomitant self-instruction. *Journal of Psychology,* 1950, **29,** 417–447.

Prien, E.P. Dynamic character of criteria: Organizational change. *Journal of Applied Psychology,* 1966, **50,** 501–504.

Pritchard, R.D. Equity theory: A review and critique. *Organizational Behavior and Human Performance,* 1969, **4,** 176–211.

Raia, A.P. A study of the educational value of management games. *The Journal of Business,* 1966, **39,** 339–352.

Randall, L.K. Evaluation: A training dilemma. *Journal of the American Society of Training Directors,* 1960, **14,** 29–35.

Raser, J.R. *Simulation and society: An exploration of scientific gaming.* Boston: Allyn and Bacon, 1969.

Raynor, J.O. Relationships between achievement-related motives, future orientation, and academic performance. *Journal of Personality and Social Psychology,* 1970, **15,** 28–33.

Raynor, J.O., & Rubin, I.S. Effects of achievement motivation and future orientation on level of performance. *Journal of Personality and Social Psychology*, 1971, **17**, 36–41.

Report of the National Advisory Commission on Civil Disorders. New York: Bantam Books, 1968.

Reynolds, B., & Bilodeau, I. McD. Acquisition and retention of three psychomotor tests as a function of distribution of practice during acquisition. *Journal of Experimental Psychology*, 1952, **44**, 19–26.

Ritti, R.R. Work goals of scientists and engineers. *Industrial Relations*, 1968, **7**, 118–131.

Ronan, W.W., & Prien, E.P. *Perspectives on the measurement of human performance.* New York: Appleton-Century-Crofts, 1971.

Roscoe, S.N. Incremental transfer effectiveness. *Human Factors*, 1971, **13**, 561–567.

Rosen, N.A., Williams, L.K., & Foltman, F.F. Motivational constraints in an industrial retraining program. *Personnel Psychology*, 1965, **18**, 65–79.

Rosenberg, B.D. An evaluation of computer-assisted instruction in the Anne Arundel County School System. Master's thesis, University of Maryland, 1972.

Rubin, I. Increased self-acceptance: A means of reducing racial prejudice. *Journal of Personality and Social Psychology*, 1967, **5**, 233–239.

Rubinsky, S., & Smith, N. Safety training by accident simulation. *Journal of Applied Psychology*, 1973, **57**, 68–73.

Ryan, T.A. *Intentional behavior: An approach to human motivation.* New York: Ronald Press, 1970.

Schneider, B. The perceived environment: Organizational climate. Paper presented at the meeting of the Midwestern Psychological Association, May 1973.

Schneider, B., & Dachler, H.P. Personal Communication, 1973.

Schramm, W. Learning from instructional television. *Review of Educational Research*, 1962, **32**, 156–167.

Schramm, W. *The research on programmed instruction: An annotated bibliography.* U.S. Office of Education, Washington, D.C.: U.S. Government Printing Office, 1964.

Scriven, M. The methodology of evaluation. In *Perspectives of curriculum evaluation.* American Educational Research Association Monograph, No. 1. Chicago: Rand McNally, 1967.

Seashore, R.H., & Bavelas, A. The functioning of knowledge of results in Thorndike's line-drawing experiment. *Psychological Review*, 1941, **48**, 155–164.

Seiler, J. Prevocational and vocational training programs. In *Breakthrough for disadvantaged youth.* U.S. Department of Labor, Washington, D. C.: U.S. Government Printing Office, 1969.

Seltzer, R.H. Computer-assisted instruction—what it can and cannot do. *American Psychologist*, 1971, **26**, 373–377.

Severin, D. The predictability of various kinds of criteria. *Personnel Psychology*, 1952, **5**, 93–104.

Shafer, C.I. A study of evaluation in management education and development programs in selected U.S. companies. Doctoral dissertation, Michigan State University, 1961.

Sheppard, H.L. (Ed.) *Towards an industrial gerontology.* Cambridge, Mass.: Schenkman, 1970.

Shoemaker, H.A., & Holt, H.O. The use of programmed instruction in industry. In R. Glaser (Ed.), *Teaching machines and programmed learning: Data and directions*. Washington, D.C.: National Education Association, 1965.

Silverman, R.E. *Automated teaching: A review of theory and research*. (NAVTRADEVCEN Technical Report 507–2) Port Washington, New York: U.S. Naval Training Device Center, 1960.

Singer, I. CAI in the ghetto school. *CAI Newsletter of the Institute for Computer-Assisted Instruction*, 1968, **1**, 3.

Skinner, B.F. Science of learning and the art of teaching. *Harvard Educational Review*, 1954, **24**, 86–97.

Smode, A.F., & Meyer, D.E. *Research data and information relevant to pilot training*. (Technical Report AMRL-TR-66-99-Vol. 1) Wright-Patterson Air Force Base, Ohio: Aerospace Medical Research Laboratories, 1966.

Sobel, I., & Folk, H. Labor market adjustments by unemployed older workers. In A.M. Ross (Ed.), *Employment policy and the labor market*. Berkeley, Calif.: University of California Press, 1965.

Speroff, B.J. Rotational role playing used to develop managers. *Personnel Journal*, 1954, **33**, 49–50.

Stake, R.E. The Countenance of educational evaluation. *Teachers College Record*, 1967, **68**, 523–540.

Stein, K.J. Digital computers to aid flight training. *Aviation Week and Space Technology*, March 4, 1968, 61–67.

Stewart, L. Management games today. In J.M. Kibbee, C.J. Craft, & B. Nanus (Eds.), *Management games*. New York: Reinhold, 1962.

Strauss, G. Related instruction: Basic problems and issues. In *Research in apprenticeship training*. The University of Wisconsin, Center for Vocational and Technical Education, 1967.

Strauss, G. Management by objectives: A critical view. *Training and Development Journal*, 1972, **26**, 10–15.

Suppes, P., & Jerman, M. Computer-assisted instruction. *National Association of Secondary School Principals Bulletin*, 1970, **54**, 27–40.

Suppes, P., Jerman, M., & Brian, D. *Computer-assisted instruction: Stanford's 1965-66 arithmetic program*. New York: Academic Press, 1968.

Suppes, P., & Morningstar, M. Computer-assisted instruction: Two computer-assisted instruction programs are evaluated. *Science*, 1969, **166**, 343–350.

Thorndike, E.L. The law of effect. *American Journal of Psychology*, 1927, **39**, 212–222.

Thorndike, E.L., & Woodworth, R.S. (I) The influence of improvement in one mental function upon the efficiency of other functions. (II) The estimation of magnitudes. (III) Functions involving attention, observation, and discrimination. *Psychological Review*, 1901, **8**, 247–261, 384–395, 553–564.

Thorndike, R.L. *Personnel selection*. New York: Wiley, 1949.

Trowbridge, M.A., & Cason, H. An experimental study of Thorndike's theory of learning. *Journal of General Psychology*, 1932, **7**, 245–260.

Underwood, B.J. The representativeness of rote verbal learning. In A.W. Melton (Ed.), *Categories of human learning*. New York: Academic Press, 1964.

Underwood, W.J. Evaluation of laboratory method training. *Journal of the American Society of Training Directors*, 1965, **19**, 34–40.

U.S. Civil Service Commission, *Catalog of Basic Education Systems*. Washington, D.C.: U.S. Government Printing Office, 1971. (a)

U.S. Civil Service Commission, *Computer-assisted instruction: A general discussion and case study*. Washington, D.C.: U.S. Government Printing Office, 1971.(b)

U.S. Civil Service Commission, *Programmed instruction: A brief of its development and current status*. Washington, D.C.: U.S. Government Printing Office, 1970.

U.S. Department of Labor, Manpower Administration, *Handbook for analyzing jobs*. Washington, D.C.: U.S. Government Printing Office, 1972.

U.S. Department of Labor, *Manpower report of the president*. Washington, D.C.: U.S. Government Printing Office, 1973.

U.S. Employment Service, U.S. Department of Labor. *Dictionary of occupational titles*. (3rd ed.) Washington, D.C.: U.S. Government Printing Office, 1965.

Utgaard, S.D., & Dawis, R.V. The most frequently used training techniques. *Training and Development Journal*, 1970, **24**, 40-43.

Vallance, T.R., Glickman, A.S., & Vasilas, J.N. Critical incidents in junior officer duties aboard destroyer-type vessels. *USN Bureau of Naval Personnel Research Technical Bulletin*, 1954, No. 54-4.

Van Brunt, R.E. Supervising employees from minority groups. *Education Exchange: Insurance Company Education Directors Society*, 1971, No. 111, pp. 1–5.

Vroom, V.H. *Work and motivation*. New York: Wiley, 1964.

Wallace, R.S. Criteria for what? *American Psychologist*, 1965, **20**, 411–417.

Wallace, R.S., & Twichell, C.M. An evaluation of a training course for life insurance agents. *Personnel Psychology*, 1953, **6**, 25–43.

Webb, E.J., Campbell, D.T., Schwartz, R.D., & Sechrest, L. *Unobtrusive measures: Nonreactive research in the social sciences*. Chicago: Rand McNally, 1966.

Wherry, R.J. The past and future of criterion evaluation. *Personnel Psychology*, 1957, **10**, 1–5.

Williges, B.H., Roscoe, S.N., & Williges, R.C. *Synthetic flight training revisited*. (T.R. ARL-72-21/AFOSR-72-10) Savoy, Ill.: Aviation Research Laboratory, 1972.

Author Index

Subject Index